# LEARNING ORGANIZATIONAL STAFF BEHAVIORAL AND TECHNOLOGICAL STRATEGIES

JOHN LC.

Made with ♥ on the Notion Press Platform
www.notionpress.com

# Contents

# Preface

Introduction

Why technology can improve staffs performance ? I shall explains why organizations need strategy to be implemented.I shall explain that economic recession or boom how influences consumer behavior e.g. the business had been experiencing decline life cycle stage, such as COVID -19 disease occurrence. I shall explain how to apply business development strategy to raise the educational robotic manufacturer sale number. I shall explain how to learn behavioral economy to solve social challenge as well as why some social challenges may influence customers number . I shall explain what factors influence our tourism industry life cycle stage as well as whether how strateges may influence tourism industry develops. I shall explain why to apply airport service life cycle stage improvement stratey to influence airport service performance. I shall explain what factors may influence managers feel difficult to make decisions in any organizations in general as well as how to help them to avoid the decision making challenges occurrences. I shall indicate how and why computer technological firm merger cooperational strategy may help any technological firms to develop impossible as well as what are the IBM and Apple merger strategic advantages and disadvantages. I shall indicate evidences to explain what the factors influence oil industry is experiencing decline life cycle stage. I shall explain whether electronic vehicle invention can influence gas vehicle need and how any why it may influence its life cycle stage changes. I shall explain what factors may influence public transport service industry reaches life cycle decline stage rapidly. I shall explain why and how any management ought spend time to learn organizational strategies in order to grow up their organizational development more easily.

# Prologue

Table of content

growing life cycle stage or decline life cycle stage. p.26-45

● How recession influences the role of advertising changes?

Applying business development strategy to raise the educational robotic manufacturer sale number in recession period

● How to develop organizations in growth stage?

● How to apply business development strategy to help educational robotic manufacturers to enter traditional education market ?

● Future educational robotic are applied on development teaching maths market

Learning behavioral economy to solve social challenges

● Why do some social challenges may influence customers number ?

Organizational life cycle stage decision making strategy

● Why do managers feel difficult to make decisions?

Computer technological firm merger cooperational strategy

● IBM and Apple merger strategic advantages and disadvantages

Chapter 3 Can technology improve travel service performance

● New and old economic theories explain oil is not main factor to influence tourism income

● What are the characteristics of birth life cycle stage to tourism industry ? p.46-73

● What characteristics to space tourism growth stage?

Airport service life cycle stage improvement strategy

● How can processes improvement management strategy influence airport service performance?

Chapter 4 Can technology improves oil sale

● Reasons cause oil industry experiences decline life cycle stage p.74-90

● How to raise global gas users need desire ?

● Shell energy firm mature life cycle stage strategy

Chapter 5 Technology facility how improves organizational performance

● Facility management influences airport and logistic employee performance p.91-120

● Facility management assists employees reduce maintenance service expenditure

● Facility management role in organization

● What is a facility manager's role to provide quality service to satisfy its user needs?
● Facility management benefits to service working environment
● Music (FM) environment influence consumer consumption desire
● Facility management brings departmental benefits
● What is efficient achievement of technological inputs factor in construction industry
● How organizational facility environment factor influences new and old employees long term performance
● Facility management how influences employee Psychology to raise productive efficiency

Chapter 6 Technology how assists organizational development

Human Behavioral network job brings social economic benefits p.121-151

What does human network job mean

Why human network job behavior may influence economy

Robots take our jobs behavioral and economy influences

Robot job behavior brings economy influences

Intellectual human economic behaviors

What does intellectual human economic behaviors mean ?

The relationship between social change and human behavior

How human productive behavior may influence economic development

● New Zealand farmer individual wine productive behavior
● America high technological productive behavior
● China share market investing behavior

Why has any individual country have many people invest share behavior which can influence the country's macro consumption desire?

Can technology influence human shopping behavioral change?

Why and how human behavior may influence the country's economic growth or recession?

Technology how impacts human behavior changing?
How and why employees behaviors may influence economy development?
Robots invention whether they can help organizations to raise efficiencies or inefficiencies?
Why social behavior may influence organizational strategy needs to be changed ?
Reasons why human behavior may influence economic recession or growth ?
How employee behavior influences organizational development?
Artificial intelligent Human clever and art creating ability methods
Why does technology raise online products sale demand and reduces shops products sale demand?
Does car technological development reach mature stage to help economic development?

CHAPTER ONE

# Strategy function to organization

● Explaining what strategy means?

What does concept of corporate strategy mean ? Why does organization need corporate strategy ? The reasons may include : reducing cost, making reasonable or the most beneficial decisions or actions, earning above average returns etc. strategy may be a set of key decisions made to meet objectives. A strategy of a business organization is a compenhensive matter plan stating how the organization will achieve its mission and objectives.

A successful strategy may have these four perspectives, a plan, how do I get these; a pattern , in consistent actions over time; a position, it reflect markets, a ploy is a maneuver instead to outwit a competitor, a perspective is a vision, direction, a view of what the company or organization is to become. For minimizes or competitive disadvantage strategy example, company realizes merging with companies advantage . Although, it may not make its market leader , but it may venture into retailing will help it increase profit.

Strategy also may provide a clear understanding of purpose, objectives and standards performance to employees at all level in all functional areas. Usually, every firm competing in an industry as a strategy, because strategy refers how a given objectives will be achieved. For example, computer industry uses a differentation competitive emphasizes innovative product with creative design. For example, coeporate strategy, Coco Cola Inc. has followed the growth strategy by acquition. It has acquired local bottling units to become as the market leader. For function strategy example, pocter and Gamber spends huge amounts on advertising to create customer demand . They aim to maximize resource productivity. It is concerned with developing a distinctive competence to provide the firm with a competitive advantage. Thus, strategy may have different functions. It depends on whether the organization needs what strategy to achieve its objectives or aims.

● Why does organization need strategist

However, any organization needs one or more strategist (s) . strengths are individuals or groups who are primarily involved in the formulation, implementation , and evaluation of strategy. In a limited sense, all managers are strategists. Strategists may include: Consulants, entreprensurs, boards of directors, chief executive officer, senior management, corporate planning staff, strategic business unit level executives, middle level managers, executive assistant titles in any organizations.

Organizations needs outsourced consultants service because many organizations do not have a corporate planning department, owing to small size . Thus, outsource consultancy firm can provide this kind service to them.

Entrepreneurs are promoters who conceive idea of starting a business for getting maximum returns on investment. They are awaiting for an environment change and for an opportunity in the best interest, for example, a biotechnology firm's managing director needs to implement policy formulation in research and development department.

Board of directors are professionals elected may by the shareholders of the company as per rules and regulation of the company act. They are responsible for the general administration of the organization. They are supposed to guide the top management .

CEO is the top man, next to the directors of the board the occupies the most sensitive post, being held responsible for all aspects to strategic management right from formulation to evaluation of strategy.

Senior management from the chief executive to the level of functional or profit centre heads. They are involved in various aspect of strategic management .

Strateic business unit is diivided into different independent units and allowed to form own respective strategies. Middle level managers are operational planners, for departmental plans, as implementers of the decisions as well as executive assistant is a person who assists the chief executive in the performance of his duties in various ways, e.g. data collection and analysis, suggesting alternative, where decisions are required. preparing briefs of various proposals, projects and reports, helping in public relation. All of above positons may be any organizations‘ role in strategic plan.

● Why do SWOT ( strengths, weaknesses, opportunitites and threats) analysis can remain a major strategic tool to any organizations?

It is one straight formed methodology for making a structured analysis of strengths and weaknesses into core competences and core problems by using the core-competence tree and the current reality true. The core competences and core problems are then linked into a plan of action aimed at preserving the organization's core competence. It supposes that any organizations ought have internal strengths and weaknesses both. So, if the organization has strengths , it also ought have weaknesses. Any organization, itself ought have ability to control or avoid or threaten its any weaknesses cause as well as finds any method to arise strengths to bring itself competitive ability. Otherwise, due to external environment factor, it can not control. So, it supposes any organization can not control any opportunities ot threats when they will occur or encounter to influence weaknesses, eliminate all weaknesses that do not satisfy the following criteria.

The weaknesses that do not satisfy the following criteria: The weaknesses must exist over a period of time can not be a one-time phenomenon, the weakness must be expressed in undesirable terms, the weakness must be under the firm's control or influence . So, any firm hopes to eliminate weakness, it depends on how it causes significant damage to the company. For example, when one firm discovers that the project ought may be finished within five months. But, after four months, it discovered that this project can not be finished, if it hopes staffs can cooperate to finish this project before five months, it needs to find whether what its main weaknesses are influenced this project will delay, e.g. lack of innovation, lack of growth, insufficient attractive profits to excite staffs to work. Hence , SWOT is a strategic management tool, it consists of the analysis, decisions and actions, an organization undertakes in order to create competitive advantages. However, the next phases of the strategic management process is external and internal organization's strengths and weaknesses analysis, by conducting an external analysis , an organization also needs to identify the critical threats and opportunities in its competitive environment. It also needs to examine who external competitive environment influences its business develops in long term.

In fact, any organizations need to make the most reasonable strategic choice with vision, mission, objectives and the external and internal analysis of its external environment influence. Hence, the strategic management process may include this steps:

From vision to mission to objectives to ( SWOT analysis, external analysis and internal analysis both ) to strategic choice ( the most reasonable choice) to strategy implementation to achive competitive advantage . So, any organizations must need to spend long time to gather data to analysis whether which it has actual internal strengths and weaknesses as well as what the present external envioronment brings opportunities and threats to influence its business development, if it hopes to implement effective strategic plan. So, it seems that SWOT ought be one step to any organization's strategic plan management process. Thus, managers have responsibilities to help their organizations to try to " fit" the analysis of externalities and internalities, to balance the organization's strengths and weaknesses as well as environmental opportunities and threats . For one car sale manager hopes to find methods to solve its car low sale problem. In the SWOT analysis, it may have these questions: Why does the performance of the car firms in the same motoe sale service industry, operating under the same competitive environment? Which tangible resources of the high performance motor sale service firm provide sources of competitive advantage and subsequent superior motor sale service firm performance? How do the identifical tangible resources actually create value for a motor sale service firm in the motore service industry and provide the motor sale service firm with source of sustainable competitive advantage?

Thus, assumption of questions are needed in order to help organizations to attempt to seek the main factors influence their short or long objectives can not achieve in the SWOT analysis process. Then, they can evaluate the different factors to make the reasonable analysis to decide whether which is the main factor to influence their objectives can not achieve satisfactory . Then, they can revise their errors as well as find the most reasonable or the most right solutions methods to achieve their objectives more successfully. Because some factors influence the business actions its objectives succussfully. They may include: poor organizational behavior, e.g. worse staff performance, working attitude, lazy , they do not enjoy or feel bore to so their work, they feel salaries are not reasonable; poor strategy, e.g. the business ought not expand more branches at this moment rapidly, the business ought chose partnership , it is more suitable to compare sole trader formation, the organization ought advertise to raise its brand awareness to let public to acknowledge etc. wrong strategy implementation. So, SWOT stragegy role may also help any organizatons to revise whether they have errors in order to find the most reasonable factor to cause their poor performance or low profit etc. effects.

● What is strategy and strategic management to future managers in organizations?

Are they understood and recognized? However, I believe that the development of organizational strategy depends on understanding the perceptions of their managers on what strategy and strategic management actually is. The identifications of perceptions of future maangers will need have some insights , opinions and knowledge on the organization's this matter reflect the efficiency and effectiveness of the strategy related learning proces in themsleves organizations. So, I believe that, the manager needs have enough knowledge about how to manage the kind of business if he/she hopes to become the organization's proficient leader, for example, one supermarket business CEO ought own part supermarket operation experience, when he/she has practised supermarket operation experience to know how to manager teams cooperation efficiently, e.g. cashiers, food promoters, food warehouse delivers, grocery shelf putters, fresh fish and fruit pick up keepers, family daily e.g. tooth paste, bath daily products, washing cloth products shelf putters staffs. Then, the supermarket store manager ought have excellent managing ability to manage the supermarket different sale teams to cooperate efficiently. So, owing the kind business managing experience to the manager will be one main factor to influence the business to grow or expand more successfully. Thus, how management develops strategies to guide how an organization conducts its business and how it will achieve its target objectives . The manager himself/herself managing ability and the organization's target objectives can be achieved, they will have close relationship . It is management's responsibility to adjust negative conditions by undertaking strategies defense and managerial approaches that can overcome adversity. However, the essence of the good strategy-making is to build a positive strong and flexible enough to provide successful performance despite unforeseeable and unexpected external factors.

Thus, the five tasks of strategic management may include as below: First step, developing a vision and a mission. It means that any firm ask is " What is our business and what will it be ? What is our business and what will it be ? " Managers need to develop the next five to ten years a clear mission to his organization needs to achieve. A clear mission can establish the organization's future effects and outlines " Who we are, What we need to do and where we are going ? "

Next step. setting objectives, or mission statements can achieve performance targets more easily . Objectives serve as for tracking an organization's performance and progress . A desired performance can pushes an organization to be more incentive, how to improve its financial performance, and its business position. Objectives may have short, middle and long time. Objectives may have two kinds. One is financial objectives, e.g. measures as earning's growth, return on investment and cash flow. The another is strategic objectives, it provides consistent direction in strengthening a company's overall business positon. They relate more directly to a company's overall competitive situation, such as growing faster than the industry's average and making gains in market share.

Then, crafting a strategy step, it is a SWOT analysis to find how to achieve organizational mission. Thus, strategy will be the most important part in order to let the organization to achieve its short, middle and long objectives more easily. For motor industry example, global competitor is competitive environment to motor manufacture industry, if the motor firm can not innovate its any kinds of motors, then it can not attract car buyers to choose its cars to drive. So, in vehicle manufacturing strategy aspect, if the vehicle firm hopes to raise its any kinds of car sale number. How to innovate to manufacturer " new design cars" which may be one important factor to influence any one motor firm sale growth in success. Then, car industry strategy ought concentrate on how to improve the car design to be more attractive. It is " the growth of motor design techniques concep strategy to any nowadays car manufacturers ". It seems that is SWOT analysis to car industry internal strengths and weaknesses analysis have more influential to compare external environment opportunities and threats to any one car manufacturer seller ought not only consider how to train car salespeople sale skill. They ought consider how to provide the useful opinions from car customers' design feeling to car manufacturers, in order to assist them to attempt to design any the most attractive car design to satisfy car buyers' needs in this global car competitive market. So, car design will be one important factor to influence car sale growth. Strategy ought focus on " how to innovate car design" to satisfy car buyers' car design pursue.

On conclusion, any kinds of businesses must have themselves characteristics or features. So , management ought need to consider how themselves business features or characteristics to decide the most reasonable ot the most right strategy implementation in order to achieve their objectives or missions more easily. So, lacking any strategic organizations ought be difficulty to achieve their missions or objectives to compare owning any strategic organizations in nowadays business environment.

- What does business development strategy ?

An effecting business development strategy ought have these five steps: The first step is market analysis. Who are your clients , knowledge of your market? Second step is how to adopt for each penetration, your business needs to learn how to adopt for each group of clients, your first need to review your own capacbility. It is important that you are realistic and honest with yourselves over where clients truly sit, learn how to classify your clients into similar groups relative is the scale of the opportunity. Third step learns how to review your performance , market matrix to plot your results to help you determine your market penerstion. In addition, it will help you then discuss and consider various strategies for growth. By potting your clients you will get a sense of where your strengths and weaknesses are against the opportunity that total market offer.Fourth step learns how to consider alternative growth strategies on the market matrix. The final step , you need to consider these questions in order to decide whic is the most effective strategy for your business. For example, which model is the most ( least effective? Why? which model work best for line managers, HR are finance, why? How might we most effectively progress from one model to the most reasonable questions? ) Then, you will need to decide how to launch new services, new products, opening new markets, how accessing new geographic territories.

- What is business model?

It is logic and provides date and other service evidences that demonstrates how a business creates and delivers values to customer. It also help how to predict revenues, costs, and profit with the business enterprise delivering that value. How does on build a competitive advantages and a super normal profit ? How the enterprise creates and delivers value to customer, and receive payments to profit easily .

In essence, a business model is a conceptual, rather than financial model of a business. An effective business model may help you to decide how to create value for customers, receive payment to profit more easily. For example, driving factors include knowledge economy, the growth of the internet and ecommerce, the outsourcing and offshoring of many busness activities, and restructuring of the financial services industry, i.e. the enterprise simply need to learn packed its technology and intellectural property into a product which it sold, either as a discrect item or as a bundled package.

The existence of electronic computers that allow low cost financial statement modeling has facilitates of assumptions about future revenues and costs. Also, the concept of a business model has no established theoetical in economics or in business studies. Economic theory assumes that trades take place around tangible products : intangibles are the best. For example, inventions are often assumed to create value naturalty and enjoying protection of patients, firms can capture value by selling patients to market, i.e. the publisher sells the another's books, the books can help it to earn high level of royalty income. In economic theory explains the publishers can create intengible value, e.g. royalty as well as tangible value, e.g. selling books.

However, business mides are necessary features of market economies, it is consumer choice, transaction cost, amongst consumers and producers and competition. It meets invention and consumer wants of new product value need and the opportunity to satisfy their needs. So, good designs are likely to be highly siutational, and the design process is likely to involve processes. New business models can both faciliate and represent innovation. For example, in te sport apparel business, sponsorship is a key component of today's business models, Nike, Reebook, Adidas and other sponsor football and rugby clubs and teams as well as royalties from sale sport related products, e.g. sport shoe, spot cloth. Moreover, business models must be over times as changing markets , technologies and legal structures to adopt the kind of business market change.

A business model achieve the logic the useful and reasonable data and evidence thst support a value decision for the customer. In practice, successful business models very often become to some degree, "shared" by multiple competitors in possible . Strategy analysis is this an essential step in designing a competitive business model, i.e. low cost strategy for newspaper advertising ( including classifieds) helps cost of generative content is easy to replicate and of many different geographically separate newspaper market in the world. So, when a country's newspaper publisher may have a differentiated and hard to initate low cost advertising strategy, but it can achieve the same time effective and efficient. Its business model will be successful in newspaper publishing industry. Hence, it seems that business model will be any businesses' essential part in their growth strategies. If the business has none a successful business model, it will not have successful growth strategy consequently.

Growth strategy is different to business development strategy, why ? Growth strategy will mark afresh start, by having all economic actors in the private sector activity and dynamically undertake efforts to promote growth with a determination to take on challenges, when the business feels that it is the right time to grow its business. Otherwise, business development strategy is not the businessmen's feeling whether it is the right time to develop its business . It is essential part to any business expects to start.

- What does business climate development strategy ?

What are the different between business growth and business development and business climate development strategy ? In fact, business growth strategy refers any businesses start up in beginning from earlier stage to nature stage of life cycle. Otherwise , business development strategy must not start up from beginning. It is common on the middle stage, the business hopes to develop its market share or new market to be more. So, it needs to find whether what its SWOT in order to develop its new niche market more successfully.

Hence, it brings this question? Business climate development strategy is on the beginning or middle or mature stage in life cycle? I shall explain as below:

A business climate development strategy means that it is one targeted policy tools appear to favour medium-sized , well established industrial enterprises over younger, small enterprises with high-growth potential operating in the services. Hence, any governments may attempt to follow the business environment to implement any methods to help small size businesses to grow up easily in the beginning stage. In general, implement to business elimate development strategy challenges may include: Lacking of coordination means that there is a disconnect between business and innovation support policies on one hand of investment localization on the other. However, to solve this challenge, governments may encourage these organizations to participate , such as technical centres, laboratories and training facilities can act as catalysts for industry, sector aggregation and support the establishment and specialized investment zones. Hence, the difference between business climate development strategy and the other both strategies. Business climate development strategy is any countries' governments attempt to follow the business environment at the moment to find the most effective methods to help any small size businesses to grow up more easily in the beginning stage.

How to implement business climate development strategy more successful? The key recommendations may include: To emergy from the workshop was further strengthened in an effort to close the policy gap and create synergies between programmes. Building on the experience of regional investment centres, the context points would identify an small middle size's (SMS) organization, and help enterpreneurs to establish a network of SMS bisiness centres across the country. So, they could not as single -window contact points, storing and channelling information abour all the government's SMS business programmes. However, a successful business climate development strategy should build on the analyzed risks and rewards of informal business operations and aim at modifying the behavior of economic agents ( enterprises, employees and customers) through a combination of incentives and penalties.

Any governments may attempt to develop a number of measures to promote and suport innovation and upgrade technology in the private enterprise sector. In order to enhance business climate development strategy to implement in success. They may include: establish a system of communication and cooperation between the institutions and private sector organizations operating in the area of technological upgrading, innovation, financial, technical standards, public education and training . It would be useful to conduct an evaluation of the enterprise Europe network's impact in order to learn from the lessons of the country's more successful sector-specific centres. It is the national strategy for innovation, technology upgrading and investment encouragement. Finally, a critical element in an effective innovation strategy is the establishment of links between support services and programmes and access to funding to support any business founder hopes to develop himself business in success in order to adopt business environment climate change more easily.

However, in general, small or medium size business will encounter these challenges when they hope to adopt the business environment climate change to grow their businesses more easily. Their challenges may include: The lack of economies of scale, which limits their ability to invest in fixed capital and technological development, proportionally higher costs,, which increases the impact of the legislative and regulatory framework, information lacking which limit access to external financing, limited resources for internal training and human capital developments. In general, any governments need to help the new business to solve these challenges in order to develop business climate development strategy more easily. They may include: innovation technology centres and networks as well as financial support for innovative SMES. Hence, business climate connection with larger foreign enterprises through active government support, the policy objective is to enhance SME access to international markets, skills development, finance and technology to any businesses' beginning stage in order they can grow up their businesses to nature stage in their business life cycle successfully.

Hence, whether which firms hace real need to get government's business climate development strategy assistance. I believe that the government needs to assume the firm has these challenges in order to ensure that the firm can achieve the requirement to get this business climate development strategy assistance. They are needed to assume on basic these factors: A company must grow and pass through all stages of development or die in attempt, second the models fail to capture the important early stages in a company's origin and growth. Third, instead of annual sales , although some mention number of employees whether it is more or less factor, government can not ignore other factors to decide whether the firm can be accepted to implement climate business development strategy assistance, such as value added, number of locations, complexity of product line and ratio of change in products or production technology etc. factors to decide whether the firm is suitable to be accepted to get business climate development strategy assistance from the government in order to avoid waste time and resource and money to desing any kind of business climate development strategy to assist the firm to develop in the beginning.

- How to implement successful organizational downsizing strategy?

What are the effects of downsizing on organizational performance? What is the most right time to downsizing to the organization ? When one organization has grown to the bigger size , e.g. more revenues, this year than last, a larger workforce, greatest market share, downsizing strategy ? If an organization did not grow, it was viewed as stagnating and upproductive in the non-growth life cycles stage, it implements downsizing strategy to influence its performance to be worse.

Organizational downsizing strategy is one part of the management of an organization and designed to improve organizational efficiency, productivity and/or competitiveness. Downsizing means to reduce organizational size, e.g. staffs number reduces expenditure reduces, cost reduces . Downsizing is an intentional set of activities, it differentiates from loss of market share, loss of revenues or unwritting loss of human resources organizational decline. Also, downsizing usually reductions in personel, such as transfers outplacement, retirement incentives reduction, byout packages, layoffers. This reductions in personnel may occur in one part of an organization, but not in other parts, e.g. in the production function, or not in the engineering function. Finally, downsizing may effect work processes, e.g. fewer employees are left to do the same amount of work, and this has an impact on what work gets done and how it gets done. However, instead of downsizing of reduction employees number aspect, it may also occur on other accepts, such as selling off, transferring out, merging businesses or altering the industry structure. It aims to improve organizational performance. Labeled workforce reduction strategies, focused mainly on eliminating headcount or reducing the number of employees in the workforce. It aims to early retirements, transfers and outplacement, by-out packages. This kind downsizing strategy whether it can bring performance improving benefit to organization or not in long term? Less employees work whether it will still improve performance, although the organization can reduce salary expenditure . Otherwise, if the organization does not reduce staffs number, it chooses to workforce reduction, work redesign and systemic strategies , whether it will be better than staffs number reduction strategy ?

What are critical success factors influence any organizations' strategic downsizing success implement ? Addresses the rationale utilized by firms to downsize, the expected outcomes in terms of economic and human consequences, and specific strategy. Also , downsizing tactics, human resources as assets to cost planning, participation, leadership, communications and support to victims . survivors are examined to any attempt implementing downsizing organizations.

In past organizations, when many blue-collor workers are also to trade off wage freezes for jobs security. White-dollars workers in the lower ranks of white-collar workers are often dismissed by downsizing, due to firms are increasingly forced to cut costs, restructure, and reduce their labor force. Instead of western countries firms are popular to accept downsizing . Downsizing has even become common in industrialized countries, such as Japan and Sweden, restructing in the 1990s led to employment reductions in industry and thus, increases in the levels of unemployment. Hence, downsizing may cause low ranks of white-collar workers feel job security

lose in any time when they are working in any organizations, because white-collar workers are different to blue-collar workers have unions protection.
However, there are three perspectives from when downsizing can be reviewed : The industry level, the organization level and the individual level in terms of industry or global perspective, it may include , mergers, acquisitions, joint ventures, the organizational and strategy level may include how to implement downsizing and the expected bebefits of downsizing on the firm's performance, efficiency , and at the individual psychological level, it includes employee himself/herself stress, negative emotion feeling , due to he/she is dismissed. Hence, any organizations need to considerate how downsizing brings negative emotion to influence every dismissed employees. Because , their leave which will influence the continue working employee's emotion feel fear to be dismissed in next. If the present employees often feel stress to work, then their performance and efficiency will be influenced to worse. So, any organizations can not neglect to care the current working employees individual emotin in order to avoid low efficiency and poor performance to their organizations. Becaus every employee will have possible to be unreasonable dismiss, due to downsizing organizational influence.
On possible reason for this occurrence, is that firms poorly planned or carried out earlier downsizing projects and hence must remedy past facilities. So, one planned downsizing strategy will avoid negative emotion to influence current employees' works. But, factory workers will have possible to encounter dismiss , due to technological improvements, e.g. robotics can reduce to have additional workers rather than replacing the existing employees. So, when the factory begins to apply robotics , then employees number will be reduced. It is technological manufactuer causes downsizing to factory workers reason. It is due to raise productive efficiency factor , more than reducing cost reason to cause downsizing need to any organizations.
The term downsizing was first used reforcing to strategies to reduce personnal. However, it was become more and more relevant , its scope has been expanded and noe refers to a wide range of management measures towards better adopting on organizations to its environment ( Gandolfi & Hanson, 2011).
reference
Gandolfi , F. & Hanson, M. (2011). Causes and consequences of downsizing : towards an integrative framwork, Journal of

management & organization , 17(4), 498-521.

In general, it is needed to implement strategies, due to the organization feels that without achieving the required organizational changes, this failing toobtain the desired results ( Magan & Cespeses, 2012).

The downsizing methods may include: retrenchment specialized production, concentrating activities until economies of scale have been achieved. Downscaling strategy is toward again reducing in a smaller differentiation of activities in the value chain , it aims to keep the organization to reduce complexity in the organization. For some organizations had begun to implement robotic factory, because they expect that manufacturing robotics can help they to specialize production, raise productive efficiency. Hence, they only concentrate on keeping the proficient workers, they can cooperate to robotics to work in order to raise more products number efficietntly every day. So, the low skillful workers will be dismissed and they will re-employ the owning control manuacturing robotics skillful new workers to replace them. So, future manufacturing robotic manufacture plants causes downsize, it will be one good example for specialized production, concentating activities until economies of sale reasons to cause downsizing factory workers need to the owning manufacture robotics plant organizations. So, downsizing has an impact on raising productivities on specialized production and concentrating activities until economies of scale aim more than reducing cost to the owning manufacturing robotic factories organizations.

Thus, downsizing activities aim to improve organizational efficiency, productivity and/or competitiveness that affect the size of the firm's workforce, costs and the work processes. Downsizing may include: building-down , de-hiring, de-recruitment, reduction in force, re-sizing and right -sizing. So, in macroeconomic factors view, global competiton , technological innovations ,a change in business strategy retains competitive advantages may cause why some organizations decide to implement downsizing strategy.

However, one successful downsizing strategy implements to any organizations, organizations can not only consider themselves benefits, they also need to consider the psychological contract between employer and employee as new mutual expectations on workplace environment. Frequently described as re-organization, restructing, downsizing or real sizing, the human resource effects of these changes have often been very destructive to individual lives, employment relationships and organizational efficiency. If mployees recognized that their company was creative and consistent action to pressure their employment ( security, trust could be reestablished and the success of the adoptive strategies. They can feel that their organizations decide to achieve the downsizing strategy is very reasonable more than unreasonable strategy in the right time. For example, when the organization decides to implement downsizing srategy before, they may enquire to their staffs opinions and acknowledge what their emotions, e.g. information on when change provided, staff views on the change are sought and are acted upon, staff have the opportunity to voice disagreement, support from manager during the change, to let they feel that change process seen as fair and equitable to let staff feel job security during the change process, and staff are trained to meet new job roles. So, all these factors may influence present employees have confidence to continue to work in your organizations after downsizing strategy is implemented. So, any organizations can not neglect to consider their present employees' feeling or emotion in order to avoid many staffs decide to leave their organizations after downsizing strategy in implemenation later.

reference
Magan , A. & Cespeses, J. (2012). Why are Spanish companies implementing downsizing. Review of business 32(2), 5-22.

● Business growth strategy

What factors cam affect the performance and growth to small businesses? Why and how obstacles are problematic for growth? How these differ between micro, small and medium sized businesses? How the obstacles are shaped?

Any businessmen had a substative growth ambition, but it can not represent that growth ambitin must sicceed to grow up their businesses. However, they must need to solve challenges when they expect grow their businesses successfully. The unpredicted external environment , include market changing and the vision of the owner and their attitudes towards growth will influence whether their businesses can grow up in success.

Hence, if the new business can keep negative growth, it ought may suceed. Some strategies , business owners need to consider that these factors will obstacle to their growth, such as during a recession, their businesses ought be difficult to growth, strategic planning is only useful when the business has a definit objective in mind, investment in research and development is too risky, expensive and difficult for a small business, there is no way,we can improve cashflow situation, factoring is only useful, if you ave in trouble, employees do not want formal, pay-related incentives and they are no use in helping business grow, we do not need to engage the staff in a structured, involving way, we can not get recruits to fit our needs, our business don't need to restructure our management as our business grow.

● How whether what obstacles can affect small business growth?

I assume small businesses have general staffs number with 50 or less than 50 staffs . Also, growth ambition was higher among younger business owners. The business owner personal poor time management factor may be one obstacles, for example, a lack of management time was rated to be the most difficult obstacle for potential exporters, which is something of an obstacles for the significant exporters, little knowledge of how to export and difficulty in finding customers also attract higher ratings from potential exporters, e.g. the fear of payment problems, the cost of exporting and being too small to export are rated as being less significant obstacles by potential exporters and their perceptions are not to distant from the significant exporters. So, lack of management time and little knowledge of how to export may be the business ower's significant obstacles.

However, many small businesses are facing values number reducing challenges. How adoption to improve sale performance? Sale improvement strategy may include: appreciated new customers, more advertising, devised a new marketing strategy, dedicated sales/ marketing manager, undertaken training in marketing sales.

Overall, making this transition from being a micro business to a small business clearly requires a greater confidence in dealing with such matters, though, undertaking activity more frequently or simply the earger scale of the business necessitating increased familiarity and competence. Also, employing a professional manager can be seen as generally enabling a company to improve.

The aim of focus groups was to explore a company to improve owners' views on growth, including how they conceptialize growth, perceived barriers,the consequences of growth and personal cirsumstances and evidence of mindsets among owners which may restrict their potential business growth. In general, family owning-business strategies may include: maintain quality and higher prices, rather than lower prices raising the value added of products and shifting into a less marketplace and the emphasis towards areas where they sold direct to end clients, rather than acting as subsontractors, whose margins were being squeezed, up-selling in terms of volume or value to existing customers , e.g. a catering establishment noted then they tried to encourage customers to return, or an accountancy practice and a range of extra services.

Many owners did also acknowledge that the would likely more if they were more actively intending to grow business or if they saw evidence of potentially opportunities. Several those lacking a current plan were aware of a growing need to develop both a more strategies outlook and more formal systems, because of a general neglect of strategic thought, with a number noting that years of unplanned growth has left them realizing that the development of the busines, needed to catch up with the situation that they had found themselves in.

- What can impact on growth strategies on business?

Overall, making this transition from being a micro business to a small business clearly requires a greater confidence in dealing with such matters, through undertaking activity more frequently or simply the earger scale of the business necessitating measured familiarity and competence. Also, employing a professional manager can be seens as generally enabling a company to improve.

The aim of the focus groups was to explore in depth business owners' views on growth, including how they conceptualize growth, perceived barriers, the consequences of growth and personal circumstances and evidence of mindsets among owners which may restrict their potential business growth. In general, family ownin, business strategies may include: maintain quality and higher prices, rather than lower pruces raising the value added of products and shifting into a less marketplace and the emphasis towards areas where they sold direct to end clients, rather than acting as subcontractors, whose margins were bring squeezed, up-selling in terms of volume or value to existing customers , e.g. a catering establishment noted that they tried to encourage customers to return, or an accountancy practice and a range of extra services.

Manyowners did also acknowledge that they would likely plan more if they were more actively intending to grow business, or if they saw evidence of potentially opportunites. Several of those lacking a current plan were aware of a growing need to develop both a more strategic outlook and more formal systems, because of a general neglect of strategic thought, with a number noting that years of unplanned growth had left than realiaing that the development of the business needed to catch up with the situation that they had found themselves in.

- What can impact on growth strategies on business ?

Growth is important and key on survival of any business profit venture. Formulating and implementing effective growth strategies may enhance business pforit to any dynamic organization . Developing growth strategies to attract human resources, including increase in the sales volume per annum, an increase in the production capacity, increase in employment, increase in production volume and increase in the all of material, increase energy and power, these factors may influence the business's strategy is implemented effectively in order to achieve growth aim.

Growth strategies that a business enterprise may wish to adopt include: understanding customer expectation, service, positioning, market segementation, setting measuring market standards, relationship marketing, human resource strategy and successful communication strategy these factors may influence business growth success. When one organization ensures that it can achieve growth, it may evaluate to measure its overall performance by these several aspects, they may include sales, assets base, employee retention goodwill and increase business profits that drive investment and economic development. Business growth may introduce new products and services, or adding new features to existing products. Growth could also mean expansion of an organization in order to buy new assets develop new products or service to enhance new investments in the economy. I shall refer some growth strategies as below:

Market penetration strategy focuses on expanding sales of a company's existing products or services in an existing market. It may attract new customer for the products and increase the usage or purchase rate of existing customers , it is often achieved by increasing activities through more intensive distribution and competitive pricing promotion.

Market expansion or market development means to move it into a completely new market. This strategy is about existing product which are offered in a new market when a region business wants to expand, or when new markets are opening up, or new use is found for the existing product.

Product expansion or product development strategy means introducing a new idea into a company's existing market. It offers new products to an existing market. It tried to grow by developing improved products for the present market.

Diversification means companies with sell new products or new market. It is very risky strategy . It needs to research market to determine if consumers in the new market will potentiallu like the new products. Acquisition means the purchase of one company by another company. It may be private or public.

The new growth strategy can be used as an alternative channel. It involves pursuring cutomers in different ways for instance selling a company's products or services online . Through the use of the internet a customer can access products or services of a particular company in a new (alternative). It goes beyond envisioning a long-term success. It has to be follow these steps: establishing a value for the company, identifying an ideal customer , who is loyal to the company, defining a company's key indicators, verifying revenue streams for cost reduction, seeking competition in the external environment, focusing on company's strength ( internal), investing in talents ( effective human resources who are creative and innovation). So, managers must achieve on growth strategy to enable stakeholders not only to plan, but also to track organic growth in their revenue and allow effective and efficient allocation of resources toward a more centered effort to adapt to frequent changes in the company and the industry occasioned by technology and the differences in competition.

Hence, of growth strategies are effectively formulated and implemented according to indicators and plan, it will lead to increase a profit in that organization . Growth strategies are often called the master business strategies, they provide the basic direction for strategies action. They are the coodinated and efforts indirected towards achieving long term business objectives and profit. Growth strategies have played central roles in the expansion and profit. They have enabled organizations to increase market shares, develop new markets, and develop new products and services, so business profit will continue to increase economic development.

- Why and how can organizational life cycle models influence organizational performance?

What does organizational life cycle mean? Must any organizations have life cycle? What do the influences when the organization reachs the organizational life cycle stage? Can the organization implement any useful strategy , if had ability to known whether what stage is its organizational life cycle? I shall explain as below:

In general, organizational life cycle has three stages: Birth, young, and maturity or decline. The related goals of profit, growth and survival seem to have overall goal structures of most organizations. IN general, most organizations will experience all three stages. However, not all organizations pass through all three stages. In fact, only about one-half of all new busness, organizations survive longer than one and half years. Relatively few for profit or not -for-profit organizations survive long time to experience all three stages. I assume that profits growth is one main factor to influence any organizations whether it can experience long whole three stages in their organizational life cycle.

What is the three stages chacracteristics of organizational life cycle? In birth stage, a merger or a point venture may occasionally lead to the creation of a new organization. A organization may be either a single person expands or an entrepreneur cooperates people to help promote a new idea, product or service. The motive in both cases is usually the desire for profit. In youth stage, when professional management is taken over by a family with a controlling interest, the organization's primary goal often changing from profit to growth. The new management team wants to demonstrate its competence and growth is the most obvious aim. For example, a manager of a large organization must consider how much company's return an investment in the organization's growth stage in this new growth stage. It has these characteristics: goals become less specific, less measurable, increasing emphasis on marketing, hoping for the increases sales that will justify the expansion of plant anf acquisition of new, more effecticient tools and equipment. Finally in the maturity / decline stage, as an organization matures and starts to decline, a desire to survive which will be the organization's goal in this stage. Why does organization may experience this stage, the organization can evaluate whether it is experiencing this stage, depends on these factors, e.g. when organization increases large , its technology is complex, its structure is bureaucratic, it is financially oriented, it is greatly affected by market and social forces and it is so complex when it grows up its organization, it will increases more new departments and it will employ many extra staffs and it will create many new positions. Hence, it explains why the organization can survive long time, and it can experience all three stages, it must be more succefful to compare the another organization can not experience all three stages , because it is common that when the organization can experience all three stages. It must survive long time. Also, it means that it can earn profit growth . Otherwise, when the organization can only experience birth stage or youth stage , then it can not survive long time and without profit growth in possible.

Hence, when one organization can experience all three stages. It may be one successful profit growth organization, e.g. although one sale trade earn less profit, and its organization size is small, but the jobb trader's business can survive a long time. So, he/she sole trading organization may experience birth, young, and mature or decline stages. So, organizational life cycle model can be applied to large or middle or small size organization, even sale trader, partnership organization to help them to evaluate whether their businesses are experiencing which stage in order to implement the most suitable or reasonable strategies to help them to solve present challenges more easily.

● What is the essential elements of life cycle model to assist business development ?

Although, when one organization feels it encoounters the decline stage, it means that its organization has possible that it can not continue survive. But if it has good strategy to help itself to solve present challenges. It has chance to renew or continue to develop its business functions to be better. Then, it has chance to continue survive. Usually, when the business is experiencing decline stage, it ought decide to change its business direction in order to continue survue . For example, raising its capabilities of organizational learning and innovations, creating new profitable and vision into the renew survival stage, and increasing its competitiveness in cost. However, the decline stage is characteristics by deterriorating profits and a loss of market share. The renewing firms have a rebuild their learning and innovative capabilities and shape a new profit direction for business. The contribution links interactions of development more effective business functions to provide a tool to help the experiencing decline stage organizations to learn how to implement new strategies to solve their present challenges in order to continue survive.

Hence, what is the essential elements to help the experiencing decline stage organizations to have possible to continut survive. I shall explain as below: In old economic society, manufacturing firms whose main driver to standardize production, products and busines processes. By constrast, the new economic society, we are experiencing information business, utilize information to differentiate, personalize and dispatch over networks at an rapid speed, small as e-commerce. It is obvious tht old economy's traditional shop business model is not popular to be accepted by consumers. Consumer shopping behaviors have been changed to choose online shopping to replace visiting shops shopping behavior. So, it seems that why some businesses will experience decline stage within one year. It is possible that their traditional business visiting step shopping method is not popular to be accept to themselves businesses, it is right time.

They need to design website store to let customers can choose online shopping when they visit themselves website stores from internet. So, e-commerce can influence some businesses to experience the decline stage in short time rapidly. It may be one factor to influence any organizational life cycle stge to be shorten in short time. It is one technological innovation element to shorten any organization's life cycle in short time. So, any businessmen ought not neglect technological innovation new influence their businesses development as well as they need to continue pursue their new sale method direction, e.g. payment by smartphone shopping method, electronic commerce payment transaction payment method, in order to keep high technological or payment channel to attract customers.

The another element is how to deliver customer focused to feel differentiation, to fight for survival in the global market, a company needs to implement innovation function to cope effectively with the changes in the customers' needs. So, it is innovation element to the experiencing decline stage organization to help it to attempt to solve challenges in order to continue survive in possible . Innovation may include service, e.g. sale service, client service, delivery service etc. as well as product innovation ,e g. design change to the cup, mobile technological improvement, car style, design, engine, chargeable battery charge etc. or individual innovation, e.g. the fundamental assumption of operate culture changes, mindset of the top manger, CEO midset change and questioned by the capability of execution of the operations function to himself organization. How to innovate organizational learning, whether and what experience or knowledge applied in the operations function can be executed for the next innovation in order to renew the experiencing decline stage organization strategy to continue survive. So, innoviation is also one element to influence organization's survival.

- What can learn from the organizational life cycle theory?

The next element is whether organization can continue keep on learning element. In fact, there are many different factors to influence whether our organizational survival. They may include organizational internal factors as well as outside factors. In general organizations can control themselves internal to be better, but they can not control outside environment, because they can not predict when environments, e.g. economic environment, customer shopping desires, when new competitors enter market. According to organizational life cycle theory, during the firm's growth from inception to high growth, to maturity firm characteristics differ and the internal resources and capabilities of the firm develop.

Organizations encounter an unpredictable business environment which is constantly pressured by the changing effects of globalization , competition and technological advancement within the context of the knowledge economy ( Thoumrungroje & Tansuhaj, 2007).

reference

Thoumrungroje, A. & Tansuhaj, P. (2007). Globalization effects and firm perferences. Jounral of international business research, 6 (2),43-58.

During the first stage, any organization will up in a new business environment with much adaptation and try to develop a niche through, learning and innovative practices. Given the success of that survival, the organization becomes aggressive in the second stage in how to managing internal resources, effectiveness and efficiency, learning workflows, and corporate structure to accommodate the increased complexity of operations, policies are needed to implement in second stage. The third stage, business efficiency is the core, and the organization keeps resolving workplace problems and defining clear objectives of what to achieve short and long term in the business. In this stage, revenue is the key pursue aim or objective. The final stage, as a nature stge, the organization tends to maintain the business stability and spend time focusing on the status of how organizational structure, management departments cooperation strategy implementation and organizational culture in order to help the organization itself and the CEO leader himself/herself how to manage her/his organization successfully . So, whether the organization can continue keep on learning , it may be one important element to influence the organization to develop in business.

- How to develop organizations in growth stage?

Theoretical development of the organization life cycle has description of distinct stages of organization growth, Little attention to the dynamics of organization growth, such as how to grow the organization? Why can the organization grow rapidly ? I believe any organizations expect that they can grow rapidly, but the organizations expect that they can grow rapidly, but the question concens: What factors influence the organization can not grow rapidly, e.g. lacking proficient staffs, lacking high technological manufacture, lacking creating mindset or innovation, lacking suitable strategy implementation, strong new competitors enter, customers taste change etc. different organizational internal and external environment etc. factors. So, any organizations expect to grow rapidly, they need to solve the challenges to threaten their grow. For example, one mobile manufacturer only concentrates on manufacturing new technological smart phones products . So, at this stge, it ought pursue a niche strategy, presenting a very narrow smart phone product time, often a single smart phone product to a single smart phone user market. The new different design and function of smart phone products venture generally undertakes major and frequent smart phone product innovation. Major investments are needed to make in smart phone products development, robotic plant and manufacture robotic equipment is needed. So, this smart phone product manufacture firm expects to grow its smart phone share market rapidly. It must often need to innovate itself manufacturing technology , e.g. manufacturing robotics as well as designers need have good creative mindset to attempt to design any kinds of smart phones and change kind functions and smart phone design in ordeer to satisfy smart phone users' needs. When , it often have different kinds of new smart phone products design. I believe that it can grow itself smart phone productive speed rapidly, when it can attract many smart phone users to choose its any kinds of smart phone products to buy to use in preference . Hence, this smart phone manufacturing firm needs have good design mindset to attract smart phone consumers‘ attention if it expects to reach the growth stage in short time. If it feels that it has not increase smart phone customer number significant in this time, it may believe that its busines can not reach growth stage in the moment. Hence, the life cycle theory offers expected obstacles for each stage, which can help the firms to solve the problems and help them to attempt to find any useful strategies accordinglyly.

Hence, organizational life cycle can help any organizations to revise whether what obstacles can influence or threaten the organization itself can not grow easily, due to consumers demand have become more complex, as well as arket trends are harder to predict and competition is severe than ever, in order to survive companies, shoulf need to learn how to reach growth stage rapidly in order to raise its competitive ability to reach mature stage rapidly in short time. Becuase of the organization can reach mature stage from birth to young stage in short time rapidly. Then , it will have enough ability to avoid to reach decline stage rapidly. If it expects to continue survive or it does not need to review its organizational strategy ocnsequently. Because different stage, it will have different kinds of challenges to the organization will encounter, e.g. in the birth stage , challenges may include lacking cash flow, less customer number, without building attractive or famous product brand or image, in the young stage challenges, may include strategy is not suitable to implement effectively, customer growth speed is slow, product development or promotion challenges when the organization reachs mature stage, its challenges may include clients number begins decrease or loss old clients, product sale number begins reduction from the top level, customers feel its products are not attractive and they begin to choose to buy other similar feature of products to replace its products in market. Hence, when the organization can know whether it reachs which stage in its organizational life cycle model. Then, it may attempt to find the most suitable or the most reasonable strategy to implement in order to keep its long survival to stay on the mature stage more easily.

Learning organizational life cycle stage strategies advantages

Any organizations may experience organizational life cycle stages from birth stage to growth stage to maturity , then it may also experience decline and/or regrow stages. But this two stages, they are not all organizations must may attempt to experience. It depends on whether economic environment how changes, organizational itself SWOT strengths and weaknesses etc. unpredicted factors to influence that when the organization will experience decline life cycle stage. It means that if the organization has very poor performance, then the organization has possible to experience decline life cycle stage in short time or long time. Otherwise, if the organizationhas very good performance, it ought not experience decline life cycle stage in short time, when it can reach mature stage in its the topest level. Even, when the organization has poor performance, so it is experiencing decline stage, but if it may implement effective strategies to help itself organization to develop . Then, if its strategies are very effective , in consequence, the organization ought may experience regrowing stage to re-experience its mature life cycle stage again. So, it seems that if the organization can have very good performance. Client number can increase significant as well as profit can also growth rapidly. Then, the organization ought may experience long time in mature life cycle stage or it means that it will be difficult to reach decline life cycle stage. Unless, some sudden inpredicted economic environment, or strong competitors etc. influence its performance, then they will have chance to cause it experiences to decline life cycle stage from mature stage suddenly. Hence, all organizations must need to experience birht life cycle stage in beginning to this stage.

However, when the business founder starts to set up his/her business. He/she needs time to deal any difficulties,e.g. how to advertise his/her products to let customers have much knowledge, promote them to sell to market, how to implement strategies to solve organizational challenges. So, in birth stage, any organizations ought feel difficult to improve its whole performance or evaluate whether its future performance can improve to be better or can not improve or worse. Then, when the organization operates one period, it ought experience to growth stage, but it still depends on external factors to influence whether when it may experience growth stage, the factors may include: Whether strategies can be effective, economic environment is good or bad, customers purchase desire level is high or loe, cost expenditure is high or low etc. difficult factor.

So, before any organizatons may experience growth stage, there are many different complex factors to influence whether they can succeed to experience this stage easily. If the organization can not implement any effective strategies to solve its customers purchase emotion challenges, then its business is difficult to continue grow, also it means that the organization can not growor expand its business easily. Due to it can not continue to develop its business easily. It must not reach mature life cycle stage easily. Thus, any organizations can reach mature life cycle stage. It represents that its business has good strategies to solve any challenges in order to its products can attract customers to choose to buy or it can provide good service performance to satisfy clients needs to compare irs competitors in this market successfully.

In fact, it is not all organizations can attempt to experience the mature life cycle stage. This stage is any organization individual the topest stage. In this stage, the organization may have many clients increasing number significantly every year, its market can continue expand, profit can continue increases . All is the best to any organizations, if it can reaches this stage . All many organizations may only experience birth stage or growing stage . They reach this either birth or growth stage, then they have none good strategies to compete their clients number can not increase, but only decreases, profit reduces , even loss. They can not know how to change strategied to improve their performance or competitive effort to fight this competitors. Then, their businesses can not continue grow or expand. So, they have more chance to experience decline stage after either birth or growth stage only. They can not reach mature life cycle stage to attempt the topest level in whole business ( organizational) life cycle stage or process. Thus, it brings these questions: Why do organizations need to learn organizational life cycle stages? What advantages to bring if they can attempt to learn how to reach growth or mature life cycle stages easily? I shall explain as below:

● Why do organizations need to spend time to learn how may experience different business life cycle stages?

The business life cycle is the progression of a business in phases over time and is most commonly divided into five stages: Launch or birth, growth, maturity and decline or regrow. Each company begins its operations as a business and usually by launching new products or services. Because any organizations will encounter challenges in every stages . If they know what factos may help them to enter another new stage of business life cycle or what challenges may threaten them can not enter another new business life cycle stage easily. Because businessman need to learn and how adjust their business model to ensure profitability. That is why an awareness of what stage of the business life cycle , you are currently it can be helpful. Hence, how to maximize each stage of the business life cycle, the businessmen might still need to learn how to work in order to improve performance when the businessmen are experiencing any one life cycle stage. Moreover, each business life cycle stage comes still need to learn how to turn a profit and the first outlines of their governance and compliance and this is one big reason why most businesses fail at this stage.

So, I assume that business life cycle stage is similar to school examination, the student needs to spend time to learn in the birth learning stage, then he needs to test in the growth learning stage, next is examination in the mature learning stage, if the student fails, t is decline learning stage to the school. It may be due to the teachers can not teach students to learn easily. So, these are many students fail in tests or examinations. So, if the school teachers can improve teaching methods to let many students may earn high grades in tests or examinations. Then, the school may experience growth, even mature teaching life cycle stage in short time rapidly . Hence, teaching quality can improve or not , it will influence any school organizations ought feel to schools to learn how to improve teaching methods or strategies in order to let students can experience the maturity learning stage or it can also experience the maturity teaching stage. It means that it ought learn how to improve its teachers teaching service performance to satisfy students learning needs if it hopes to reach maturity learning and teaching life cycle stage in short time for itself school organization benefit.For example, the organization founder may ask himself/herself why he/she wants to start this business, learns how to manage exployees strategies? It is the learning needs in the third stage, such as maturity stage. Otherwise, in the first stage of the business entity birth life cycle is sometimes called the seed stage and a matter of iteraing, testing an learning , and trying again, knowing that the businessman is unlikely to have.

What advantages may bring to the organization if it can attempt to learn how to solve different challenges in different business life cycle stages ? What advantages to the organization, if it can know how to experience every business life cycle stage?

In fact, the business life cycle is the progression of a business in phases over time, and is consumer segments by advertising their comparative advantages and vale. For example, when the business is experiencing growth stage , in the growth phase, the business founder needs to spend time to learn how his company can experience rapid sales growth. This learning may assist his business to develop his business to enter next mature how stage easily , for example, he can learn how the rapid growth stage takes advantage from the proven sales model, e.g. online sale or traditional visiting shop sale model which is more suitable to his business, marketing model and operations model, e.g. how to advertise his product or promote his products can affect more audiences concern this will see the businessmen's jounrey from idea to start up, and if successful, how to keep to stay long time in the mature stage. Rememeber, when having a successful business model behind any businessmen is undoubtedly an advantage, it is not a disadvantage when the founder spends more time to learn hoe to run his business. In fact, he won't waste his time to learn how to improve his business in different business life cycle stages. So, a tactical plan will take any business strengths and reduces to avoid weakness cause to influence its development. So, knowing where you small product is in its product life cycle, it is important to continue to develop your business successfully. SO, any impacts of all life cycle stages, any businesses need to be considered comprehensively , for one new technological product firm example, its new technological product life cycle begins with the introduction or birth stage. The high technological product company must succeed at both developing new product and managing them in the face of changing tastes, competitors' technologies similar change. So, it is what it needs to learn in this stage for this new product technological firm preparing development to next growth stage.

On the conclusion, learning how to achieve in every business life cycle stage, it can bring these benefits to any organizations, such as : they can understand and redefine this role from a more, if the organization ony to learn sale frameworks what it could have picked up. It is not enough, because most organizations will only find that a majority of their total sale number which is to use solely supplier-specific data about the life cycle, but they neglect how to set targets to learn how to improve their sale to be better in the future time, it is one important factor explain why many organizations only reach the growth stage, but they can not experience to next mature stage more easily, due to they do not consider how to implement strategies in order to achieve their next targets. They feel often implment targets which will help them to know whether they need to how to do in order to improve their businesses to satisfy clients needs. As with any effort in your organization, communication plays a critical role, craft machine learning to predict and manage human for remote teams to work through the innovation lifecycle, serve them well. Any organizations need to learn how to satisfy any customer individual purchase jounrey ( called purchase experience) which the customer has with the organization, because when the organization can learn how to satisfy any client individual real need in any life cycle stage. On consequence, its clients number with have possible to influence increase. Thus, any organizations can bot neglect to learn how to satisfy client individual real purchase experience need in any life cycle stages because improvement to salepeople sale performance, they need spend time to learn in every time sale experience . When the organization can build excellent sale teams, then they may help it to build famous loyalty and good client relationship in order to expand its business more easily. Hence, in any businesses' life cycle stages, they must need to spend time to learn how to improve product quality service performance to bring customers' satisfactory emotion in order to expand their business developmenr more easily. So, i recommend that all small organizations expand to large size, they must need time to learn and attempt to find the best methods to solve any difficulties when they are facing in any one business cycle stage, if they want to expand their businesses successfully.

● The relationship between learning change management and rapid reaching mature life cycle

It is one good question: Can the manager or CEO help whole organization to develop rapidly if he/she attempt to learn how to help his/her organization to implement different strategies to solve different challenges in different business life cycle stages? Does it easy to help the organization to grow up when a learning CEO or learning manager accepts to learn anything to compare a non learning manager in different business life cycle stages? Has it relationship between learning or non learning manager and rapid experiencing business life cycle stage and rapid developing business growth? I shall attempt to explain as below:

In fact, it is not essential to any managers or CEOs need to spend time to learn how any why what factors may influence their organizations to grow up to next business life cycle stage, but in comparison one learning how to change organizational life cycle stages manager and non-learning how to change organizational life cycle stages manger. Can learn attitude or strategy to help the manager to develop or expand his organization to next life cycle stage more easily or rapidly? I shall attempt to explain as below:

In fact, any organizations expect to change to next life cycle stage in success , can the manager(s) learn how to implement strategies to achieve to change management to their organizations‘ development in success? How the organizational management learns how to adapt organizational management change, it may be one important factor to influence whether the organization needs to spend how long time to reach growth life cycle stage from birth stage or reach mature life cycle stage from growth stage. So, it seems that how management spends time to learn how to change his/her organization. It will have relationship to the organization needs to spend long time to reach next life cycle stage successfully.

Hence, learning how to train employees in each life cycle stage, it is the important factor to influence any organizations succeed, the employee lifecycle is an ongoing process that starts and ends with competent employees in any managers' organizations. There are nine elements ofa successful change management process, if the organizational management expects whole organization can real reach to next life cycle stage in success. The nine elements of a successful change management process, any management needs to spend time to learn. They may include: readiness assessments, communication planning implementation, sponsor activities and sponsor roadmaps organizing, organizatons need to provide change management training for managers to learn how to achieve effectiveness as well as providing training development and delivery learning methods to them, resistance management learning and learning employee feedback and corrective action. Moreover, managements also need to spend time to learn change management steps in order solve any challenges in order to reach next life cycle stage easily.

The change management learning steps may include: Step 1: Urgency creation , step 2: Building every team serves to every department efficiently, learning how to create avision, how to communication of division, how to remove obstacles, going for quick wins, let the change mature, integrate the change. These elements are incorporated into change management phases process. For example, some elements of communication planning occur early in the lifecyle. At this stage, change management is not fully achieved effectively, so management needs to spend more time to learn how to achieve effective communication planning in order to achieve effective communication planning in order to keep whose organization employees can communicate to work efficiently. Also, it will help client service employees to know how to build good communication management method to deal or answer or satisfy their clients' sale service and improving service performance absolutely.

Because organizations are nor statis, they change , if one organization still stays long time in birth stage, it represents that the organization feels difficulties to continue develop . So, the management needs to find whether what challenges threaten its organization can not reach growth stage more easily. One failure changing management organization, it has these characteristics: failure to change, inexperienced management, not enough revenue, inadequate leadership. Hence, it has close relationship between employee life cycle and organizational life cycle . If the organizational management expects its organization can continue develop or reaches next life cycle stage in success, it needs to learn how to let employees to adapt when its organization is changing in order to keep efficience and improving service performance absolutely . So, I believe that it has relationship between learning change management and reaching to mature business cycle stage rapid and achieving long time staying in business cycle mature stage .

The question concerns that how management can learn to implement change management strategy in order to let his organization can reach mature cycle stage in short time as well as keep to stay in this mature life cycle stage in long time?

Firstly, we need to know what change management life cycle means ? For information technological industry example, it may be explained that the change management process is designed to help control of the life cycle of strategies, tactical and operational changes to IT services through standardized procedures. The goal of change managent is to control risk and minimize disruption to IT service and business operations. So, IT industry, the process change management maturity model presents five levels of organizational maturity in change management: The five level may include: from the lowest level 1 to the highest level 5, level 1: Absent or Ad hoc, level 2: Isolated projects , level 3: Multiple projects, level 4: Organizatinal standards and level 5: organizational competency. So, for IT , software manufacturing industry, if the management knows how to manage and change software manufacturing quality in order to satisfy manufacturing organization can follow software users' needs to change old function to new function and improve their qualities to achieve the highest level 5 organizational competency level.

Then, I believe that due to this organization's software management can learn how software user needs change and change its any kinds of software functions ( software life cycle), when its all softwares can be often changed to more new functions to create many different kinds of new software functions to satisfy software users needs and fight its software compettors in this often changing needs market. Due to software product may experience often changing life cycle stages. So, for often one learning software manager example, I believe that he can help this software organization to reach growth life cycle stage, even mature life cycle stage more easily in short time as well as he can also help his software organization to stay in mature life cycle stage long time if this software organizational manager can keep learning attitude to continue to create any new kinds of different functions software to satisfy software clients' changing needs for long time . Then, I believe that this software organization may experience or reach growth life cycle stage, even mature life cycle stage as well as continue staying long time on mature life cycle stage or avoid to encounter decline life cycle stage occurrence chance, if this software organization's softeare management can learn how to change software organization operation and software manufacture and sale strategy in order to satisfy this software users' needs in this software users' need often changing market . So, it is one example to explain why it has close relationship between learning organizational management method and business life cycle stages. As this software organization case, the software management needs often to create and change any new kinds of software functions in order to satisfy software users' needs . So, the software managers need to spend time to learn software life cycle stage , it can help the software organization may reach products life cycle stage, even mature life cycle stage in short time,even the software product organization may also stay long time in mature life cycle stage , when it can reach this stage. Hence, learning how to change organizational management or strategy, which is one important factor to help any organization can reach growth or mature life cycle stage eadily in short time.

As Lewin describes that the change as a three stage process of unfreezing, change and freezing . In this phases of change model, Lewin emphasizes that change is that a series of individual processes, but rather one that flows from one process to the next . So, in general, services mature firms pace greater emphasis on more bureaucratic form, control systems might need to change throughout the life cycle to fit in with. He explains they have relationship between both organizational life cycle stage and management control.

Effective management control may help the organization to reach mature life cycle in short time rapidly. So, leadership managment and the way of thinking are required to balance control and through several stages of growth, maturity , decline or re-grow changes in the external environment influence. Hence, managers position in each of the stages of life cycle and providing practical solutions are, however world where environment changes have proven a rapid growth, the management of varios , they also need to implement how to change their organizational cultures, strategies in order to let their organizations to reach mature stage with a distinction-oriented rapidly. Hence, to successfully implement change initiatives, for each phase of life cycle. Any organizations need to produce resistance to change ( the old model wins out over management boils down to improving the relationship ) learning the relationship between leadership style and the organization life cycle were important. The change from one organizational life cycle phase to another, it depends on how the manager‘c capacity to learn and change.

However, organizations at any stage of the life cycle are impacted by external environment, for example, threats in the start up stage differ from those in the maturity stage. So, managers must need often to learn when the right time is to be needed to change the goals, instead he also needs to learn types of changes in the maturity stage, comparisons with other, having strong personal and professional relationships in the organizaton's maturity stage. Hence, I believe that it has close relationship between learning change management and reaching maturity life cycle and staying long time in this stage.

● How to achieve the experience of mature life cycle reaching stage rapidly for product and service ?

Any businesses expect they can have chance or possibility to attempt to experience this nature life cycle stage, but it is not guarantee any kinds of businesses must may experience this the topest stage, the question is that: Have any methods may help any kinds of businesses to reach this the topest level of business life cycle, when their businesses had been developing or expanding in a period, e.g. after five years? So, it has no absolute to guarantee any kinds of businesses must may experience this the topest stage in one fixed time. How businesses can adapt to birth and growth life cycle stages in order to reach this the topest mature stage in their business life cycle stages? I shall attempt to explain whether it is possible that achieving what strategies may help businesses bring high successful chance to reach the business life cycle mature stage as below:

Product life cycle with maturity stage, it foucs as an important strategic inflection point. A number of techniques can help their businesses to attempt to reach this stage more easily. In fact, the product life cycle contains four distinct stages: introduction, growth, maturity, and decline. Each stage is associated with changes in the product's marketing position . Any firms can use various marketing strategies in each stage to try to proplong the life cycle of their products.

How do the firm extend the maturity stage of a product? I shall recommend change price , place or promotion extension strategy , what does change price extension strategies mean? Change prices mean proces can be lowered to allow ew customers to buy it as well as change place means that products can be sold in different countries or territories to gain more sales, change promotion means different advertising or sales promotion techniques can proplong the life of the product, giving it a new image. So, any organizations can attempt to achieve this extension strategies in order to adapt in different birth, growth and maturity stages for ther product sale easily. This extension strategies' characteristics is at the product;s price, sold places and promotin methods can be changed in order to adapt clients needs when their products are selling in birth, growth and maturity three stages in order to achieve the most effective sale effort and clients growth increasing for long time.

In fact, any product is like human beings, products also have a limited life-cycle and they pass through several stages in their life cycle. A typical product moves through five stages, namely, introduction or birth, growth, maturity or saturation and decline stages. So, when the product needs the maturity life cycle stage, in this maturity stage, it has these characteristics: The maturity stage of the product life cycle shows that sales will eventually peak and then slow down. During this stage, sales growth has started to slow down, and the product has already reached widespread acceptance in the market, in relative terms, utimately, during this stage, sales will peak . Hence, any businesses ought need to consider what key strategies can be implement to achieve the best sale performance throughout the different product life cycle stages and how to make the most of each stage. For example, when the product is selling in the birth stage, e.g. one author's book , his book is selling to the publisher in the first year, there are not many readers knew this book existence, so this book is not popular, its price ought not change high to compare similar topic book, e.g. story book in this year, but after this year, if there are many readers know this book and readers number can grow up rapidly. This author's this topic story book does not change, either increases or decreases , but its sale number has been significant increasing after the first year . So, this author's this story book ought be raised book price to attempt to sell easily. It is one good example of extension strategy to this author's this story book in its life cycle stages. So, such as ths publisher book sale case, it may attempt to achieve extension strategies to every author's book sale, it can follow every author's book prices, publishing places and promotion methods to help every author to sell in the most competitive book sale price, sale place choice and promotin methods in order to earn their readers growth aim . So, any book , it is as product to book shop, it will experience introduction, growth, and maturity life cycle stages. Some books may attract many readers to consider or some books may not attract many readers to consider to read . So, it causes their reading life cycle stages staying time will be different. So, extension strategies can help any books to be sold easily.

In fact, instead of product has life cycle stage, any service also has life cycle stage. There are five stages in service lifecycle. Thay may include: Service strategy, service design, service transition, service operation and continual servce improvement five stages. The service strategy phase of the service lifecycle provides guidance on how to design , develop and implement service management. Because any service business needs to manage to any employee service performance in order to provide excellent service quality, e.g. property management service to building tenants or property owners , if the peoperty management furm can train employees to provide excellent property management service to let their managing building clients to feel satisfactory. Then, the property management firm ought may keep long time property management service to this building. So, service provider will also experience service performance different stages.

In different service performance life cycle stages, such as this property management service case, they ought implement dfferent strategies in order to let their employees to know how to achieve service performance improvement to let their servicing building clients ( tenants or builgin owners) can feel their property management service can be continue improved to avoid to choose any property management service provider to replace it easily.

The purpose of the service strategy stage of the service life cycle is to define the perspective, position plans and pattern that a service provider needs to be able to execute to meet an organization business outomes. The objective of service strategy may include: An understandng of work strategy is thus either the concept of the product life cycle or the concept of the service life cycle is today at about to give a propsed new product or service , how and to what extent. This generally requires important changes in marketing strategies and methods, because any learning kinds of service or product lif cycle stage why and how to change to any organizational management, it may be an important tool for marketers, managers, and product and service providing designers alike, If specifies four individuals stages of a product's or service's life and offers guidance for developing strategies to make the best use of these stages and promote the overall success of the product or service in the marketplace.

Reasons managment needs to spend time to learn how to manage his/her product or service life cycle development stage? They may include: The product or service life cycle is determined by how long its marketable . Product or service life cycle also plays a critical role in marketing strategy . So, learning how to adapt your product or service to meet the coming trends , this is the stage what will occue in which differentiation when the kind of the product or service will have possible to reach the another new experience life cycle stage in order to adapt its business development more easily.

Hence, each stage is associated with changes in the product's or service's marketing postion . The organizational management can use various markting strategies in each stage to try to prolong the life cycle of your products or services . Any product or service reaches the marketplace, it enters the service or product life cycle . This product cycle typically has for stages: Introduction or birth, growth, maturity and decline ( and possibly deaths stages for product as well as service strategy stages includes service strategy. service design, servic transition, service operation, and continual service stages four service stages. So, the organization management can spend time to learn how to develop its business product or service needs to change in order to adapt marketing change in its product or service different life cycle stages. It can bring these benefits, such as: true benefits of product or srvice life cycle management may include, reduced time to makret, reduced market entry costs, more efficient and profitable distribution challen, higher return on investment from promotional cappaigns in possible, extending the lifetime of your product or service by adapting your approach as it moves through the lifecycle , for example, any management needs to learn what can make its products or services move from growth to maturity. After the introduction and growth stages, a product or service passes into the maturity stage. IN the first two stages , companies try to establish a market and then grow sales of their product or service to achieve as large , a share of that market as possible. Hence, marketers must be sure that a product or service has moved from one stage to the next before changing its marketing strategy. At each stage, marketing strategy varies. Strategy for the different stages of the product or service life cycle strategies may include: such as more benefits may be provided to the customers, e.g. extending the warranty period, guarantee period etc. However, company's market strategy depends on which stages the product or service is in its life cycle, for example, when one software manufacture company expects to expand its software sale market to overseas from local in growth stage. If it expects that it can reaches maturity stage in short time rapidly. It needs to implement technology innovation strategy for competition advantage reasons in global software sale markets development. Thus, the software organizational manager needs to spend time to learn what its present organizational characteristics are what resources and skills it owns or lacks, that gives it to comparative advantages over different countries to the operating changes that result in the learning curve to prepare this software product sale organizational maturity life cycle stage development more successfully. So, it needs to look at the advantages of focusing on what kinds of software manufacture and sale services in this software development industry whole life cycle stages and find the best or the most suitable competitive straregy, e.g. a discountinuous change to the software product development marketplace, what the global software product development industrial stage is and the tertiary or sale services sector durig the maturity life cycle stage to this softare manufacturer and sale organization strategy to this software firm during this growth stage may include example of it how changed its software product sales channels to which countries will be its another expanding sale market choice.

On conclusion, any organization management ought spend time to learn whether which strategies are the most suitable or the best to implement as well as how to implement when it is experiencing in the prodiuct or life cycle stage in order to spend less time to reach the maturity life cycle stage and proplong its maturity life cycle stage more success.

CHAPTER TWO

# How technology helps staff cooperation

● COVID -19 disease how influence businesses may experience either growing life cycle stage or decline life cycle stage.

Nowadays, we are facing global economic recession period, since COVID 19 human mouth disease effect can bring economic crisis. Can it influence businesses feel difficult to adapt how global economic recession change after their decline life cycle stage? However, the effects of COVID 19 spreading will have wider implication , not just on how economies function, but also on how consumers behave, across china, Asia-pacific and around the world. Another effect of China;s economic rise is its influence in the adoption and adaption to new technological invention to manufacture , e.g. manufacturing robotic products had sold to China factories to replace workers to manufacturer products. It also will influence many China manufacturing workers lose jobs, when many China factories apply manufacture robotics to replace them in nowadays economic recession period.

Considering the adoption of online-offline shopping and home online office tasks, they are influenced by COVID-19 human disease influence, it also influences on regional travel in China, even global travel income is also reducing, because many travelers feel afraid to catch air planes to avoid to get COVID 19 human disease when they are sitting in close window airplanes by air . HOwever, COVID 19 also influences global consumer behavior changes to online shopping, because many people are afraid to enter crowd shops to avoid get COVID 19 human disease easily. So global shops will lose many visiting shop consumers, if they do not decide to attempt to open online stores to let customers to apply internet to buy their products. So, COVID 19 human mouth disease induced changes in consumer behavior. Shop online will be one new trend to influence young and old consumers make shopping from online stores. They will enquire whether the kind of product is worth to choose to buy by social media, e.g. facebook, online post . Hence, COVID19 human mouth disease may influence global economic recession, but it also brings e-commerce boom chance, when many consumers are fear to enter any crowd shops , when they need to stay long time in any shops. Then, they get COVID 19 human mouth disease chance will increase. Hence, it will influence many customers reduce to visit shops times, but it also creates online-shopping new business model . For example, China families are renewing their joy in home cooking. Onlins cooking videos are helping with the discovery od new recipes, new ways to create dishes , and new influences. So, opportunities are opening for more cleaning products, new ways to clean and new home hacks from online videos will bring global home consumers spend more time on their wellness or beauty routines ? So, COVID-19 disease also influences many families choose to cook dinner at homes at nght. Restaurants will lose many eating clients, because they are fear to enter restaurants to eat together to avoid to get COVID19 human mouth disease. But, it also creates home cooking products sale chance, e.g. rice cookers, dishes or any cooking tools because many families choose to cool at home. Hence, in some situation, economic recession will create new business chance , such as online store or rice cooker sale increases, they may be influenced in this COVID 19 human mouth disease occurrence environment.

Economic recession also influences business strategy changes. Many companies seem to be applying many aspects of a retrenchment approach , e.g. reduced fixed costs, narrower product offering, reduced staffs, but also there are some aspects of an investment approach which can be observed , because customers number will be influenced to reduce in economic recession environment. Companies have felt the robustness and quality of the approaches being applied had been allowed to decline. As a consequence of the challenges of a recession, urgent improvement have needed to be made because factories will reduce workers number to avoid salary expenditure spending more , but customers umber reduced in recession environment .

Hence, they will choose to buy manufacturing robotics to replace workers. If robotics can be improved to be proficient manufacture. Then, they won't need to buy many robotics to help them to replace to replace many workers to manufacture any products efficiently. So, manufacturing and improvement to robotics number demand may increase to any factories , e.g. vehicle manufacture, electronic products, e.g. computer hime cooking electronic products , e.g. rice cookers, heaters etc. products may be manufactured by manufacturing robotics. It creates the manufacturing robotic sale improvement quality chance in recession environment. It may impact on medium, or long term, it depends on how long time of recession. So, economic recession may bring robotic manufacture industry boom , when electronic products manufacturers need many improved robotics to replace workers in factries in order to reduce spending too much salaries expenditure in recession.

It is one external environmental factor to influence sudden manufacture robotic industry boom absolutely ,because electronic manufacturer's manufacturing robotic needs increases in recession environment. So, robotic manufacturers' strategy need to change , such as how to improve any manufacturers' needs in recession, e.g. manufacturing robotic product categories, market segments, geographic areas, core technologies, reliability , price, customisation, robotic manufacturing efficiency how to be improved of business.Change strategy to any manufacturing robotics manufacturers. So, recession may influence some kinds of manufacturing robotics' needs raise in robotic manufacturing market.

- How recession influences the role of advertising changes?

Advertising plays a key role in a dynamic economy. It may provide valuable information about products and services in an efficient manner, communicates client value, builds brand awareness and creates demand. However, when one country is experiencing recession, how it influences the country's businessmen spending on advertisement behaviors? Due to clients number reduces, a company usualy cuts come from the advertising budget than companies begin to cut back on advertiseing during an economic recession, they become less visible to the public because they predict clients number ought reduce next three months, even half year or one year. It depends on how long economt recession occurs. So, economic recession many impact any companies' advertising budget expenditure to be reduce . How much on the reduction on advertising budget expenditure, it depends on the company predicts how many clients number will reduce.However, due to advertising number reduces, it can influence consumer behavior changes indirectly.

In economic boom environment, consumers can watch to different kinds advertisement from television. Advertisement may bring positive alternative evaluation phase of biying decision-making process is bring exposed to buy several communication messages. In such an economic boom environment, any organizations may be clearly heard by the consumers, after any advertisement programs are broadcasted on television. Therefore, advertisemtn can persuade clients to choose to buy the kind of product after the kind of product advertisement is broadcasted from television absolutely.

However, when recession occurs, any companies; advertisement time is shortened , even number is reduced . Hence, they can not receive any client's positive or negative feedback immediately in short time afer advertisements are broadcasted from television . So, recession may influence advertisement time is shortened and number is rediced . On consequence, companies can not have any repsonse to know whether how market or customers' demand is changing to themselves products in shor time.

However, recession may bring worse advertisement effect to influence any businesses . On one hand, there is a negative economic recession environment because of the negative media reporting, these would be a decline in demand for the products and services and eventually companies would want to save more than they spend , But in the other hand, when the companies cut back advertiseing expenditures, they become less visible to public. Hence recession may influence many companies brand image will be lost, due to spending on advertisement expenditure wil reduce. Then, clients number may be influenced to reduce, because they can not watch the kind of product advertisment from television home often.

When one country is encountering recession, how are the various components of household consumption affected ? How is the impact of the recesion distributed across socio-demographic group? How does the recession compare to previous recessions? When book will boom? In fact, any country's recession may impact consumer behavior changes, it depends on these factors: age, race, education and wealth groups resulted in a decline in consumption inequality. The rich group is the " wealth effect influence group" when recession comes, it may influence their wealth reduces, so their enjoyment dsires will be influenced to reduce, e.g. purchase expensive cars driving enjoyment desires, purchase expensive house living enjoyment desires. If one rich person loses jobs , it may influence him to spend less time to drive themselves cars, so consumption of gasline will be influenced to reduce.

Economic theory ( e.g. consumer behavioral economic theory) predicts that when economic recession occurs, it will cause many businesses may experience decline cycle life stage rapidly, that link between income shocks and consumption has close relationship, such as rich person consumer group, if his income reduces, then he will buy less gas to drive himself car, even if he loses his job in recession environment, he will choose to sell his car to exchange cash. Hence, consumption may fall as a direct consequence of a fall in income induced by job loss, reduced hours or productivity and negative returns from assets, if there are long term changes to a household's econmic resource in recession environment. Hence, in recession environment, job loss or income reduction factors that may affect consumers and their shopping attitudes in the recession period. Otherwise, for low income group, recession may influence food consumption to low income consumer behavior changes to worse. Because low income person may reduce income ot lose job, then cheap food consumption will be influenced to worse to low income consumer group.

In recession period, if the food price is raised , due to the cost increase of food, it will lead to change in the reductin on quantity and type of food being purchase to low income food buyers. This may lead to a reduction in the quantity of food consumed and/or the substitution of high-priced food for cheaper food, which is often less nutritous and of worse quality. Hence in recession perios, low income food consumers will consider whether the kind of food price has how much increase or decrease. They won't consider the quantity of food consumed for maintaining energy balance and the quality of food consumed for maintaining ample intakes of protains, fats and micronutrients, such as vitamins, minerals and trace elements on food issue. So, if the kind of food price reduced in recession period, it ought may attract many low income food consumers number, even its food nutritious is worse. Hence, if the kind of meat price can be reduced in recession , the cheap types of meat consumption to low income consumer may be increased, even its nutritious is worse to compare the recession occurs before period.

On conclusion, in either economic recession or boom period, in general, consumer behavior will be influenced to change. Some products may be influenced to have higher sale in recession period, e.g. home electronic rice cookers , due to COVID 19 human mouth disease influenced many households choose to cook dinner at home at ight. Otherwise, some products may be influenced to have lowr sale., e.g. expensive cars sale in recession period, many high income people may lose jobs or reduce salaries , then it will influence their car purchase desires to be reduced. But if COVID 19 human mouth disease has medicine to kill this kind of disease. Then, economy will boom, many households will choose to go to restaurants to eat dinner. The, the electronic rice cookers sale number may reduce, when they reduce time to cook at home at night. Hence, it explains why economic recession or boom period may have impact to influence consumer behavior in behavioral economic view.

Applying business development strategy to raise the educational robotic manufacturer sale number in recession period

● What does business development strategy ?

An effecting business development strategy ought have these five steps: The first step is market analysis. Who are your clients , knowledge of your market? Second step is how to adopt for each penetration, your business needs to learn how to adopt for each group of clients, your first need to review your own capacbility. It is important that you are realistic and honest with yourselves over where clients truly sit, learn how to classify your clients into similar groups relative is the scale of the opportunity. Third step learns how to review your performance , market matrix to plot your results to help you determine your market penerstion. In addition, it will help you then discuss and consider various strategies for growth. By potting your clients you will get a sense of where your strengths and weaknesses are against the opportunity that total market offer.Fourth step learns how to consider alternative growth strategies on the market matrix. The final step , you need to consider these questions in order to decide whic is the most effective strategy for your business. For example, which model is the most ( least effective? Why? which model work best for line managers, HR are finance, why? How might we most effectively progress from one model to the most reasonable questions? ) Then, you will need to decide how to launch new services, new products, opening new markets, how accessing new geographic territories.

● How to apply business development strategy to help educational robotic manufacturers to enter traditional education market ?

Many thinkers concern robots that are used in manufacturing workplaces, homes, roads, hospitals and care centre aspect, but they don't feel robotics may be possible to apply on social service aspect, e.g. educational service aspect . In fact, robotic may have both functions. Industrial robotics, e.g.

manufacturing function as well as service robotics, e.g. professional robotcs, medical robotics, entertainment robotics, e.g. toy and education robotics and service robotics , e.g. personal and domestic robotics.

Educational robotic is on the birth stage in its industry life cycle. So, any educational robotic products will need time to persuade schools or any educational institutions to buy their products to assist teachers to teach students in classrooms. The question is how to apply business development strategy to help the educational robotic manufacturer to develop its educational robotic products to persuade educational clients to choose to buy ? I shall attempt to explain as below:

Due to educational robotic product is one new educational tool to assist any schools to buy to assist teachers to improve teaching service performance to let students to feel more learning satisfaction, so any educational robotic products must need time to introduce whether what it can bring schools benefits to let students and teachers to feel. When robotic can be popular to use on manufacturing, educational service industries aspect, e.g. warehouse , factory, shopping center, even restaurant's kitchen cooking robotics, office environment's accounting, law draft etc. clerical robotics may be invented to replace human 's general simple tasks. However, if future robots can be applied to educational aspect, e.g. classroom, school teaching students. Can educational robotic may assist or replace teachers to teach students in clasrooms? Will future teachers be replaced by teaching robotics . I shall attempt to explain whether it is possible that educational robotic can be developed to global educational organizations successfully as below:

Robotic technology has been invented to own " mind " ability, e.g. writing words, writing song, simple calculation tasks reading tasks . So, future robotics can be invented to own " mind " ability, when robotics' mind ability can be improved to own how to " communication" ability and " analytical" ability. Then can it be possible to apply robotics to do teaching tasks in classrooms, e.g. learning any books , the it applies the book's contents to analyze any "knowledge" in order to follow the logic mind to teach students in classroom. It is one major factor to influence any schools to explain why they need to buy any educational robotic in schools in any educational robotic product business development strategy. So, they need to find whether what their educational robotic strengths , any competitors won't own or their product weaknesses, they need to improve their educational robotic products in order to attract educational organizations to choose to buy.

Can future teaching robotics learn to do teacher individual same education tasks? It will be absolute competitive point to any educational robotic product manufactures. If it is true, can teaching robotics may be trained to exceed teacher individual teaching skill? It is another competitive point to any educational robotic product manfacturers. Is it ethic to apply robotic to teach students to replace teachers if teaching robotic can perform better teaching service to compare teachers? If the eduational robotic manufactuer can persude the school can accept eduational robotic ethic issue to assist or replace teachers to do teaching tasks, then it's sale chance will raise. So, ethic to educational robotic will be another factor to develop the educational robotic business. Can teachers be teaching robotic's teaching assistant role if teaching robotics can have teaching ability to teacher in the school? So, if the educational robotic manufacturer can persuade the school to feel that its products can be teacher's assistant to improve their performance to let students learn more easily. The educational robotics manufacturer may develop its product to sell in this educational market more easily, in business development strategy view.

All of these will be future any one educational robotic development challenges if they hope their products can sell more easily. They also need to know to let schools to know these disadvatages to their products to become advatanges in order to attract they to choose to buy their producte more easily. Such as what potential harmful consequences may come from the inventing of teaching robotics? What happends to important education moral, such as teacher or school privacy then robotic are starting to become an teaching tool to the school? Do such robotics hace any roght and responsibilities if the class has many students learning ability are influenced to poor or examination results are poor when the educational robotic has been bought to assist the school teachers to teach their students? Why does the school need to buy educational robotic to do teaching tasks? Any school organizations must need any one educational robotic product seller to answer any one of above questions, before they decide to buy their products. So, they must need to ensure teaching robotics will be used to help the school to teach students to learn more understanding to compare teachers only.

- Future educational robotic are applied on development teaching maths market

In the future, business development to educational robotic market may be teaching maths. I shall explain as below:

It is possible that students can use mobile robotic to learn mathematics subject to compare teachers more easily. Why? For example, young age from 4 to 14 age, they may apply mobile robotics to learn add, multiple, divided, simple math equation more understanding than math teaches. Robotic kints and apps is currently available on the maket for teacher of 4 to 14 age students,due to mobile , kits app price is cheap. So, they can be popular to be accepted by any primary schools , even in secondary schools, robotics may be applied to teach computer science, statistical methods subjects of one robotic kit for teach team of 2 to 3 students, short theory lessons , and tutorials to link theory and practice, realistic but affordable tasks linked with curricular subjects, teachers at ease with the robotic etc. So, future primary and secondary , even university teachers may need to choose the more suitable robot kit for their students,and carefully design where and how to use it and with which role.In fact, children will be possible to raise interest to learn when they can contact for any kind of teaching robotic to learn maths in classrooms together. So, teaching robotics may help 4 to 14 children students to raise learning interest instead of learning about ability.

In the future, robotic role is school may be one tool to engage the students as teachers role may be transfer base knowledge when teachers teach maths, geography, statistics, computer science subjects to promary , secondary even university students. This is one good example , whether what subjects robotic may be applied when it is invented to own human mind and anlaytical skill and communication ability. Robotics can perform more better to be applied to teach these subjects. It can let students to understand easily, e.g. understanding how to create equations that describe numbers a relationship understanding solving equations as a process of reasoning and explain the equations and inequalities in one variable, helping students to find different solutions, then best solves the problem , given the criteria and the constraints, helping students have more understanding how science knowledge is based upon logical and conceptual connections between evidence and explanations, even robotc can ask questions that can be investigated within the scope of the classroom, outdoor environment, and museums and other public faciltities with available resources and when appropriate frame a hypothesis based on observation and scientific principles. Even, robotics may help students to learn how construct, use and present oral and written arguments supported by evidence and scientific reasoning to support or refute an explanation or a model for a phenomenon, or robot can hep students to learn how obtain, evaluate and communicate information in 6-8 builds on k-5 and progresses to evaluating the merit and validity of ideas and methods, integiate qualitative scientific and technical information in written text with that contained in media and visual displays to clarify cliams and findings, helping students to anlyze data from texts to determine similarities and differences among several design solutions to identify the best characteristics of each that can be combined into a new solution to better meet the criteria for success, even helping students to learn how analyze data in 9-12 builds on k-8 and progresses to introducing more detailed statistical anslysis, the comparision of data sets for consistency and the use of models to generate and analyze data, analyze data using tools, technologies , and/or models e.g. computational, mathematical in order to make valid and variable scientific claims or determine and optinal design solution more easily than human teacher. So, there are human-made educaton machine advantage to students more than human teacher.

Educational robotic has been introduced as a powerful, in fact, flexible teaching / learning tool stimulating learns to control the behavior of tangible model using specific programming languages ( graphical, or textual and involving them actively in authentic problem -solving activities. Howeverm in future educational robotic development, it may be divided two separate categories as below:

Robotics as learning object: This first category includes educational activities where robotics is being studied as a subject on its own. It includes educational activities aimed at configuring a learning environment that will actively involve learners in the solution of authentic problems, facing on robotics -related subjects, such as robot construction, robot programming and artificial intelligence as well as robotic as learning tool: In the frame of this second category, robotics is proposed as a tool for teaching and learning other school subjects at different school levels. Robotics as learning tool is usually, seen as an interdisciplinary, project -based learning activity drawing mostly on science, maths, informatics and technology and offering major new benefits to education in genera at all levels. However, I believe the role of teacher is crucial for the successful industry of technological and innovations in classrooms, when robotics are been particiapted to any education tasks in classrooms. Schools can focuse on the training of prospective and in-service teachers in the use of robotics technologies through courses.

In future electronic learning environment, robotics can be participated, such as recognised their active participation in all sessions of the course and their creative involvement even in the theoretical parts introducing principles and methodology for designing robotic-enhanced projects, very much liked the activity-orientation of the educational content, acknowledged the central role of the e-workspace during the face-to-face meetings and beyond ehem in enhancing sense of community, acknowledged the potential of educational robotics as a teaching tool but also as a subject, in different disiplines , such as technology, informatics and engineerinfg, highly appreciated the opportunity to create their projects.
How to develop robotic in technological subjects on teaching, learning and educational aspect? Learners can be encouaged hen robotics participate actively in the learning process. Through robotic learners build something on their own, preferably a tangible object, that they can both touch and find meaningful. In robotic learners are invited to work experiments or problem-solving with selective use of available resources, according to their own interest, search and learning strategies. Robotics can help them to seek solutions to real world problems, based on a technological framework meant to engage students' movitation. So, when students can have control of specific robotc in a rich learning environment, the construction of robots and programs to control them the emphasis might move on interesting learning actiities in the frame of specific learning areas , such as science and technology. Thus, the design of robotic construction activities is associated with the fulfillment of a project aimed at solving a problem. In such a learning environment, learning is driven by the problem to be solved. To engage students in activities requiring to design and manufacture real objects, i.e. robotic structures that make sense for themselves and should devise activities that will encourage students to support in order experiment. So, robotic participation any science experiments, they may encourage students to create problem solving and combining interdisiplinary concepts from different knowledge areas,: science, mathematics , technology and research educational tasks, the role of students will change, when preparing a work with a programmable robotics studies experiment with simple programmable sobotics devices , e.g. a car-robot, motors, sensor etc. Students are asked to synthesize their finds and reach conclusions and solutions to the problem uner investigation. SO, robotic is educaional participation to any scientfic technological or research experiments, they may help students to work with creativity , imagination

and independence and finally organize the evaluation of the activity in collaboration ith studens. Also robotic participation to any technological or scientific research experiemtn, it also change teacher role . The teacher is such a constructist theoretical framework, like that teacher 's role that does not transfer ready knowledge to students, but rather acts as a organizer, coordinator and facilitator of learning for students. when educational robotics participate to any science or technological any research experiments, students may be organize the learning environment, raise the question , problem to be solved by students allow students to work with creativity, imagination and independence and finally organize the evaluation of the activity in collaboration with students. So, any educational robotic manufacturers must let their school clients to feel all these benefits which can bring to let students to raise learning abilty and learning interest to compare that are only taught by teachers, if they hope their educational robotics can be sold successfully in business development strategy view.

Learning behavioral economy to solve social challenges

- Why do some social challenges may influence customers number ?

In our societies , we shall have different challenges to our every day. However, in general , the challanges seem that they do not have relate to influence businessmen profit, but in fact, these social challenges have relationship to influence business profit and clients number. I shall indicate some social challenges to explain why these social challenges may influence any business profit indirectly as below:

In investment or raving individual preference decision aspect, for some people , it may be interesting or fun to think cbout the best investments or the right health care plan. But, for other people, these choices are unpleasant, they may be persuaded to buy anythings, e.g. car, computer. So, if car seller can have persuasive methods to influence many people feel the health care plan or investment plan is not prefereable choices, driving car enjoyable feeling or material enjoyment is the most preference choice. Then I believe that the car seller's car selling number may increase, because some people greatly enjoy thinking about their pension and the best investment or health care insurance preferable decision, their decision had been influenced to choose to buy the car seller's cars. When they feel driving car enjoyable feeling is more important than future benefit.

Hence, in behavioral economy view, they had felt the driving car benefit is much to compare pension investment or health care insurance future benefit. The question is how to car seller can persuade these investment

ot pension plan or health care preference decision individual to change purchase car driving decision>
I suggest that the car seller may have discount or cash coupon or installment payment method to attract them to consider , instead of advertisement promotion method. because this preference investment or pension saving or health care plan decision individual customer group will be more difficult to persuade them to choose to buy car immediately at this moment. Hence, if the car seller can not implement cheap car discount strategy, it will be difficult to attract this prefeence long term future benefit consumer to make purchase ca r decision easily. Because they think pension or investment or health care plan ce help them to bring long term future benefit, also it means that purchase car may only bring short term present benefit. It is general social behavioral consumption model to influence their purchase choice. Hence, I assume that general social long term future benefit product or service, e.g. insurance, investment , pension may influence th scocial shor tterm present benefit product , e.g. car consumer. It is the main reason, it can explain why car sellers can not persuade this long term future benefit consumers to make decision to buy their cars easily, when they have no enough money to spend to buy car and make investment, saving , medical care insurance , pension plan in the same time. They must need to make either purchase car or insurance etc. decision in our nowadays societies.
So, in behavioral economic view, it explains why consumer individual purchase choice behavior has relationship to himself/herself spending budget. I assume that it has two kinds of behavioral economic consumers. One kind if long term future economic benefit in preference more than short term present economic benefit, such as purchase car and investment or health care plan insurace saving term present benefit consumer, he / she considers to earn driving enjoyment at this moment is not preference than purchase insurance or investment future benefit decision . So, our society, any business will encounter these two kinds of behavioral consumer. They persuade either long term futuer benefit consumers or short term present benefit consumer to change himself/herself products or services more easily. Otherwise, such as if car seller can not implement coupon or cash reward or discount or installment cash payment strategy to attracr the long term future benefit consumer. Then, it will lose this group car customers number absolutely. So, it explains why businessmen need to learn consumer behavioral consumption model in order to increase client number more easily.

" Social welfare" usually measured by people's prefences, and it also focuses for the conventional economists, on how to maximize social welfare. What then is the task of behavior law and economics? Such as, this cate seller case example, whether what social welfare the car seller can bring to society when the individual decides to buy its car to drive or when the individual chooses to buy health care insurance or pension plan or investment . When he/she chooses to buy health care insurance or make pension plan or buys any companies' shares. Then, these investment service companies will bring what benefits to our society? So, instead of consumer benefit, we also need to consider whether the kind of product or service will bring what long term social benefit . However, I think that when global many people own cars, then many cars are driven on the roads, it will bring serious air pollution to influence our health. Then, when many people are got lung diseases by air pollution. Then, many people will need to pay more medical expense. It will be long term negative medical cost increasing expense to future us, but it also bring possible income for insurance firms, when many people plan to buy medical care plans when they feel air pollution will influence them to need to pay future medical expense. So, it seems that the effect on many people own cars and their driving behaviors will bring serious air pollution, but it will also create the health care medical insurance need to be increased due to many people feel air polluton will bring lung disease and they need to pay long time medical expensein the future long time in possible. So, many people driving behavior may bring air pollution, but it also bring medical insurance need increases in our society in possible. It means that air pollution may create medical insurance market develops in possible, such as most smokers say they would prefer not to smoke, and many pay money to join a program or obtain a drug that will help them quit.If many smokers forgive to smoke, then the medical care insurance need for smokers number may be influenced to reduce.

In social benefit view, medical insurance for smokers insurance will be influenced to reduce, due to many smokers forgive to smoke. Although, many smokers may get health, when they do not smoke, they do not pay to buy any cigeratte often, they can save more money, but cigeratte sellers and medical insurance service providers , their income must be influenced to reduce. Hence, when our society government's advertisement concerns smokers often smoke cigeratte, it may bring poor drug health or many cars air pollution, these two messages may influence or dissuade many smokers forgive to smoke or many people do not buy cars. They choose to catch public transportation, or owning car people who do not often drive cares, then car gas or fuel suppliers income will be influenced to reduce, due to many car owning people do not often drive cars or many people do not choose to buy cars. Then, car sellers' income wil be influenced to reduced. Moreover, in long term social influence, when many people do not feel lung disease . Then, the medical care insurance need will also influenced to reduce.

It may bring insurance industry develops in difficulty for lung dissease medical care insurance. So, it explains why consumer behavior may also influence our social economic development in long term . They have cause and effect close relationship. When many consumers individual forgive or dislike to do the behavior in habit, e.g. driving car behavior or smoking behavior. Then, it will influence car seller market and cigeratte seller market to be poor in any countries , even global market.

Hence, in our society, when one individual feels that he.she has individual challenge, it may be economic or emotion or health problem, such as smoking influences health case, driving influences air pollution case. These both kinds of individual behavior may influence the individual may need to spend money for lung disease if he/she has continue smoking habit every day or he/she often drives car . Then, the individual will seek methods to solve these possible occurrence of problems before they do not occur. As it occurs in the natural environment, e.g. air pollution or lung disease is caused by cars or smoking. When individual begins feel these negative effect may case, if he/she continues to do smoking or dirving car behavior. He/she will begins to find methods to solve problem, problem solving is defined as the self-directed cognitive -behavioral process by which an individual , couple or group, such as smokers and drivers group in our society, they attempt to identify or disciver effective solutions for specific problem encountered in everyday living. More specifically, this cognitive -behavioral process ( a) makes available a variety of potentially effective solutions for a particular problem and (b) increases the probability of selecting the most effective solution from among the various alternatives ( D'Zurilla & Gold field 1971).

reference

D' Zurilla, T. J. & Goldfield, M.R, (1991). Problem solving and behavior modification, Journal of abnormal psychology, 78, 107-126.

As this definition implies social problem solving is conceived as a conscious, rational, effortful, and purposeful activity. Depending on the problem solcing goals, this process may be aimed at changing the problematic situation for the better, reducing the emotional distress that it produces or both.

Hence, it implies that when any one feels he/she will have individual problem, e.g. health problem , economuc problem,emotion problem. He/ she will avoid to continue to do the kind of behavior often every day ,e.g. smoking behavior or driving car behavior .When our society has many people make to forgive to do above themselves behaviors, such as smoking or driving habit. Then, it will influence cigeratte sale number and car sale numner to be reduced. So, when our society has any consumer groups, they forgive to do themselves behaviors in habit. Consequently, the kind of product seller or service provider may lose man customers. So, in our society , when one kind of product or service consumers , their habital behaviors are changed to reduce, then it may influence the kind of product sellers or service providers their income or clients number to be either decrease or increase. On conclusion, it explains that why social behavior has close relationship to influence business income or clients number in our societies.

Learning organizational life cycle stage strategies advantages

Any organizations may experience organizational life cycle stages from birth stage to growth stage to maturity , then it may also experience decline and/or regrow stages. But this two stages, they are not all organizations must may attempt to experience. It depends on whether economic environment how changes, organizational itself SWOT strengths and weaknesses etc. unpredicted factors to influence that when the organization will experience decline life cycle stage. It means that if the organization has very poor performance, then the organization has possible to experience decline life cycle stage in short time or long time. Otherwise, if the organizationhas very good performance, it ought not experience decline life cycle stage in short time, when it can reach mature stage in its the topest level. Even, when the organization has poor performance, so it is experiencing decline stage, but if it may implement effective strategies to help itself organization to develop . Then, if its strategies are very effective , in consequence, the organization ought may experience regrowing stage to re-experience its mature life cycle stage again. So, it seems that if the organization can have very good performance. Client number can increase significant as well as profit can also growth rapidly. Then, the organization ought may experience long time in mature life cycle stage or it means that it will be difficult to reach decline life cycle stage. Unless, some sudden inpredicted economic environment, or strong competitors etc. influence its performance, then they will have chance to cause it experiences to decline life cycle stage from mature stage suddenly. Hence, all organizations must need to experience birht life cycle stage in beginning to this stage.

However, when the business founder starts to set up his/her business. He/ she needs time to deal any difficulties,e.g. how to advertise his/her products to let customers have much knowledge, promote them to sell to market, how to implement strategies to solve organizational challenges. So, in birth stage, any organizations ought feel difficult to improve its whole performance or evaluate whether its future performance can improve to be better or can not improve or worse. Then, when the organization operates one period, it ought experience to growth stage, but it still depends on external factors to influence whether when it may experience growth stage, the factors may include: Whether strategies can be effective, economic environment is good or bad, customers purchase desire level is high or loe, cost expenditure is high or low etc. difficult factor.

So, before any organizatons may experience growth stage, there are many different complex factors to influence whether they can succeed to experience this stage easily. If the organization can not implement any effective strategies to solve its customers purchase emotion challenges, then its business is difficult to continue grow, also it means that the organization can not growor expand its business easily. Due to it can not continue to develop its business easily. It must not reach mature life cycle stage easily. Thus, any organizations can reach mature life cycle stage. It represents that its business has good strategies to solve any challenges in order to its products can attract customers to choose to buy or it can provide good service performance to satisfy clients needs to compare irs competitors in this market successfully.

In fact, it is not all organizations can attempt to experience the mature life cycle stage. This stage is any organization individual the topest stage. In this stage, the organization may have many clients increasing number significantly every year, its market can continue expand, profit can continue increases . All is the best to any organizations, if it can reaches this stage . All many organizations may only experience birth stage or growing stage . They reach this either birth or growth stage, then they have none good strategies to compete their clients number can not increase, but only decreases, profit reduces , even loss. They can not know how to change strategied to improve their performance or competitive effort to fight this competitors. Then, their businesses can not continue grow or expand. So, they have more chance to experience decline stage after either birth or growth stage only. They can not reach mature life cycle stage to attempt the topest level in whole business ( organizational) life cycle stage or process. Thus, it brings these questions: Why do organizations need to learn organizational life cycle stages? What advantages to bring if they can attempt to learn how to reach growth or mature life cycle stages easily? I shall explain as below:

● Why do organizations need to spend time to learn how may experience different business life cycle stages?

The business life cycle is the progression of a business in phases over time and is most commonly divided into five stages: Launch or birth, growth, maturity and decline or regrow. Each company begins its operations as a business and usually by launching new products or services. Because any organizations will encounter challenges in every stages . If they know what factos may help them to enter another new stage of business life cycle or what challenges may threaten them can not enter another new business life cycle stage easily. Because businessman need to learn and how adjust their business model to ensure profitability. That is why an awareness of what stage of the business life cycle , you are currently it can be helpful. Hence, how to maximize each stage of the business life cycle, the businessmen might still need to learn how to work in order to improve performance when the businessmen are experiencing any one life cycle stage. Moreover, each business life cycle stage comes still need to learn how to turn a profit and the first outlines of their governance and compliance and this is one big reason why most businesses fail at this stage.

So, I assume that business life cycle stage is similar to school examination, the student needs to spend time to learn in the birth learning stage, then he needs to test in the growth learning stage, next is examination in the mature learning stage, if the student fails, t is decline learning stage to the school. It may be due to the teachers can not teach students to learn easily. So, these are many students fail in tests or examinations. So, if the school teachers can improve teaching methods to let many students may earn high grades in tests or examinations. Then, the school may experience growth, even mature teaching life cycle stage in short time rapidly . Hence, teaching quality can improve or not , it will influence any school organizations ought feel to schools to learn how to improve teaching methods or strategies in order to let students can experience the maturity learning stage or it can also experience the maturity teaching stage. It means that it ought learn how to improve its teachers teaching service performance to satisfy students learning needs if it hopes to reach maturity learning and teaching life cycle stage in short time for itself school organization benefit.For example, the organization founder may ask himself/herself why he/she wants to start this business, learns how to manage exployees strategies? It is the learning needs in the third stage, such as maturity stage. Otherwise, in the first stage of the business entity birth life cycle is sometimes called the seed stage and a matter of iteraing, testing an learning , and trying again, knowing that the businessman is unlikely to have.

What advantages may bring to the organization if it can attempt to learn how to solve different challenges in different business life cycle stages ? What advantages to the organization, if it can know how to experience every business life cycle stage?

In fact, the business life cycle is the progression of a business in phases over time, and is consumer segments by advertising their comparative advantages and vale. For example, when the business is experiencing growth stage , in the growth phase, the business founder needs to spend time to learn how his company can experience rapid sales growth. This learning may assist his business to develop his business to enter next mature how stage easily , for example, he can learn how the rapid growth stage takes advantage from the proven sales model, e.g. online sale or traditional visiting shop sale model which is more suitable to his business, marketing model and operations model, e.g. how to advertise his product or promote his products can affect more audiences concern this will see the businessmen's jounrey from idea to start up, and if successful, how to keep to stay long time in the mature stage. Rememeber, when having a successful business model behind any businessmen is undoubtedly an advantage, it is not a disadvantage when the founder spends more time to learn hoe to run his business. In fact, he won't waste his time to learn how to improve his business in different business life cycle stages. So, a tactical plan will take any business strengths and reduces to avoid weakness cause to influence its development. So, knowing where you small product is in its product life cycle, it is important to continue to develop your business successfully. SO, any impacts of all life cycle stages, any businesses need to be considered comprehensively , for one new technological product firm example, its new technological product life cycle begins with the introduction or birth stage.

The high technological product company must succeed at both developing new product and managing them in the face of changing tastes, competitors' technologies similar change. So, it is what it needs to learn in this stage for this new product technological firm preparing development to next growth stage.

On the conclusion, learning how to achieve in every business life cycle stage, it can bring these benefits to any organizations, such as : they can understand and redefine this role from a more, if the organization ony to learn sale frameworks what it could have picked up. It is not enough, because most organizations will only find that a majority of their total sale number which is to use solely supplier-specific data about the life cycle, but they neglect how to set targets to learn how to improve their sale to be better in the future time, it is one important factor explain why many organizations only reach the growth stage, but they can not experience to next mature stage more easily, due to they do not consider how to implement strategies in order to achieve their next targets. They feel often implment targets which will help them to know whether they need to how to do in order to improve their businesses to satisfy clients needs. As with any effort in your organization, communication plays a critical role, craft machine learning to predict and manage human for remote teams to work through the innovation lifecycle, serve them well. Any organizations need to learn how to satisfy any customer individual purchase jounrey ( called purchase experience) which the customer has with the organization, because when the organization can learn how to satisfy any client individual real need in any life cycle stage. On consequence, its clients number with have possible to influence increase. Thus, any organizations can bot neglect to learn how to satisfy client individual real purchase experience need in any life cycle stages because improvement to salepeople sale performance, they need spend time to learn in every time sale experience . When the organization can build excellent sale teams, then they may help it to build famous loyalty and good client relationship in order to expand its business more easily. Hence, in any businesses' life cycle stages, they must need to spend time to learn how to improve product quality service performance to bring customers' satisfactory emotion in order to expand their business developmenr more easily. So, i recommend that all small organizations expand to large size, they must need time to learn and attempt to find the best methods to solve any difficulties when they are facing in any one business cycle stage, if they want to expand their businesses successfully.

● The relationship between learning change management and rapid reaching mature life cycle

It is one good question: Can the manager or CEO help whole organization to develop rapidly if he/she attempt to learn how to help his/her organization to implement different strategies to solve different challenges in different business life cycle stages? Does it easy to help the organization to grow up when a learning CEO or learning manager accepts to learn anything to compare a non learning manager in different business life cycle stages? Has it relationship between learning or non learning manager and rapid experiencing business life cycle stage and rapid developing business growth? I shall attempt to explain as below:

In fact, it is not essential to any managers or CEOs need to spend time to learn how any why what factors may influence their organizations to grow up to next business life cycle stage, but in comparison one learning how to change organizational life cycle stages manager and non-learning how to change organizational life cycle stages manger. Can learn attitude or strategy to help the manager to develop or expand his organization to next life cycle stage more easily or rapidly? I shall attempt to explain as below:

In fact, any organizations expect to change to next life cycle stage in success , can the manager(s) learn how to implement strategies to achieve to change management to their organizations' development in success? How the organizational management learns how to adapt organizational management change, it may be one important factor to influence whether the organization needs to spend how long time to reach growth life cycle stage from birth stage or reach mature life cycle stage from growth stage. So, it seems that how management spends time to learn how to change his/her organization. It will have relationship to the organization needs to spend long time to reach next life cycle stage successfully.

Hence, learning how to train employees in each life cycle stage, it is the important factor to influence any organizations succeed, the employee lifecycle is an ongoing process that starts and ends with competent employees in any managers' organizations. There are nine elements ofa successful change management process, if the organizational management expects whole organization can real reach to next life cycle stage in success. The nine elements of a successful change management process, any management needs to spend time to learn. They may include: readiness assessments, communication planning implementation, sponsor activities and sponsor roadmaps organizing, organizatons need to provide change management training for managers to learn how to achieve effectiveness as well as providing training development and delivery learning methods to them, resistance management learning and learning employee feedback and corrective action. Moreover, managements also need to spend time to learn change management steps in order solve any challenges in order to reach next life cycle stage easily.

The change management learning steps may include: Step 1: Urgency creation , step 2: Building every team serves to every department efficiently, learning how to create avision, how to communication of division, how to remove obstacles, going for quick wins, let the change mature, integrate the change. These elements are incorporated into change management phases process. For example, some elements of communication planning occur early in the lifecyle. At this stage, change management is not fully achieved effectively, so management needs to spend more time to learn how to achieve effective communication planning in order to achieve effective communication planning in order to keep whose organization employees can communicate to work efficiently. Also, it will help client service employees to know how to build good communication management method to deal or answer or satisfy their clients' sale service and improving service performance absolutely.

Because organizations are nor statis, they change , if one organization still stays long time in birth stage, it represents that the organization feels difficulties to continue develop . So, the management needs to find whether what challenges threaten its organization can not reach growth stage more easily. One failure changing management organization, it has these characteristics: failure to change, inexperienced management, not enough revenue, inadequate leadership. Hence, it has close relationship between employee life cycle and organizational life cycle . If the organizational management expects its organization can continue develop or reaches next life cycle stage in success, it needs to learn how to let employees to adapt when its organization is changing in order to keep efficience and improving service performance absolutely . So, I believe that it has relationship between learning change management and reaching to mature business cycle stage rapid and achieving long time staying in business cycle mature stage .

The question concerns that how management can learn to implement change management strategy in order to let his organization can reach mature cycle stage in short time as well as keep to stay in this mature life

cycle stage in long time?
Firstly, we need to know what change management life cycle means ? For information technological industry example, it may be explained that the change management process is designed to help control of the life cycle of strategies, tactical and operational changes to IT services through standardized procedures. The goal of change managent is to control risk and minimize disruption to IT service and business operations. So, IT industry, the process change management maturity model presents five levels of organizational maturity in change management: The five level may include: from the lowest level 1 to the highest level 5, level 1: Absent or Ad hoc, level 2: Isolated projects , level 3: Multiple projects, level 4: Organizatinal standards and level 5: organizational competency. So, for IT , software manufacturing industry, if the management knows how to manage and change software manufacturing quality in order to satisfy manufacturing organization can follow software users' needs to change old function to new function and improve their qualities to achieve the highest level 5 organizational competency level.
Then, I believe that due to this organization's software management can learn how software user needs change and change its any kinds of software functions ( software life cycle), when its all softwares can be often changed to more new functions to create many different kinds of new software functions to satisfy software users needs and fight its software compettors in this often changing needs market. Due to software product may experience often changing life cycle stages. So, for often one learning software manager example, I believe that he can help this software organization to reach growth life cycle stage, even mature life cycle stage more easily in short time as well as he can also help his software organization to stay in mature life cycle stage long time if this software organizational manager can keep learning attitude to continue to create any new kinds of different functions software to satisfy software clients' changing needs for long time . Then, I believe that this software organization may experience or reach growth life cycle stage, even mature life cycle stage as well as continue staying long time on mature life cycle stage or avoid to encounter decline life cycle stage occurrence chance, if this software organization's softeare management can learn how to change software organization operation and software manufacture and sale strategy in order to satisfy this software users' needs in this software users' need often changing market . So, it is one example to explain why it has close

relationship between learning organizational management method and business life cycle stages. As this software organization case, the software management needs often to create and change any new kinds of software functions in order to satisfy software users' needs . So, the software managers need to spend time to learn software life cycle stage , it can help the software organization may reach products life cycle stage, even mature life cycle stage in short time,even the software product organization may also stay long time in mature life cycle stage , when it can reach this stage. Hence, learning how to change organizational management or strategy, which is one important factor to help any organization can reach growth or mature life cycle stage eadily in short time.

As Lewin describes that the change as a three stage process of unfreezing, change and freezing . In this phases of change model, Lewin emphasizes that change is that a series of individual processes, but rather one that flows from one process to the next . So, in general, services mature firms pace greater emphasis on more bureaucratic form, control systems might need to change throughout the life cycle to fit in with. He explains they have relationship between both organizational life cycle stage and management control.

Effective management control may help the organization to reach mature life cycle in short time rapidly. So, leadership managment and the way of thinking are required to balance control and through several stages of growth, maturity , decline or re-grow changes in the external environment influence. Hence, managers position in each of the stages of life cycle and providing practical solutions are, however world where environment changes have proven a rapid growth, the management of varios , they also need to implement how to change their organizational cultures, strategies in order to let their organizations to reach mature stage with a distinction-oriented rapidly. Hence, to successfully implement change initiatives, for each phase of life cycle. Any organizations need to produce resistance to change ( the old model wins out over management boils down to improving the relationship ) learning the relationship between leadership style and the organization life cycle were important. The change from one organizational life cycle phase to another, it depends on how the manager'c capacity to learn and change.

However, organizations at any stage of the life cycle are impacted by external environment, for example, threats in the start up stage differ from those in the maturity stage. So, managers must need often to learn when the right time is to be needed to change the goals, instead he also needs to learn types of changes in the maturity stage, comparisons with other, having strong personal and professional relationships in the organizaton's maturity stage. Hence, I believe that it has close relationship between learning change management and reaching maturity life cycle and staying long time in this stage.

● How to achieve the experience of mature life cycle reaching stage rapidly for product and service ?

Any businesses expect they can have chance or possibility to attempt to experience this nature life cycle stage, but it is not guarantee any kinds of businesses must may experience this the topest stage, the question is that: Have any methods may help any kinds of businesses to reach this the topest level of business life cycle, when their businesses had been developing or expanding in a period, e.g. after five years? So, it has no absolute to guarantee any kinds of businesses must may experience this the topest stage in one fixed time. How businesses can adapt to birth and growth life cycle stages in order to reach this the topest mature stage in their business life cycle stages? I shall attempt to explain whether it is possible that achieving what strategies may help businesses bring high successful chance to reach the business life cycle mature stage as below:

Product life cycle with maturity stage, it foucs as an important strategic inflection point. A number of techniques can help their businesses to attempt to reach this stage more easily. In fact, the product life cycle contains four distinct stages: introduction, growth, maturity, and decline. Each stage is associated with changes in the product's marketing position . Any firms can use various marketing strategies in each stage to try to proplong the life cycle of their products.

How do the firm extend the maturity stage of a product? I shall recommend change price , place or promotion extension strategy , what does change price extension strategies mean? Change prices mean proces can be lowered to allow ew customers to buy it as well as change place means that products can be sold in different countries or territories to gain more sales, change promotion means different advertising or sales promotion techniques can proplong the life of the product, giving it a new image. So, any organizations can attempt to achieve this extension strategies in order to adapt in different birth, growth and maturity stages for ther product sale easily. This extension strategies' characteristics is at the product;s price, sold places and promotin methods can be changed in order to adapt clients needs when their products are selling in birth, growth and maturity three stages in order to achieve the most effective sale effort and clients growth increasing for long time.

In fact, any product is like human beings, products also have a limited life-cycle and they pass through several stages in their life cycle. A typical product moves through five stages, namely, introduction or birth, growth, maturity or saturation and decline stages. So, when the product needs the maturity life cycle stage, in this maturity stage, it has these characteristics: The maturity stage of the product life cycle shows that sales will eventually peak and then slow down. During this stage, sales growth has started to slow down, and the product has already reached widespread acceptance in the market, in relative terms, utimately, during this stage, sales will peak . Hence, any businesses ought need to consider what key strategies can be implement to achieve the best sale performance throughout the different product life cycle stages and how to make the most of each stage. For example, when the product is selling in the birth stage, e.g. one author's book , his book is selling to the publisher in the first year, there are not many readers knew this book existence, so this book is not popular, its price ought not change high to compare similar topic book, e.g. story book in this year, but after this year, if there are many readers know this book and readers number can grow up rapidly. This author's this topic story book does not change, either increases or decreases , but its sale number has been significant increasing after the first year . So, this author's this story book ought be raised book price to attempt to sell easily. It is one good example of extension strategy to this author's this story book in its life cycle stages. So, such as ths publisher book sale case, it may attempt to achieve extension strategies to every author's book sale, it can follow every author's book prices, publishing places and promotion methods to help every author to sell in the most competitive book sale price, sale place choice and promotin methods in order to earn their readers growth aim . So, any book , it is as product to book shop, it will experience introduction, growth, and maturity life cycle stages. Some books may attract many readers to consider or some books may not attract many readers to consider to read . So, it causes their reading life cycle stages staying time will be different. So, extension strategies can help any books to be sold easily.

In fact, instead of product has life cycle stage, any service also has life cycle stage. There are five stages in service lifecycle. Thay may include: Service strategy, service design, service transition, service operation and continual servce improvement five stages. The service strategy phase of the service lifecycle provides guidance on how to design , develop and implement service management. Because any service business needs to manage to any employee service performance in order to provide excellent service quality, e.g. property management service to building tenants or property owners , if the peoperty management furm can train employees to provide excellent property management service to let their managing building clients to feel satisfactory. Then, the property management firm ought may keep long time property management service to this building. So, service provider will also experience service performance different stages.

In different service performance life cycle stages, such as this property management service case, they ought implement dfferent strategies in order to let their employees to know how to achieve service performance improvement to let their servicing building clients ( tenants or builgin owners) can feel their property management service can be continue improved to avoid to choose any property management service provider to replace it easily.

The purpose of the service strategy stage of the service life cycle is to define the perspective, position plans and pattern that a service provider needs to be able to execute to meet an organization business outomes. The objective of service strategy may include: An understandng of work strategy is thus either the concept of the product life cycle or the concept of the service life cycle is today at about to give a propsed new product or service , how and to what extent. This generally requires important changes in marketing strategies and methods, because any learning kinds of service or product lif cycle stage why and how to change to any organizational management, it may be an important tool for marketers, managers, and product and service providing designers alike, If specifies four individuals stages of a product's or service's life and offers guidance for developing strategies to make the best use of these stages and promote the overall success of the product or service in the marketplace.

Reasons managment needs to spend time to learn how to manage his/her product or service life cycle development stage? They may include: The product or service life cycle is determined by how long its marketable . Product or service life cycle also plays a critical role in marketing strategy . So, learning how to adapt your product or service to meet the coming trends , this is the stage what will occue in which differentiation when the kind of the product or service will have possible to reach the another new experience life cycle stage in order to adapt its business development more easily.

Hence, each stage is associated with changes in the product's or service's marketing postion . The organizational management can use various markting strategies in each stage to try to prolong the life cycle of your products or services . Any product or service reaches the marketplace, it enters the service or product life cycle . This product cycle typically has for stages: Introduction or birth, growth, maturity and decline ( and possibly deaths stages for product as well as service strategy stages includes service strategy. service design, servic transition, service operation, and continual service stages four service stages. So, the organization management can spend time to learn how to develop its business product or service needs to change in order to adapt marketing change in its product or service different life cycle stages. It can bring these benefits, such as: true benefits of product or srvice life cycle management may include, reduced time to makret, reduced market entry costs, more efficient and profitable distribution challen, higher return on investment from promotional cappaigns in possible, extending the lifetime of your product or service by adapting your approach as it moves through the lifecycle , for example, any management needs to learn what can make its products or services move from growth to maturity. After the introduction and growth stages, a product or service passes into the maturity stage. IN the first two stages , companies try to establish a market and then grow sales of their product or service to achieve as large , a share of that market as possible. Hence, marketers must be sure that a product or service has moved from one stage to the next before changing its marketing strategy. At each stage, marketing strategy varies. Strategy for the different stages of the product or service life cycle strategies may include: such as more benefits may be provided to the customers, e.g. extending the warranty period, guarantee period etc. However, company's market strategy depends on which stages the product or service is in its life cycle, for example, when one software manufacture company expects to expand its software sale market to overseas from local in growth stage. If it expects that it can reaches maturity stage in short time rapidly. It needs to implement technology innovation strategy for competition advantage reasons in global software sale markets development. Thus, the software organizational manager needs to spend time to learn what its present organizational characteristics are what resources and skills it owns or lacks, that gives it to comparative advantages over different countries to the operating changes that result in the learning curve to prepare this software product sale organizational maturity life cycle stage development more successfully. So, it needs to look at the advantages of focusing on what kinds of software manufacture and sale services in this software development industry whole life cycle stages and find the best or the most suitable competitive straregy, e.g. a discountinuous change to the software product development marketplace, what the global software product development industrial stage is and the tertiary or sale services sector durig the maturity life cycle stage to this softare manufacturer and sale organization strategy to this software firm during this growth stage may include example of it how changed its software product sales channels to which countries will be its another expanding sale market choice.

On conclusion, any organization management ought spend time to learn whether which strategies are the most suitable or the best to implement as well as how to implement when it is experiencing in the prodiuct or life cycle stage in order to spend less time to reach the maturity life cycle stage and proplong its maturity life cycle stage more success.

Organizational life cycle stage decision making strategy

Every company must have strategy to make any important or not important decision. Any decisions must be very important because they may influence any companies‘ future development. So, our company management can not neglect to cosider whether all strategies are reasonable to influence any organizations success. However, we need to consider how to achieve effective decisions to avoid wrong decisions to cause our companies' development in long term.

The question is how to implement effective decision making to achieve every consequence to gain the best benefits to any organizations? Any organization managers ought need to follow these steps in order to make effective decisions. Acknowledge and compensate for your biases, use positive and negative lists, experiment by reversing your live of thinkin, create a scoring system. Any organizational decisions have four decision making styles. They may include these four basic categories for decion making, these being: Directive, conceptual, consultative, and consensue. So, strategic decisions usually mean managers must plan for change and risk.

Many factors are unknown, since managers are planning for future changes. Another example for a major change is the decision to modify the company's culture. For instance, the firm may be having trouble with increased employee turnover. It may be the company's culture needs to be changed in order to employees can adapt to work together. Hence, when one company's working environment and employees attidude is poor, because they feel unhappy to work, so working environment will be caused poor. It may be influenced whole organizational culture to be more poor. Hence, the organizational ought need to change its organizational culture to be more happy in order to let whole organization's employees can feel happy to work in this enjoyable working environment . Hence, any entrepreneurs or managers ought need to consider employees' emotion issue how to let they have good working emotion to do their tasks every day, e.g. get comfortable with the cost of deciding , teaching employees hoe to control themselves emotion, understand that logical decisions have a secret emotional intuitive is one of the simplest, and arguably one of the most common ways to make a decision, rational decision making is the type of decision making many people want to believe what they do.

The first stage model to any making strategic decisions, they may include: defining the problem, consider these questions, gathering information, seeking information on how any why the problem occurred, developing and evaluating options, generating a wide range of options, choosing the best action, selecting the option that best meets the decision objective. Hence, decision including strategies are the ways, we use information to make a choice, in this case, managers need to make strategic choices as muually exclusive options, start with the most apparent options, generate alteratives, specify the conditions under which each option is attractive, identify barriers to each option, design and run tests to prove or disprove each of the conditions, finally using the data, make a decision. Hence, business leaders use strategic decision-making when they plan the company's future strategic management involves definingl long term goals, responding to market forces and carrying out the firm's mission, so making strategic decisions managers look at the big picture.

In psychology view, decision making is regarded as the cognitive process , knowledge necessary to know when to use any strategies. They do posses to change their approach to decision making. Rather, think of it is a decision making process that keeps you from making the same mistakes year after year. Making-judgement-based decisions among a variety of variable options is made easier when a systematic process is utilized. So, decision making strategies are the structured method and operational guidelines followed by decision makers. So, any strategic decision making process is needed in the procedural rationality stage, if the organization expects to do the most reasonable decision making to solve any challenges. So, strategic decision making is essential on how top managers use process and tools to implement long-term goals. Also, decision making is a process that reduces uncertainty to a considerable level.

In most decisions, uncertainty will be reduced, when the manager had prepared one good strategic decision making method, the most difficult decison making suitation is that when the manager needs to implement a multi-perspective strategic decision making. It is the process of making long-term decision's that helps or helps the organization t build long term benefits. However, any organization's managers ought need to spend time to learn a large variety of decision making techniques, it can help improve decisions of different types.

It can be useful in decision between strategies or investment opportunities with constrained resources. This is called strategic decision making, where decisions are made according to a company's goals or mission. At many organizations, it is up to managers to make the key decisions that influence business strategy. So, managers must need to learn how to implement any kinds of strategic decision making method in order to help their organizations to achieve the most reasonable long term benefits. However, with any strategic planning process, any organization will be able to know. What it wants to achieve in the long term vision is on ongoing process that involves crafting strategies to achieve goals.

- Why do managers feel difficult to make decisions?

Usually these factors may cause managers feel difficult to make decision for their organizations: Making decisions will always be difficult because it takes time and energy to weigh their options. Things like second-guessing the manager himself/herself and feeling indecisive and just a part of the process. However, decision-making is important to achieve the organizational goals/objectives within given time and budget. It searches the best alternative, utilizes the resources properly and satisfies the employees at the workplace. As a result, organizational goals or objectives can be achieved as per the desired result. Moreover, decision-making is an integral part of modern management.

Decisions play important roles as they determine both organizational and mangerial activities. A decision can be defined as a consequence of action purposely chosen from a set of alternatives to achieve organizational or managerial objectives or goals. The first step to making those decision is understanding what makes managers themselves so hard, the decisions that may include senior leaders, middle managers, frontline staffs , they many face short time or long time decision making challenge , when they need to find solution methods to solve any organizational challenges. For example, one manager needs to make decision to resolve organizational challenge before tomorrow morning time. Then, time pressure can lead to poor decision making to influence the manager feels physically, mentally ad personally pressure. He will have much chance to make poor decisions when he feels he is in a position of power. IF he can not make any decisions to help his organization to solve challenge before tomorrow morning, he will not achieve any satisfactory management effort to the company's senior management, even CEO . So, time pressure may be one main factor to cause the manager to do poor decision making to help his organization to solve the challenge.

So, if the manager hopes to make better decision making , he needs likely feel comfortable and confident making decisions, e.g. learning how to manage his senior manager or CEO expectations. However, some decisions carry enough weight that the prospect of simply making a choice can be made in short time. SO, the manager ought need to learn how to weight whether which choices may bring more benefits or advantages ro make any decision in short time frequently every day. It can train that when the manager encounter difficult problem to be solved in short time. He can be trained to judge whether which is the most suitable choice easily to do any decision more easily. So, daily learning how to solve any short time or long time decision making skill frequently, this learning behavior must help any managers to raise short time critical thinking decision making skilful effort. Hence, learning managing uncertainty and making the most reasonable choices , strategic decision making skill, it will be any organizational managers ought need to consider issue if they want to be the best strategic decision maker in themselves organizations.

Hence, any organizational managers need to know that decision making is difficult to taugh, particularly when there may not be one right answer. It's common for managers and leaders to feel alone. Being alone as a decision maker comes with the job. However, decision making is absolute one of the toughest parts of running a business. They will feel responsible for it, compared to the management announcing the change in policy without listening to what. Hence, self confidence, time management factor, is a important part to influence any managers to do any important decision making more success. So, they can not neglect how to train themselves to attempt to find the most reasonable decision making to solve any chalenges for themselves organizations in order to achieve one strategic decision maker for their organizations.

On conclusion, managers' attitudes toward work and incentives may influence his decision making whether it can be more accurate, when reviewing upon motivation, incentives, the social psychology of work and behavior at work, it is tempting to conclude that managers are motivated when manual workers need bonus payment, between ideas , beliefs attitudes. So, any managers individual personal attitudes will influence their behaviors, also his behaviors will motivate how he can make resonable decision making. So, manager's working attitude can be one factor to influence whether his/her decision making can be made more reasonable for his/her organization.

Computer technologic firm merger cooperational strategy

- IBM and Apple merger strategic advantages and disadvantages

IBM and Apple computer firms, they merger to cooperate together, whether merger will help them to bring what advantages and disadvantages ? What is the life cycle stage to these two big computer organizations? These two computer companies IBM and Apple , they had set up abut forty years. From 1970 year, when Apple founders, they had invented new computer machine to bring human playing electronic game to entertain at home. Then, IBM founder also invented micro softword clerical software to let any office workers or students or home users can type on computers to replace typing machines . So, Micro soft word software invention also help office workers or students or home users to choose to apply computer to do typing tasks to replace traditional typing machines. So, these two firms' borth stage, is that when Apple desktop computer products are innovated as well as Microsoft IBM micro soft word softwares are also innovated to this traditional typing market.

When, 1980, there are not that Microsoft word softare functions are, so these two founders will spend long time to promote desktop computers and microsoft word software new products to let many people know what their real functions are, e.g. playing electronic entertainment game activities and clerical tasks , these two main functions to let them to know, when they may be known whether what microsoft word software and Apple brand desktop computer can help any students or clerical office workers or home users to do any clerical tasks or play electronic playing game leisure activites at homes or offices. Then , many people begin to accept these both new products to use for their daily clerical tasks or electronic playing game lesiures activies .

However, in their birth life cycle stage time needs about two years short time only, because their advesrtisement strategies are effective to let global many people feel computer product can belp us to fo any clerical tasks or bring exciting electronic playing game leisure feeling when students feel bore, they may spend some times to apply computer to play any games at homes. Even they may turn on computers to apply Microsoft word sofware to help them to do any homeworks or assignments. Students can use computers to replace typing machines to type any clerical documents at homes or schools conveniently.

After1982 year, global IBM computer and Microsoft word software buyers number had been increasing rapidly. So, from 1982 year, these two firms are experiencing life style growing stage period. Till to 1988 year, these two firms may ensure global computer and software products main suppliers their computer and software technological products had high market share. So, in global computer and software technological market, these are not many competitors to win them. So, they do not need long time to enter life cycle growing stage. They only need four ro five years time to attract many global computer and software buyers begun to accept their products and also choose to buy their IBM and Microsoft computers and softwares to use. Hence, then 1988 year, these two high technolgical computer and software product firms had been experiencing life cycle mature stage till to 2000. Although, in this forty , IBM and Apple computer firms number had been increasing rapidly globally. But, other computer and software competitors number is also increasing, e.g. Dell computer brand had be familiar to global computer buyers. Dell's market share is also high. So, their computer and software buyers may have many kinds of computers and softwares brands of product choices in global students and office clerical workers and home users computer and software product market.

In fact, IBM and Apple began to enter life cycle decline stage , due to laptop products need increase and many different brands of laptop computers may be supplied to let computer users to choose to buy in global computer market. So, after 2000 , these two computer firms began to change to new technologial product or service market, e.g. apply also invented Smart mobile products because it felt desktop and laptop products competitors number had been decreasing , due to they had many laptops and desktops competitors' products to choose to buy. So, Apple brand computer begun to invent smart mobile phone and small flat laptop , it has or has none phone function products in order to earn high market share to smart mobile and flat laptop product user market ratio in order to avoid life cycle decline stage reachs rapidly.

In fact, IBM smart mobile strategy may be effective to absord global some smart mobile customers. But IBM is skill desktop same smart mobile competitors. Also, IBM laptop and desktop products may also face different similar computer function products to choose from competitors.So, IBM will may enter life cycle decline stage rapidly. Also, Microsoft brand computer may be its main competitor, Microsoft can attempt to apply interest technology to help it to sell electronic book, because it felt desktop and laptop product market has reached mature stage.

It is common that global every family had own at least one laptop or desktop or both computer product. So, it means that product needers number begins to decrease, when global every family own at least one computer product to use at home, even global every office also wn at least one computer in offices. Unless, their computers are broken , thwy ill feel need to buy another new. Otherwise, they use computers about three to five years when they feel too old,then they will choose to change another new. So, Microsoft applies internet to help it to sell electronic book, it can bring another electconic publish business chance, instead of selling laptop, desktop, Microsoft software products only, because it also feel that when computer market had reached mature period. Global many people had owned computers, their needs will also decrease. Since internet invention, it creates e-commerce chance, electronic publishing is also popular to let global readers to read any books from desktop or laptop computers or mobile computers tools anywhere. So, Microsoft is attempting to enter this electronic publish market . this electronid publishing reading service market does not need readers to buy paper books to read, they won't need feel heavy if they need to bring bags to carry many heavy books to go to schools, libraries , students only need to bring laptops to read any Microsoft publish electonic books from computers anywhere conveniently. So, Microsoft electronic book pubishing new market help it to avoid to experience the life cycle decline stage rapidly. But, these two firms are still main competitors , if they choose not to merger or coopeerate to do technologic product, e.g. laptop, desktop , software or electronic book publish online reading service together. They may influence their clients number to reduce. Otherwise, if they can merger or cooperate , then it is possible that their clients nu,ber may increase or profit increase, even fight other computer and software companies competitors easily. Then, their computer and softare market share may raise when other competitors number reduces, e.g. Dell may be their main computer competitor, but if they cooperate or merger , then Dell's clients may be influenced to choose to buy their any desktops, laptops, softwares products. They can help themselves invention high technological products , if they can attribute their unique computer technology to help to invent any new kinds of more advanced computers or softwares , e.g. even high technological electronic reading platform to be improved to publish high reading quality of electronic books to attract many readers to read their electronic books from their publishing webstores.

IBM and Microsoft merger or cooperation can help them to raise market share or fight competitors in this often changing high technological computer product market. What are the disadvantages and advantges when they choose to merger or cooperate together? I shall explain as below:

Can IBM and Microsoft merger can keep their computer , software , even electronic book publish market in the mature life cycle stage in long time in order to avoid decline life cycle stage occurs. IBM's global strategy is based on three aspects: cloud , data and engagement . IBM's strategy imperatives may is business growth on cloud, analytics, mobile, social and society . So, it has changed its old strategy only concentrates on computer sold aspect. Since internet technology had been invented. However, IBM's primary generic strategy is cost leadership.

In Michael Porter's model, the generic strategies are what companies use to ensure competitive advantages . The cost leadership generic competitive strategy supports IBM's competitive advantages through cost-effectiveness of its operaton. However, if IBM can operate or merger to Microsoft, then Microsoft ought may help it to reduce more cost , when their technology can assist to develop their products, e.g. IBM's clouds , data technologic strengths can be brought to Microsoft 's product or Microsoft's electronic book publishing technology or software manufacturing technology strengths can bring to IBM' s products to assist themselves to raise computer, smartphone phoe, electronic publishing reading technological service business competitive effort in global computer , smartphone and electronic book publish markets. Then, when IBM can own Microoft 's technology , it may help it to reduce manufacturing cost in possible.

In fact, instead of IBM may merger to microsoft to reduce its cost to be more. It may also merger to Amazon, Amazon is us one online electronic book sale provider, it help global different businesses to apply itself online platform to sell their products. It is middleman role, it helps any sellers to sell their products from its online store platform. Any one can turn on computer and click to Amazon website to buy any products . Amazon will help any buyers to deliver their products to their homes by flight , after they pay visa card, because Amazon is global the topest online product sale service middleman provider. It's cloud technology is very proficient. If Amazon and IBM can merger to cooperate to do themselvers cloud service high technological business. IBM can apply Amazon's cloud high technological platform to help itself to grow its business and increase its cloud service clients number more easily. So, IBM ought choose Amazon's cloud platform to assist itself to continue to develop its future cloud service business, e.g. electronic book publish, because Amazon's electronic book publish market has have high reading market share.

Hence, IBM needs to find, e.g. Amazon or Microsoft to expand its high technological product or cloud strategy or cloud technology may be IBM's main competitors. If Amazon and IBM and Microsoft can merger or cooperate to expand themselves unique computers or softwares ot smart mobiles or electronic book platform sale markets to be merger together, then global computer buyers , smart mobiles buyers , electronic book readers, electronic platform product buyers must may enjoy the most benefits, because they can attribute their unique computers, smart mobiles manufacture, cloud service platform technology to be applied to themselves unique computers, smart mobiles, electronic book reading flatform and ebooks ale mix together, t means to improve these products or services unique function or improve themselves technology in order to let global computer , smart mobile or electronic book readers or electron platform product buyers feel that their these products or cloud platform products sale or reading service performance can br improved. Hence, their merger ought bring advandages more than disadvantages.

However , I shall also indicate some possible disadvantages to IBM merger strategy. Higher prices to IBM products, A merger can reduce competition and give the IBM more monopoly power with less competition and greater market share to IBM, but when IBM chooses to merger to Micrsoft and / or IBM chooses to merger to MIcrosoft and/or Amazon , they may influence IBM's computer or smartmobile phone products can usually increase prices for consumers. Then, consumers may also compare IBM's products to other computer and smart mobile phone sellers. If they feel its price is not reasonable, they may choose to buy other smart mobiles or choose to buy other brands of laptops, desktops to replace IBM's product. Because IBM's any products prices may be controlled or dominated by Microsoft or Amazon after they merger. So, IBM can not change itself products prices more easily. It is its weaknesses . Another risk's associated with mergers and acquisitions to IBM, it may be differences in culture between Amazon and Microsoft and IBM. It may bring inefficient communication and lack of transparency to IBM organization when Amazon and Microsoft staffs may participate to IBM any important decisions. It may bring miscalculations in the evaluation of assets to IBM. For example, merger may bring disadvantages when the main drivers behind the Lenovo and IBM merger. The drivers behind the merger between China's Lenovo and US IBM was inspired by several moves. The main one being the loss that the latter incurred to IBM itself pc division after a change of business strategy.

On conclusion , before IBM decides to implement merger strategy to any technological firms, it needs to consider whether what risks they may bring and what benefit they may bring after IBM itself chooses to merger to the firm in order to avoid miscalculation consequence to influence IBM's business continues to develop or reachs life cycle decline stage rapidly.

CHAPTER THREE

# Can technology improve travel service performance

Our global tourism development had been developed from birth cycle stage to decline life cycle stage nowadays. From 1960 beginning, when airplanes were popular to be increased need to global travelers. Hence, from 1960 to 1970 is whole global tourism industry birth cycle stage. Till to 1971 beginning, many Asia, e.g. Singapore, Japan, China and Western, e.g. UK, UK etc. countries people, they have jobs to do ,and they have more extra money to prepare to choose any leisure activities. From 1971 to 1980, it is growth life cycle stage to global tourism industry. Many airplane manufacturers had been beginning to manufacturer many airplanes because they felt global traveler number would increase. In fact, in this ten years, global traveler number had been increasing every year. Then, from 1981 to 2019 this fourty years, it is global tourism industry nature life cycle stage. It means that every year travel number had been increasing more significantly to compare past. Also, many travelers feel need to travel every year. So, global travel tourism industry may reach the most top travel clients level in this fourty years. However, till to 2020 , due to COVD19 human mouth and disease occurrence, it influences global travelers feel fear to catch air planes to travel because this kind COVD 19 human mouth disease may cause lung disease from air. When many travelers are sitting in the close window air plane, if one person has ths kind COVD19 human mouth disease. The sick person may contact air to let the persons to breath to cause lung disease in possible in airplane. So, global travelers number is decreasing after 2019 . Also, it implies that tourism industry is facing decline life cysle stage.

It brings these questions: IS it right time to develop space tourism? Can space tourism help future tourism industry to re-grow its life cycle stage from nowadays decline life cycle stage? Can space tourism develop to nature stage from birth life cycle stage ? I shall attempt to give evidence to explain whether space tourism may be developed to let human has more one kind tourism . It may be future leisure new trend for travelers, instead of earth travel. Because one day earth tourism destination may not bring leisure interesting to global traveler, then space tourism may be attempted to replace this kind of travelling activity . So, space tourism is birth life cycle stage. However, our earth tourism may define moral tourism, nature tourism, green tourism, responsible tourism in future new travelling leisure trend.

It bring these questions: Can our future tourism industry meet the expectations with the terms " ecological tourist"? Which factors affect the product life cycle of eco tourism? Nature and green tourism may be our earth new kind of travel activities, when many young and old age travelers like to climb mountains, they feel life nature scene more than non-man made) nature scene in their journeys, they do not like to visit cities to travel. It is possible that they often work in offices, this office working factor may influence many travelers like green tourism in the future. So, green or nature tourism will be our future popular tourism leisure activities. It may influence nowadays our tourism decline life stage to re-grown to nature life cycle stage in possible in this COVD19 people mouth disease influential environment.

New economic development in Tourism and oil industries

- How to develop new economic tourism industry

How to develop tourism industry in new economic environment? Any examination of the new economic development of travel and tourism requires definitions of the subject and its components, which are suitable for economic analysis. However, in new economic development to tourism industry, it is also important to look at tourism conceptually, in order to set the scene for a deeper understanding of the future new tourism industry development.

Tourism is neither a phenomenon nor a simple set if industries, however, in new or old economic development environment. It is a human activity which encompasses human behavior, use of resources, and interaction with other people, economies and leisure enjoyment environment. It is also involved physical movement of tourists to locales other than their normal living places.

In future new economic environment, traditional travel needs to include these element in order to satisfy traveler enjoyment and leisure feeling: They may include: Tourist needs and motivations, tourism selection and behavior and constraints , travel away from home , market interactions between tourists and those supplying products to satisfy tourist needs and impacts on tourists , hosts, economies and environments.

In new economic environment, the tourism products may include: carriers, in any forms of transport for tourist travel accommodation, man-made attractions, which could also include the managed areas of natural attractions, private sector and public sector support services, middlemen, such as tour wholesalers and travel agents.

The tourism resources may also include: Natural resources, lands , minerals, water and biological; labor resources, human work, and enterprise; capital resources, manmade enhancement and other resources. The travel and tourism resources problems may include: As there is frequently a mismatch between producer and consumer perception of what constitutes the tourism product , there may be conflict in ideas of which resources are properly involved as well as many of the resources likely to be in demand for tourism are public goods , or even free resources.

In new economic development to tourism industry view, we need to consider that tourism and travel has the reputation of being a relatively clean and pleasant industry in which to work or invest in order to attract a greater number of resource suppliers than as less well-perceived industry, which therefore keeps rewards prices down by competition, how to attract those retiring from or travel business for example, if their finances are already sound, income from travel is not expected to be optimal , travel and tourism is frequently highly seasonal , offering rewards that are competitive with other industries only some of the time, destination products are often in locations which are of little use to other industries, so that competition for resource use if minimal and hence rewards are low.

In general, tourist purpose may include: recreational purpose : holiday, health and sport and religion as well as business purpose: company business , e.g. conventions and sales trips. So, in new economic tourism development aim, tourism industry need consider hoe to achieve incentive trips to let these both tourists to feel. For example, the overall type of tourism required, destination arrangement, travel mode, accommodation and attraction visiting and purchasing method or distribution channel. The purchasing method choices may include: whether to buy an inclusive package or separate service, whether to buy direct from suppliers, such as airlines or hotels or use an agent , which tour wholesaler or operate or agent to use.

I predict the tourism development in new economic view, it may have these characteristics: Few enterprises in travel and tourism are large, highly cashed-up and have a large asset base, enterprises within travel and tourism that are not in a financial position to diversify, and those do well success to the above –average growth obtainable in travel and tourism compared with many other industries, they would therefore tend to expand within the sector. The result of individual enterprise growth and integration within travel and tourism is an increase in the concentration of that industry. The degree to which output is produced of fewer and fewer enterprises. This can be only be accounted for realistically with the context of an individual economy, Levels of concentration in any part of travel and tourism in the future are likely to depend on two opposing factors: The constant demand by many tourist market segments for new experiences and products, which encourages the development and survival of more and diverse enterprises, and therefore leads to the reduction of concentration as well as technology, which in travel and tourism frequently calls for large capital outlays and requires mass markets for efficient use, promotes integrations and large scale enterprise, especially in air travel and non-personal services ( marketing and information communication, travel insurance , tourism payment methods). IN these areas, concentration will undoubtedly increase in future new economic development environment.

HOW TO PROLONG TOURISM LEISURE MATURE LIFE CYCLE STAGE AS WELL AS AVOID DECLINE AND DEATH LIFE CYCLE STAGE OCCURENCE FROM COVID 19 HUMAN DISEASE

Any businesses expect to reach the mature life service cycle stage and they also hope to prolong to stay in this stage and avoid to have chance experience decline life service cycle stage, even death stage in future whole business life cycle stages. However, in fact, there are many businesses need to spend long time to have effort to reach mature life cycle stage from birth and growth both stages, even when they have effort to experience this the topest level stage, many can not stay to prolong time in this stage, then they will reach next stage, such as decline life cycle stage, even final death life cycle stage possibly. Hence , research whether how can reach the mature life cycle stage in short time and prolong to say in this stage. It is one common researching value question to any businesses. Such as COVID 19 human disease had been occurrence in 2019 end , it bring global tourism industry traveller number began to reduce. I shall attempt to explain how airline organizations implement strategies to avoid to enter decline service life cycle stage as below:

- How to avoid to reach the decline service life stage rapidly to global airlines tourism service industry due to COVID 19 human disease occurred

Strategies for growing and maturity a product or raise service performance, and increasing profit margins and prolonging to stay on the mature service life stage. I believe that it is any service businesses final aim. However, in any service life cycle stages, when the service , e.g. airline tourism leisure service industry will experience the decline service life stage , due to the COVID19 human disease influences to global travelers began to feel fear to catch airplanes to avoid air contact to give this kind of disease from 2020. So, nowadays, airlines ought have the suitable or right strategies to help them to solve travelers reducing number to influence their profit growth to encounter decline life service cycle stage later.

Life cycle strategy is based on product or service life cycle thinking from marketing, the factors may influence when the business can reach the mature life cycle stage, but some unpredicted factors may influence their clients number reduce, such as this airlines organizations traveler number reduces is due to COVID 19 human disease influences they feel fear to catch airplanes to travel case, their strategies may include: market growth rate, market growth potential, breach of service lines, number of competitor, distribution of market, share among competitors, customer loyalty , barriers to entry and technology improvement etc. factors to influence the global airlines tourism service industry can continue develop or expand to future overseas tourism market, when COVID 19 human disease may be killed by new medicine later.

Such as this COVID 19 human disease influences travelers feel fear to catch airplanes to avoid get this kind of disease and it influences global travelers number is decreasing in 2020 case, when the airline organization reaches the growth life service cycle stage from the birth stage, if it expects to spend short time to reach the mature life service cycle stage. Before COVID 19 human disease had not been killed by new medicine, if they hope to attract many travelers to choose to catch their airplanes to fly , the extension strategies that any airline organization can attempt to achieve, they may include, rebranding, establishing airline service in order to differentiate the other airline competitors tourism service , ticket price discounting and seeking new marketers, rebranding is the creation od a new look and feel for an established airline tourism service from the airline's competitors.

The airline service life cycle extension strategies also may include these methods to help the airline organization to grow or grow up or develop its airline tourism market rapidly, e.g. repackaging and new sizes, the appearance of airline tourism service can be crucial gaining a passenger's attention and developing tourism interest , new formulas or additional airline tourism features to the tourism country, lower ticket prices to maintain interest or liquidate surplus stock new airline tourism service advertising campaign, altering the new airline channel of destination, such as online ticket purchase.

Hence, after COVID 19 human disease had been skilled by new medicine , any airline organizations need to consider how to choose the most suitable strategy from different kinds of key strategies to expand their airline new tourism channels throughout the different airline tourism service life stages, in these four distinct stages: introduction, growth, maturity and decline or possible death stage, when this COVID 19 human disease had occurred from 2019 end, it may influence global travelers number had significant been reducing to bring any airline organizations may enter the decline life service cycle stage rapidly, even death life service cycle stage comes consequently.

Any airline organizations can use various marketing strategies in each stage to try to prolong the life cycle or attempt to reach the mature life cycle stage in short time. Avoiding to experience decline life service cycle stage, such as the COVID 19 human disease occurrence causes global travelers number began to reduce. It is ensure that any airline organizations do not expect to experience or reach the decline service life stage due to this COVID 19 human disease influences. The question is that how the airline organizations can maintain a strategy in the decline stage , such as COVID19 human disease influences global travelers number reduced and it brings many airlines income began to reduce, for example, reducing the airline promotional expenditure in this COVID 19 human disease occurrence period, reducing the number of airline distribution outlets , e.g. Hong Kong to New York airline flight channel reduces implementing ticket price cuts to get passengers to but the maintaining the airline tourism service and waiting for airline competitors to withdraw from the global airline tourism market.

Thus, following the initial growth, in this COVID human disease occurrence period, when the new airline organization enterprise enters the expansion stage during which the routing operation succeeds. The new airline organization can either reach the mature life service cycle stage either it can prolong to stay in this stage or it can not prolong to stay and enters to decline service life cycle stage , even death service life cycle stage. So , how to avoid the decline service life cycle stage comes to the new airline organization in this COVID 19 human disease occurrence period. It is any airline organizations concerning question when they are experiencing in the mature life cycle stage, but when COVID 19 human disease occurs to influence global travelers number began to reduce. May the airline organization experience the decline service life cycle stage rapidly when the COVID 19 human disease occurs ? It depends on whether it's strategies implementation are effective , its' strategies are effective, it may avoid to reach the decline life service cycle stage in short time easily due to COVID 19 human disease influences.

For this COVID 19 human mouth disease case , since 2019 had occurred, it brought serious tourism industry economic loss to any countries, many people loss jobs, many people feel fear to enter any shops when they are in crowd shop environment, e.g. restaurants can not permit to allow many people to sit closely, because when one person has COVID 19 human mouth disease, he can bring this disease to another person from air. So, many restaurants lose many clients in morning, lunch and night busy eating time, even ships also can not permit many people to enter their ships, because they avoid many people may contact, if one or some people has/have COVID 19 mouth disease, when he/she talks to the salespeople in the shop. It has high chance to cause many people get COVID human disease by mouth. So, any shops can not allow crowd in themselves shops to avoid any people have COVID 19 human disease occurrence. So, this COVID 19 human mouth disease may influence many businesses are experiencing decline life cycle stage, because clients number is continue decreasing, unless drug invention succeeds to fill this kind human mouth disease. Otherwise, on the consequence, many businesses will face death life cycle stage in short time possible. So, it is good example to explain unpredicted external environmental factor to bring global businesses will face decline life cycle in 2020 or next year, even after two years latter. So, COVID -19 human mouth disease may also influence any businesses had been experiencing long time in the mature life cycle to change to decline life cycle stage in possible.

Instead of the businesses are experiencing in either birth or growth life cycle stage. for example, UK Cathay airline had been experiencing long time in the mature life cycle stage from 2000, when its clients number had been increasing, but when the end of 2019, COVID-19 human mouth and air contact disease had occurred in global to influence any people feel fear to catch airplanes to travel or business travel frequently, due to airplanes have none windows, its none window environment will bring COVID-19 disease to any passengers when the airplane has many passengers are sitting together closely, if anyone has COVID-19 disease, he will cause any one airplane service waiter, passenger , even pilot to have COVID-19 disease easily.

So, global airline industry is experiencing decline life cycle stage. even Cathay airline is one big UK developed airline , it's passengers number is large in the past, but when COVID-19 disease occurs to cause travelers number had been decreasing. Hence, Cathay airline is experiencing decline life cycle stage from mature life cycle stage. It needs to implement dismissing staffs to keep salaries expenditure reducing strategy in global, e.g. HK will have 4,000 front line airline service staffs or airport check in service staffs , they will be dismisses in HK Cathay airline market. Although, HK government had given money to support it to continue to alive in order to avoid dismissing employees decision . But, Cathay airline had made decision that it will dismiss many airline service staffs in different countries. In fact, if Cathay airline expects it would not reach to the decline life cycle stage later, this dismissing employees strategy aims to avoid spending much salaries expenditure , it may be one good method to avoid decline , even death life cycle stage occurs in this year or latter.

On conclusion, it is difficult to predict what factors may cause the business itself will face decline life cycle stage occurrence in any time. Hence, any businesses ought to spend time to research whether which methods or strategies can help them to continue to expand their market or fight any kinds of threats in those four identified business life cycle stages. To avoid business can not continue develop or die, when the business is experiencing in the decline life cycle stage, the strategy is that , the organization needs to spend time to observe or learn how and why its market environment is changing in order to make the most accurate or effective strategies decisions to solve any challenges in any one of these four life cycle stages successfully.

- How new economic development in oil industry

The future global economic growth, it will influence personal incomes and GDP rise. They would carry different weight in different countries at different times. Starting from low levels of incomer and economic development. Household consumption will change from being dominated by basic heat to rapidly rising energy use for higher levels of comfort in space heating and cooling ( and large dwellings), and greater use of electrical appliances, finally to a degree of saturation influenced by the income distribution patterns of the country concerned. Income distribution typically changes very slowly, so that the technical market for heart will never be saturated because there will always be a proportion of poor people living in small spaces less comfortably than the average. Industrial energy consumption will be influenced by technical efficiency within each sector, and by changes in the structures of the economy, e.g. changing proportions of agriculture, heavy and light industry, and services. One may eventually see evidence of diminishing marginal returns to additional energy inputs compared to other inputs. Energy consumption in the energy transformation sector may be influenced by income, which drives the demand for electricity to influenced by income, which drives the demand for electricity to grow faster than the demand for heat, but is also subject to the chosen technology of transformation, which is influenced by the cost and availability of primary energy inputs ( fuels) in new economic development environment.

IN new economic development environment, it will influences that fuels do not compete in all sectors; for example, the transport sector is dominated by oil. Nuclear and hydroelectric power ( and most renewables) reach the user through electricity; electricity itself competes with the direct burning of fossil fuels. Electricity provides the means by which other fuels can compete with oil and gas in sectors, such as space heating and process heat. It also is the only means of powering applications such as motors, computers and lighting: these subsectors are difficult to analyze. However, there is strong evidence that higher incomes do not weaken the demand for electricity so much as the demand for energy in total ( in contrast to the effect on the demand for non-electric energy forms).

Econometricians look at the historical record of change in fuel prices and quantities to distinguish several factors between the new economic development and old economic development to oil industry in the future. An income effect. Increasing ( reducing) fuel prices reduces ( increases) the purchasing power of consumers' income: higher incomes caused by lower prices will increase energy consumption; the consumers' allocation of the increased income to energy purchases may reduce as income rises. Thus income may be heading in a different direction from fuel prices that the effect of fuel price changes when incomes are rising means simply that rising incomes have increased demand. Reducing the cost of using energy through win-win efficiency measures causes a similar problem . On the consequence, in future new economic development environment, it may influence in both cases demand will be less than if the future oil price or efficiency has not changed. The other effect is that an efficiency or substitution effect. An increase in fuel prices may cause consumers to spend more on new equipment, building materials and management operations, which will reduce the amount of fuel required to give the same energy result to the user. The extent of the efficiency effect depends on what happens to the price of the new equipment or building: if those price s rise in line with the fuel price, changes in the balances between fuel and capital or management will not occur. A new user technology , such as the development of the combined cycle gas turbine generator may increase efficiency and thus greatly reduce the quantity of primary fuel needed to produce the required output in this case electricity. If electricity prices had remained sticky, and the electricity and gas markets were not competitive, some of this advantages could have accrued to the gas suppliers in the form of an increase in price, because th4 unit of gas produces more output of electricity, it would have a higher value. In reality, the development of new economic competitive environment in both gas and electricity has tended to ensure that the benefits of such technical advanced accrue to the consumer through lower final prices. The same many apply in the case of improved efficiency in future non-manual driving auto vehicle development: the consumer's cost of motoring is reduced in new economic non-manual driven auto vehicle (Artificial intelligent vehicle) can replace manual driven vehicle , even electricity battery can replace oil energy to be used in vehicles. So, oil price may be influenced to reduce in future new economic development environment.

New and old economic theories explain oil is not main factor to influence tourism income

- Can economic theory explain old price change to influence tourism income?

I shall attempt to apply old and new economic theory to explain whether oil changing price has direct relationship to influence global tourism indusry development or tourism income as below:

Is oil changing price the main to influence tourism income or tourism development or economic growth ? If oil price rises ar falls, it will or won't cause tourism income decreases or increases? If they have cause and effect relationship, what are the main factors to influence tourism income changes by oil price rises or falls ?

I aim to investigate how any why among oil price shocks will influence tourism income variables. We may distinguish between these oil price shocks: Supply-side , aggregate demand and oil specific demand shocks. I assume that oil specific demand shocks affect inflation and the tourism sector equity index. By constrast, I also believe that aggregate demand oil price shock exercisr an effect, either directly and indirectly tourism generated income and economic growth. So, in old economic theory, supply-side , aggregate demand view to oil specific demand shocks will influence tourism income varies. So, governments ought implement strategies against future oil price movements or plan for economic policy development.

In fact, instead of oil price changes will influence tourism income, it could also harm economic growth and tourism activities, due to the effect they expert on transporation, production cost, economic uncertainty.Because tourism activities is one important sector to influence any country's leisure consumption GDP income source. So, sudden fluctations in oil prices may also influence economic growth. It is based a hyphthesis known as the tourism led economic growth. So, it seems that they have direct or indirect relationship to case effect between oil price and tourism activities and development. So, increase on tourism income, the called " economic-driven tourism growth". In addition, high oil prices are affecting certain tourism industry segments , e.g. airlines, cruises lines, hotel, rent travelling car services etc. for oil, importing countries example, with reference to macro economic effects, higher oil prices generally lead to higher inflation, when they negatively influence to country's income.

Hence, from a micro-economic perspective, positive oil price shocks lead to a decline in disposable income. for low income people, it will bring an immediate and negative impact on tourism, mainly due to they feel tourism leisure is regarded as a luxury good, when oil price shocks to rise suddenly . It influences any airline or cruise entertainment service providers' costs are influenced to raise. Then, they need to increase air ticket or cruise ticket price. It will bring on negative tourism leisure demands-side the oil price increases low income group, potential tourism leisure consumers. Hence, it seems that oil price may have indirect relationship to influence tourism leisure consumers' needs.

● How the price of oil changes influences global tourism industry growth or recession?

In macro-economic view, sudden mid and long term oil price shock can influence global torusim industry growth or recession. For example, a oil price of US$180 per barrel was considered only a few years ago, now this has a realistic scenario to which all plaers in the T&T sector have to adapt. At such a high level, the price of oil will become even more critical to almost every part of the tourism value chain. Although, weak global demand, caused by global economic recesson, resulted in a steep oil price decline to US$45 per barrel by the fourth quarter of 2008 in the past low oil price occurrence history, this won't change the mid to long -term oil forecast.

In fact, the past oil price occurrence history of the dramatic structural had changed a high price imposed on airlines, travelers, and destination countries, all of which will have to navigate through times of shifting or even declining travel demand. I assume that a high oil price scenario is assumed in the long term in order to highlight the changes , such a senario would mean for consumer behavior and the competitiveness of several destinations.

Low oil price in the 1970 and early 1980 did not bring significant growth of international air travel, but its growth has been strongest between 1980 and 2004, a period with stable and relatively moderate oil prices. Also, the rapid development of the low-cost carrier business model in the 1990s further fueled air travel growth by capturing tourism leisure demand , such as weekend leisure travel to cities using mostly secondary airports in any big area countries, such as UK, US . However, the tourism growth is whole influenced by high oil prices, due to oil price had been continue rising in possible.

Basis of oil is shortage supply product, oil is assumed to be the main energy source for the aviation sector for the nest 30 years. Although, second-generation biofuels seem to be on the horizon, the economics as well as the production scalability and aviation biofuel shortage will be a main challenge to airline industry. So, I assume that oil price will continue rise up, if there have none any aviation biofuel can be reflected to oil to use for air plane energy.

Until 2004, the only factors to have affected air travel growth, negatively were in external shocks , such as 9/11, causes catching air plane crisis or US regional geopolitical conflicts. It brings some travelers feel fear to go to US travel, as well as until recently 2019, human mouth disease can influence air to have disease to anyone from mouth. So, global travelers number had been continue decreasing, because they arc fear to get disease by air when many themselves every stranger travelers are sitting on the without windows air planes. Although, mouth human and air disease and US 9/11 air attack both matters may influence oil price falls effect, because air planes flying times will reduce. They won't need frequent to fly, to cause aviation oil energy need reduce. Consequently, oil price will decrease, due to travelers number reduces and air planes flying times are also influenced to reduce. ( oil demand decreases cause oil price decrease). Although, air lines ' cost will also be influenced reduce, but oil price decrease can not bring travelers number increase , when air ticket price reduce because global many leisure and business trip travelers feel fear to catch air planes frequently when human mouth air disease occured in 2019. So, oil price decreases can not grow up tourism industry growth or rise tourism income.

However, the obvious impact of a high oil price is an increase in the operating costs of airline. Moreover, fuel cost as a percentage of airline operating costs vary significantly based on the length of the flight. The longer the flight, the higher the fuel costs as a percentage of the airline operating cost. So, from an online's perspective, long -hauel flights represent the most criticial challenge to profitable operation because the share of fuel on these flights, compared with other cost items, is largest, because of the unfacorable fuel economics, due to fuel costs even at high-load factors. For example, Thai airways dropped its non-stop Bongkok to US flights in the summer of 2008 for commercial reasons, because fuel reached operating cost levels of 55 percent on this route, a cost burden that could not be passed on to their customers. So, the estimated price elacticity of passengers demand at this Bongkok to US flights route is high, if Thai Airways rises less air ticket price, it will influence many travelers to choose other airlines to catch air plan to fly. Hence, due to Thai Airways can not make decision to rise air ticket price, because it believes that it will lose many travelers, so it only chooses to drop this non-stop Bongkok to US flights to avoid fuel cost rising economic loss.

However, although micro and macro economic theories may also that oil price variable or change, it may influence global tourism income. But, recently, on 2019, human mouth and air diseases, it can influence global individual leisure and business trip travelers feel fear to catch air plans to avoid their bodies get this kind of death sickness when they sit in the no fresh air supplying air planes. They feel that they reduce leisure travelling flying times or business trip flying times with strange travelers to sit in crowd air planes together. Then, they must many avoid human moth and air disease to avoid death crisis. Hence, in this global human mouth and air diseases threat environment occurrence, even oil price sudden reduces to low price, it brings airline's cost reduces and air ticke price reduces. However, when air ticket price reduce to be very cheaper, it can not still attract global many leisure or business trip travelers to buy air tickets to fly frequently. Why does air ticket reduction, it can not attract many leisure or businee trip travelers to buy air ticket to fly ? The main reason is because human mouth and air disease influences global many travelers feel fear to catch air planes frequently. In psychological view, this kind of human mouth and air sickness will bring long time negative influence to global traveles do not want to catch air planes for business trips or travelling leisure frequently. So, it implies that oil price changing to influence air ticket price reduction factor ought not main factor to influence tourism income. It may include traveler individual negative emotion psychological factor, such as human mouth and air disease or 2019 9/11 attack both cases, they can influence global travelers feel fear to catch air planes to fly to avoid death threat. So, oil changing price ought not be only one absolute main factor to influence global tourism income significantly.

On conclusion, in economic view, it seems that oil chang price may have indirect or direct relationship to influence tourism income, instead of some unpredicted external environment factors influence, such as US 9/11 attack crisis and human mouth and air disease factors, they may be main factors to influence travellers number to reduce in non-economic external unpredicted environment view.

How can artificial intelligent tools predict travelling consumer behavior in airline and air agent travelling market

I believe that applying (AI) big data tool to predict vehicle buyer consumption choice behavior, it is similar to predict traveler consumption choice behavior. In this chapter, I shall indicate how to apply (AI) big data gathering tool to predict vehicle buyer consumption choice behavior. Then, I shall its what its similar points to be applied to predict traveler consumption choice behavior.

Nowadays, many vehicle manufacturers hope their vehicles can attract to vehicle buyers to choose to buy their vehicles. However, there are many different brands of vehicles to provide to them to choose, so the vehicle market competition is very serious.

How to judge their different kinds of vehicle price which is reasonable acceptance to attract vehicle buyers to choose to buy the brand of vehicle manufacturers' any kinds of vehicles, e.g. fast speed sport style vehicles, comfortable and slow speed common cars, for four passengers common small size or more than four passengers common large car size?

How to evaluate the vehicle prices issue is important factor to influence vehicle buyers' choices. Either if the brand of vehicle price is too high to compare other brands of similar vehicle price, it will influence many vehicle buyers choose to buy other brands' vehicles or if the brand of vehicle price is too low, it will influence vehicle buyers feel this brand's vehicle machine quality or safe driving level or manufacturing steel material or speed or not comfortable sitting etc. different factors is worse to compare to other vehicle brands' similar vehicle products.

Thus, if the brand of vehicle manufacturers can predict how to design vehicles which can attract many vehicle buyers to choose to buy whose any vehicle products. What are future vehicle buyers' favorable vehicle styles? Then, the vehicle manufacturer can concentrate on manufacturing the kind style of vehicle products to sell already. It will reduce its vehicle manufacturing investment risk.

How to apply (AI) tools to predict vehicle buyers' behavioral consumption model? Whether artificial intelligent tools can predict automotive buyers' behavioral consumption model and predict future vehicle design trend. In fact, automotive brands and dealerships are facing an increasingly competition when attempting to manually gathering the vast quantities of data required to create customer focused programs that increase retention, ultimately new sales and service automotive business.

Building a based on that client's intrinsic needs and interests to any kinds of automotive vehicles at any given time. This is especially true in the automotive industry where the time span between purchases is measured in years. Because vehicle buyers would not like often to change their old vehicle to another new one. So, their decisions to buying another new vehicle, the time is usually after one year, even longer time. Hence, it seems any vehicles won't be frequent consumption products to the owned at least one vehicle family consumers (vehicle buyers). It implies that why vehicle manufacturers ought need to spend time to predict future vehicle buyer design choice for whole year vehicle buyer number growth because they won't often change preferable vehicle design to change another new vehicle more easily.

Hence, how to predict vehicle consumers' taste or preferable which styles of vehicle choices issues is very important. If the vehicle manufacturers can not manufacture any attractive vehicles to sell easily in this year. Then, it will lose time, money in this year because it won't know when the owned least one vehicle users or non-owned any vehicle users who will decide to buy one new vehicle or change another new vehicle ensure. The different brand vehicle dealers will possible wait more than one year to attract them to buy their vehicles if their styles are not attractive to compare other brands of vehicle competitors.

However, artificial intelligence and machine learning can help any vehicle manufacturers to find solution to solve patterns in highly to solve patterns in highly complex data-sets that are beyond the capability of a human brain, and then building and automatically acting on the customer insights it generates.

Given the automotive customer need for individualized communications, this technology is positioned to become a critical component of any successful vehicle retailer's domestic or/and overseas vehicle markets. How can vehicle manufacturers and retailers use (AI) to enhance their vehicle marketing campaigns? How will (AI) affect their vehicle sale marketing strategy? What criteria would they use when selecting on (AI) solution?

Vehicle consumers today are able to quickly access different brands of vehicle information, research vehicle products and reviews, negotiate prices and compare one vehicle brand or retailer to another resulting of the brands of vehicle customers. At the same time, the rise of " big -data mining", wearable devices that track user's every move and preference and greater contextualization in advertising and social media has resulted in consumer expectations of individualized. Thus, it seems that (AI) tools can be used to gather " big-data" and then they can make human's mind to analyze how to

design kinds of vehicles to satisfy vehicle buyers‘ needs.
As automotive vehicle marketers can apply (AI) tools to achieve messaging strategies to meet the needs of this new generation of informed vehicle consumers, using data from a variety of sources to move from a variety of sources to move from mass- messaging to more personalized messages aimed at particular vehicle buyer segments, e.g. fast speed sport vehicle buyer segment, slow speed comfortable small size or large size of buyer segment. However, when 90% of vehicle marketers believe having a single vehicle buyer view is important, only 6% have achieved it.
However, one of the main issues vehicle marketers are facing the lack of capacity to efficiently sift through and analyze the massive vehicle buyer amounts of data required to create vehicle buyer individualized vehicle customer experiences easily. This is especially difficult for automotive dealers, the long periods between purchase cycles, and the highly considered nature of the vehicle purchase means that each vehicle dealer needs to not only track a large number of potential vehicle customers for an extremely long period of time, but each of those vehicle customers will generate a huge amount of different kinds of vehicle behavioral consumption data as they research their next vehicle purchase. However, by choosing the right (AI) technological tools and programs , vehicle dealers can solve this big data gathering challenge into a major advantage.
For Forrester vehicle brand example, vehicle consumers have more power over the Forrester vehicle brand's reputation than ever before. Mayne, L. (2014) indicated that Forrester calls this new (AI) tools is the " age of the vehicle customer", a 20 year business cycle in which the most successful vehicle enterprises will reinvent themselves to systematically understand and serve increasingly powerful vehicle consumers. To win in this new age, Forrester declares companies must become vehicle customer obsessed and the only sustainable competitive advantage is knowledge and engagement with customers, such as (AI) gathering data knowledge.
Thus, the biggest challenge vehicle businesses currently face is not the collection of a large quantity of vehicle consumer data, but what to do with that data once they have it. Even at a large vehicle data research firm, the data sets are often too big for a single analyze, or even a team of analysts to sort through and draw conclusion from. However, enter artificial intelligence and machine learning , an efficient technology solution that can continuously find patterns in highly complex data sets that are way beyond the capacity of a human brain and then automatic drive action based on the

customer insights is generated.

What is (AI) machine learning tool? Machine learning is a type of (AI) that learns from data and is not explicitly program. Think Amazon, face book. Machine learning serves up relevant content based on an individual vehicle purchase behavior and experiences. More simply, machine learning is a computer program that can learn relationships between data, subject those learnings to errors functions, and then learn from its errors. The program in effect, trains itself.

Lee, T. (2016) explained that "Thus, (AI) tools can learn deep a more advanced branch of machine learning inspired by how our brain's nervous function, has also been found to be especial effective in identifying patterns from data."

When this way sound is complicated from a vehicle dealer perspective, the implementation of a marketing program driven by artificial intelligence can take care of these tasks in an automatic vehicle fashion with little to no manual intervention required from the staff at time vehicle stores.

In practice at a vehicle dealership, the program will continue track vehicle customer behavior online, merging that data with any offline source ( like CRM or DMS data) and then analyze this aggregated vehicle buyer data set to predict what vehicle customer may be shopping for and what information they might like to relevance from different kinds style of vehicle design photos.

Why does travelling market seem to similar to vehicle market which can apply (AI) learning tool to predict travellingconsumer behaviors?

Artificial intelligence refers to complex in vehicle market and travelling entertainment market which is very seem to be applied to predict consumer behaviors.

(AI) machine learning that posses the same characteristics of human intelligence and that have all our sense, all our reason and think just like human vehicle buyer who prefer vehicle purchase choice or travelling consumer who prefer travelling package or travelling destination and airline choice. Besides, machine learning is the practice of using algorithms to collect and examine data, learn from it, and then make a determination or prediction about something in the world.

So, it can be attempted to gather data concerns that travelling consumer past travelling destination choice and air ticket price choice and different travelling package, e.g. high, middle, or low class hotel and foods supply and entertainment places choice in their past travelling journeys.

The machine is " trained" using large amounts of data and algorithms that give it the ability to learn how to automatically perform a task with increasing accuracy. Otherwise, deep learning is primarily based on artificial neural networks inspired by our understanding of the biology of human's brains.

Thus, (AI) big data can gather all these past traveler consumption behavioral choice data to make reference to analyze whether how many travelers will choose to go to the specific travelling destination in any time by the past traveler number record to different travelling destinations, then it can gather the past air ticket sale price to different destinations and past travelling package design to different destinations in order to analyze whether it is the cheap airline ticket price factor or attractive travelling package factor or attractive travelling entertainment etc. in order to predict which factor is the most potential influential factor to they choose to go to the destination to travel in different time within one year. Then, traveler agent or airline can collect these big data to judge how to design their package to attract travelers to go to anywhere to travel or what the main factor influence most of them to choose to visit the destination to travel.

For example, travel agents or airlines can apply "Deep learning" breaks down tasks in ways that enables machines to assist them to predict when travelling consumer choice will be changed and why their travelling choice will change and how their travelling choice will change with increasingly complex tasks.

So, such as why (AI) technology can be applied to predict how travelling consumer behavior changes to bring to judge whether anywhere will be many travelling consumers who will prefer to choose travelling hot destinations next year or next month.

Then, travel agents and airlines can gather overall past travelling consumer data to analyze and conclude the more accurate prediction of different travelling destinations to the number of traveler. Then, they can choose how much air ticket price is more reasonable to charge to the travelling destination or how to design the travelling package which can bring more attractive to the prediction number of different travelling destination travelers in order to achieve to raise the different travelling destination number next year.

Thus, (AI) big data machine learning can help airlines or travel agents to solve how to design any attractive travelling package challenge. A travelling package is both one of the most important and carefully considered travelling entertainment consumption the majority of travelling people will ever make in their lifetime at least one travelling time.

It is also a prediction how travelling package will be designed that tends to be fundamentally tied to a travelling person's travelling destination choice identify and travelling package view of themselves. As the same time, travelling consumers' travelling choice changing lifestyles result in changing travelling destination needs, e.g. the country's young travelers can choose to change non-extreme exciting travelling entertainment package from past extreme exciting travelling entertainment package. Due to personal feeling factor in general. However, I believe that (AI) big data can also be attempted to predict when the country's young travelers will choose to change non-extreme exciting travelling behavior.

It is similar to automotive dealers need to remember that vehicle customers and prospects are individual human beings with risk, complex and ever-changing lives factors, these factors will influence every vehicle consumer why who feels has vehicle purchase need, and how who choose to buy the first vehicle if who decided to buy the first vehicle.

It seems that travelling agents or airlines need to remember that travelling consumers and different features or designs are very traveler beings with risk, complex and ever-travelling package attitude personal changing factors in different travel season, these factor will influence every individual traveler why who feels has travel entertainment need, and how who choose to buy different feature or design travelling package if who decide to travel. The (AI) big data technological travelling customer behavioral prediction tool seems to be the best travelling behavioral prediction tool in the world are those that know every one of different country's traveler need. Their likes and dislikes which style of travelling package, preferences and travel destination changing tastes to travelling destination choices.

The capacity of the human brain, however, limits us from achieving these different type of travel package sales. In this competitive travelling destination choice entertainment environment, (AI) big data machine learning enables platforms to assist the air ticket and travel package sales team by tracking the travelling consumer behaviors of each travelling customer, learning and memorizing their preferences and predicting their future travelling destination choice and travelling package design needs.

Finally, I recommend that for a travel agent or airline travelling marketing platform to make their travelling customer engagement efficient and fully-functional, I should be able to: applying (AI) tools to track every travelling customer behavior across the web, connecting to a society of data sources, CRM, DMS, third-party, web travelling brands, social traveler email, click etc., aggregating and accurately cross-reference data from a variety of sources, leveraging this data to drive insights on a mass scale, as well as on an individualized basis, driving actions and automatically direct travelling customer engagement via multiple channels based on where each customer is in their travelling individual lifecycle.

Why is (AI) big data gathering tool better than psychological and survey methods to predict traveler individual travel choice behavior?

Prediction travel behavioral consumption from psychology and survey methods.

How to predict travel consumption? It is one question to any travel agents concern to use what methods which can predict how many numbers of travelers where who will choose to go to travel more accurately. I think that who can consider how to predict travel behavioral consumption from psychology and survey travel choice prediction method, but it is better to apply (AI) big data gathering method to predict travel consumer's destination choice more accurate. The reason is as below:

The first reason is that traveller individual travel psychological desire is difficult to predict accurate more than (AI) big data gathering method, it is due that the data is past traveler's destination choice and travel package and ticket price actual data from (AI) big data gathering method. Otherwise, survey investigation is only traveler psychological thinking method. It lacks enough past actual traveler data gathering.

The second reason is that on the weakness of traveler individual psychological thinking view of survey investigation. It has evidence to support the relationship between self-identify threat and resistance to change travel behavior to any travelers, controlling for whose past travelling behavior, resistance to change if a psychological phenomenon of long standing interest in many applied branches of psychology.

Past travelling behavior has been acknowledged as a predictor of future action. Such as travelling behavior that is experienced as successful is likely to be repeated and may lead to habitual patterns. Some psychologists differentiate habit between two concepts, such as goal oriented and automatic oriented both. Although repeated past travelling behavior is addition goal oriented and automatic oriented. Further non-deliberative nature of habit may make appeals to judge and to predict future individual traveler's behavior accurately.

However, repeated one traveler will choose the destination to repeat to travel without a necessary constraint of goal orientation and automatic oriented both. So, it seems that psychological factor can influence any individual traveler why and how who choose to decide to repeat to choose the destination to travel.

So, survey investigation is only the traveler's thinking to answer the travel firm. It is not sure that the traveler's past travel experience is real answer. Otherwise, (AI) big data gathering method is computer gathering method which gather past traveler consumption actual data to analyze and conclude future traveler possible repeated travel destination choice and travel package choice more accurate.

The third reason is that on the strength of (AI) big data gathering method computer statistic view to predict future traveller consumer's destination and travel package choice. It is structural equation modeling is an extremely flexible linear-in-parameters multivariate statistical modeling technique. It has been used in modeling travel behavior and values since about 1980 year. It is a software method to handle a large number of variables, as well as unobserved variables specified as linear combinations ( weighted averages) of the observed variable.

Can (AI) big data gather data to predict when climate will change to influence poor travelling behaviours?

(AI) big data tool can predict the flexibility of human travelling behavioral change is at least the result of one such mechanism, our ability to travel mentally in time and entertain potential future. Understanding of the impacts is holidays, particularly those involving travel.

Using focus groups research to explores tourists' awareness of the impacts of travel own climate change, examines the extent to which climate change features in holiday travel decisions and identifies some of the barriers to the adoption of less carbon intensive tourism practices.

The findings suggest many tourists don't consider climate change when planning their holidays. The failure of tourists to engage with the climate change to impact of holidays, combined with significant barriers to behavioral change, presents a considerable challenge in the tourism industry. In the future, computer (AI) big data tool can attempt to predict when the country's climate change to influence travelers to choose to go to the country to travel, e.g. next month or next half year or next year hot travelling destinations.

Tourism is a highly energy intensive industry and has only recently attracted attention as an important contributions to climate change through greenhouse gas emissions. It has been estimated that tourism contributes 5% of global carbon dioxide emissions. There have been a number of potential changes proposed for reducing the impact of air travel on climate change. These include technological changes, market based changes and behavioral changes.

However, the role that climate change plays in the holiday and travel decisions of global tourists. How the global tourists of the impacts travel has on climate change to establish the extent to which climate change, considerations features in holiday travel decision making processes and to investigate the major barriers to global tourists adopting less carbon intensive travel practices.

It will bring this question: Will tourists aware the impacts that their holidays and travel have on climate changes to influence their travelling decision?

When, it comes to understand individual traveler's behavioral change, wide range of conceptual theories have been developed, utilizing various social, psychological, subjective and objective variables in order to model travel consumption behavior. These theories of travel behavioral change operate at a number of different levels, including the individual level, the interpersonal level and community level. Whether pro-environmental behavior can be used to predict travel consumption behavior in a climate change. However, the question of what determines pro-environmental behavior in such a complex one that it can not be visualized through one single framework or diagram.

Despite the potentially high risk scenario for the tourism industry and the global environment, the tourism and climate change ought have close relationship.

However, (AI) big data tool can be applied to find what factors to influence the time of travelers' travelling choices. What are the important factors and variables which can limit tourism? e.g. money, time, family problem, extreme hot or cold weather change, air ticket price, journey attraction etc. variable factors.

Mention of holidays and travel were deliberately avoided in the recruitment process, so as not to create a connection factor to influence traveler's individual mind. However, the dismissal of alternative transportation modes can be conceived as either a structural barrier, in the sense that flying is perhaps the only realistic option to reach long-haul holiday destination, or a perceived behavioral control barriers in that an individual perceives flying as the only option open to whom.

The transportation tool factor will be depend to extent on the distance to the destination. This can also be interpreted in a social perspective as an intention with the resources available where much international tourism is structured around flying. To increase the availability of different transportation modes, tourists could choose holiday destination closer to home.

Finally, also how to predict future travel behavioral consumption. I feel that travel agents need to predict whether any country's random daily variation of weather factor is also important to influence travel behavior. e.g. in weather, temperature, rainfall and snowfall with traffic accidents factors will have relationship to cause travel demand.

Some scientists estimate suggest that when warmed temperatures and reduced snowfall are associated with a moderate decline in non-fatal accidents, they are also associated with a significant increase in fatal accidents. Thus increase in fatalities and temperature. Half of the estimated effect of temperature on fatalities is due to changes in the exposure to pedestrians, bicyclists and motorcyclists as temperature increase.

So, if any countries have rainfall, snowfall and low temperature to cause traffic accidents, whether this accident occurrence will influence the travelers who liking climb snow hills, riding bicycle, running sports who will avoid to travel to these countries' bad weather after occurs. So, why I feel that this natural climate factor will also be one serious factor to influence travel behavioral consumption. However, (AI) big data tool can predict more accurate than survey method when climate change to influence the country's climate to be poor, then it can predict when which countries are not popular acceptable to global country consumers' travel choice next month.

How can apply (AI) to provide travelling businesses with better-informed decisions ?

I shall explain how (AI) big data gathering technology can provide travelling businesses with better-informed decisions to drive top-line growth, deliver meaningful experience for travelling customers and smooth their path along the travelling consumer journey. The widely understood definition of (AI) involves the ability of machines or computers to learn human thinking, reasoning and decision-making abilities.

So, such as (AI) learning machine system can attempt to learn travelling consumer's travel destination or travel package thinking, judgement of their reasons why they choose to go to the destination to travel or why they choose to buy the travel package and learn how and why they make their past travelling decisions from their past travel big data gathering.

A Narrative science study in 2015 year identified that (AI) was being used primarily in voice recognition, machine learning virtual assistants and decision support. This study also highlighted the many branches of (AI) and that techniques and their definition are used interchangeably. It is possible that (AI) can be used to gather big data , then to analyze to help travel businesses to predict travelling consumer travel destination and travel package choice behaviors. For example, one of the most common techniques is traveler machine learning, where algorithms are used to perform tasks by learning from the airline or travel agent whose past all travelers' travelling destination choice and travel package choice historical data.

However, during 2017 year, search engines will begin to find what additional factors can influence past traveler personal travelling destination and travelling package travelling behavioral data into prediction of future travelling customer behavioral results, such as the online traveler (user's) history of travelling data searches, such as anywhere are the most popular travelling locations or travelling destinations and previously captures conservations.

Artificial intelligence will use this past travelling destinations and travelling package information to power predictive search results, e.g. predictive future travelling consumer's choice behavioral processing for where will be their preferable travelling destination choice and how to design travelling package to satisfy future travelling clients' needs.

Predictive search will improve the quality of online travelling search results, and provide new insights into travelling consumers' travelling destination and package behavior and the moments which matter to them. Search will give recommendation into tailored how travelling consumer individual travelling destination choice in travelling decision making process. Several of the largest online platforms already use (AI) travelling machine learning to improve predictive travelling consumer behavioral search results.

For example, Google's rank brain technology adds research by understanding the context in which the travelling consumer has entered it. Over time, rank brain will learn further from user behaviors Amazon's DSSTNE ( pronouned destiny) learns from shoppers' purchasing habits and consumption behavior to offer better product recommend actions, which Amazon can offer before a consumer has entered anything into the search bar.

Such as (AI) big data can gather past online travelers' e-ticket purchase transactions to conclude that online traveler's travelling choice habits and online traveler consumption behavior to offer better travelling destinations and travelling package opinions to travel agents or airlines. However, this technology is not independent of human input. For example, Google engineers will periodically retain the rank brain system to improve the models it uses.

For another example, in 2016 year , Apple computer revamped its travelling scene photos app to allow travelling consumers to search for specific travelling destinations in the travelling scene phots, they want to find anywhere travelling destination photos, not just dates and locations. Each travelling photo that an intelligent phone or intelligent pad user takes goes through 11 billion computations, so that travelling scene photos can understand exactly where is the travelling destination photography to let online travelling consumer to feel anywhere they plan to go to the location to travel. So, (AI) learning machine can make online travelling photos more attractive to influence potential travelers choose to the destination to travel after they see the travelling destination scene photos from internet.

It seems that in future, (AI) machine learning will allow online travelling search to evolve even further. Search engineers will deliver refined recommendations to airlines' online traveler e-ticket search users and use less human input to predict travelling consumers' needs from internet channel. For IBM computer example, it indicated 90% of the data that exists today has been created in the last two years.

This huge explosion of past traveler's e-ticket consumption data gives the opportunity to quickly spot and react to the latest trends, fashion and fads among its travelling clients and potential clients. This will allow airline or travel agent companies to better engage with younger travelling consumers, who gain influence access to the latest travelling destination and package trends.

They associate with to help define who they are as individuals. Thus, travelling company brands have to identify and make use of them before travelling consumers move on, but the vast quantity of past e-ticket purchase data available makes from internet channel. This a resource-intensive task. For next example, Lesara, a based online clothes store, uses this machine learning to inform its product decision often gathering information from internal and external sources.

When its trends -spotting shoes. Lesara has a range of over 20 styles and sells hundreds of pairs a day. It focus on giving consumers, the very latest trends allow Lesara to develop on average of 50,000 new items each year. It compared to 11,000 old items each year. Thus, travelling agents or airlines can attempt to apply (AI) big data gathering method to gather all past e-ticket purchase data, concerns where they prefer to choose to go to the destinations to travel and what travelling packages are the most attractive to the travelers to choose to buy. It aims to help them to predict where future travelers will prefer to choose to go to travel or what travelling package they will prefer to choose to buy next year.

For another (AI) big data prediction example, Lesara is one online clothes store, uses machine learning decisions after gathering information from internal and external sources. One of its most popular products, shoes with LED started life when its trend spotting software flagged up a blogger wearing similar shoes. Now Lesara has a range of over 20 styles and sells hundreds of pairs a day. Its focus on giving consumers the very latest trends allows Lesara to develop an average of 50,000 new items each year, compared to 11,000 for its competitor Lara.

It seems (AI) big data gathering machine learning can help Lesara business to predict what kinds of shoes design or style that shoe consumers will prefer choose to buy in future shoe market trend. Thus, Lesara can predict shoe consumers' taste successfully and it can manufacture many attractive style of shoes.

(AI) machine learning can gather global past shoe consumer's shoe shopping experiences, then analyzes to make conclusion to give lesara recommendation successfully. This will make the experience more enjoyable for shoe consumers and allow Lesara to advert whose different new style or design of shoes to deliver them move relevant messages by understanding the context of the experience.

So, online travel agents or online airline can also attempt to apply (AI) big data gathering method to predict where travelers will prefer to go to travel and how they ought design travelling packages to attract them to choose to buy next year. Hence, (AI) big data gathering technology can conclude how to design traveler agents' travelling package products to be the most attractive to excite many travelers choose to buy their travelling package, due to it has more accurate to predict travelling consumer destination and travelling package choice behaviors to compare human themselves prediction judgement effort, e.g. travelling survey or marketing research, or telephone enquire. It seems that (AI) machine judgement effort is more accurate to compare to human judgment effort in travelling industry.

Future travel consumption behavior

Can (AI) big data gathering tool predict traveler individual habitual behavior , e.g. renting travel transportation tools ?

Can (AI) big data gathering tool can predict past traveler destination and travelling package choice habit and it can be intended to predict of future traveler behavior to people are creatures of habits judgement of future anywhere travelling destination choice next year or next month or next half year destination prediction ?

Many of human's everyday goal-directed behaviors are performed in a habitual fashion, the transportation made and route one takes to work, one's choice of breakfast. Habits are formed when using the some behavior frequently and a similar consistency in a similar context for the some purpose whether the individual past travel consumption model will be caused a habit to whom. e.g. choosing whom travel agent to buy air ticket or traveling package; choosing the same or similar countries' destinations to go to travel ; choosing the business class or normal (general) class of quality airlines to catch planes.

Does habitual rent traveling car tools use not lead to more resistance to change of travel mode? It has been argued that past behavior is the best predictor of future behavior to travel consumption. If individual traveler's past consumption behavior was always reasoned, then frequency of prior travel consumption behavior should only have an indirect link to the individual traveler's behavior. It seems that renting travel car tools to use is a habit example. So, a strong rent traveling car tools useful habit makes traveling mode choice. People with a strong renting of traveling car tools of habit should have low motivation to attend to gather any information about public transportation in their choice of travelling country for individual or family or friends members during their traveling journeys.

Even when persuasive communication changes the traveler whose attitudes and intention, in the case of individual traveler or family travelers with a strong renting travel car tools habit. It is difficult to change whose travel behaviors to choose to catch public transportation in whose any trips in any countries. However, understanding of travel behavior and the reasons for choosing one mode of transportation over another. The arguments for rent traveling car tools to use, including convenience, speed, comfort and individual freedom and well known.

Increasingly, psychological factors include such as, perceptions, identity, social norms and habit are being used to understand travel mode choice. Whether how many travel consumers will choose to rent traveling car tools during their trips in any countries. It is difficult to estimate the numbers. As the average level of renting travel car tools of dependence or attitudes to certain travel package policies from travel agents. Instead different people must be treated in different ways because who are motivated in different ways and who are motivated by different travel package policies ways from travel agents.

In conclusion, the factors influence whose traveler's individual traveler destination choice behavior The factors include either who chooses to rent traveling car tools or who chooses to catch public transportation when who individual goes to travel in alone trip or family trip. It include influence mode choice factors, such as social psychology factor and marketing on segmentation factor both to influence whose transportation choice of behavior in whose trip. So, (AI) big data can be attempted to gather past traveler transportation tool choice, rent travelling car tools choice or catching public transportation tools choice to predict where destination can provide what kind of transportation tool to attract many travelers to choose to go to the place to travel.

How (AI) big data determine future travel behavior from past travel experience and perceptions of risk and safety for the benefits to travel consumers?

How (AI) big data determine future travel behavior from past travel experience and perceptions of risk and safety for the benefits to travel consumers? Why does individual traveler avoid certain destination(s) is(are) as relevant to tourist decision making as why who chooses to travel to others?

Perceptions of risk and safety and travel experience are likely to influence travel decisions. If travel agents had efforts to predict future travel behavior to guess whether travelers will feel where is(are) risk and unsafe to cause who does not choose to go to the country to travel. Then, the travel agents will avoid to choose to spend much time to design the different traveling package to attract their potential travel consumers to choose to travel. The reason is because in the case of individual traveler's tourism experience, the traveler whose past disappointment travel experience ( psychological risk) will be a serious threat to the traveler's health or life ( health, physical or terrorism risk). The past safety or unhealthy risk to the country(countries) will influence the traveler decides to choose not to go to the countries(country) to travel again in the future.

What is push and pull factors to influence any traveler who chooses where is whose preferable travelling destination ?

How to apply (AI) big data to predict individual traveler's behavioral intention of choosing a travel destination?

Understanding why people travel and what factors influence their behavioral intention of choosing a travel destination is beneficial to tourism planning and marketing. In general, an individual's choice of a travel destination into two forces.

The first force is the push factor that pushes an individual away from home and attempt to develop a general desire to go somewhere, without specifying where that may be.

The other force is the pull factor that pull an individual toward in destination, due to a region-specific or perceived attractiveness of a destination. The respective push and pull factors illustrate that people travel because who are pushed by whose internal motives and pulled by external forced of a destination. However, the decision making process leading to the choice of a travel destination is a very complex process.

For example, a Taiwanese traveler who might either choose new travel destination of Hong Kong or another old travel Asia destinations again or who also might choose any one of Western country, as a new travel destination. The travel agents can predict where who will have intention to choose to travel from whose past behavior and attitude, subjective and perceived behavioral control model. When (AI) big data gather past every country traveler number who chose to go to which countries to travel in order to judge where destinations will be the country travelers' travelling choice destinations in the future.

The factors influence where is the traveler choice, include personal safety, scenic beauty, cultural interest, climate changing, transportation tools, friendliness of local people, price of trip, trip package service in hotels and restaurants, quality and variety of food and shopping facilities and services etc. needs. So, whose factors will influence where is the individual travel's choice. It seems every traveler whose choice of travel process, will include past behavior. e.g. travelling experience, travelling habit, then to choose the best seasoned travelling action to satisfy whose travel needs. This process is the individual traveler's psychological choice process, who must need time to gather information to compare concerning of different travel packages, destination scene, climate change, transportation tools available to the destination, air ticket price etc. these factors, then to judge where is the best right destination to travel in the right time.

Hence, (AI) big data can gather past different countries' climate changing data, transportation tool changing data, destination scene environment changing etc. different data to give opinions to travelling businesses whether any country's these above factors will influence about how many traveler number will be increase or decrease in the future.

Why can expectation, motivation and attitude factor influence travelling behavior?

Social psychology is concerned with gaining insight into the psychological of socially relevant behaviors and the processes. For instance, on a global level bad influence to global warming, it influences some countries extreme cold or hot bad climate changing occurrence, then it ought influence some travelers' behavioral decision to change their mind to choose some countries to go to travel at the moment which do not occur extreme hot or cold climate ( temperature). e.g. above than 40 degree in summer or below than 0 degree in winter. Due to the extreme climate changing environment in the countries, it will cause them to feel uncomfortable to play during their trips. So, the global warming causes to climate changing factor will influence the numbers of travel consumption to be reduced possibly. This is global climate changing environment factor influences to bad or uncomfortable social psychological feeling to global travelers' mind of traveling decision. What is individual traveler expectation, motivation and attitude? Tourism sector includes inbound (domestic) tourism and outbound (overseas) tourism both incomes to any countries. According to recent article, a tourist behavior model has been developed, called the expectation, motivation and attitude ( EMA) model ( Hsu et al., 2010).

This model focuses on the pre-visit stage of tourists by modeling the behavioral process by incorporating expectation, motivation and attitude. Travel motivation is considered as an essential component of the behavioral process, which has been increasing attention from the travel; industry. The economic approach defines "tourism" is an identifiable nationally important industry. It includes the component activities of transportation, accommodation, recreation, food and related service. So, tourism behavioral consumption is concerned the individual tourist's usual habituate of the industry which responds to whose needs, and of the impacts that both the tourist and the tourism industry have on the socio-cultural, economic and physical environment.

However, travel motivation means how to understand and predict factors that influence travel decision making. According to Backman and others (1995, p.15), motivation is conceptually viewed as " a state of need, a condition that services as a driving force to display different kind of behavior toward certain types of activities, developing preferences, arriving at some expected satisfactory outcome." So, motivation and expectancy which has close relationship to any tourist before who decided to do any tourism of behavior.

Some economists confirmed motivation and expectancy which has relations, such as expectation of visiting an outbound destination has a direct effect on motivation to visit the destination; motivation has a direct effect on attitude toward visiting the destination; expectation of visiting the outbound destination has a direct affection on attitude toward visiting the destination and motivation has a mediating effect on the relationship in between expectation and attitude.

Hence, (AI) big data can gather all the country's climate environment change, transportation tool change, entertainment scene change, hotel price and restaurant price change etc. data to give opinions whether the country will attract how many traveler to choose to go to travel in the year.

What is (AI) deep learning techniques to forecast travelling environment behavioral consumption

Prediction how many travelers will choose to go to the country to travel. It is similar to apply deep-learning technology to predict how to raise the agricultural farming productivity in the agricultural export country.

The (AI) deep-learning technology leads to performance enhancement and generalization of artificial intelligent technology. It influences the global leader in the field of information technology has declared its intention to utilize the deep-learning technology to solve environmental problems, such as climate change.

So, it will help agriculture farming businesses can raise any plant food: vegetable, fruit, rice which grow up very easily if farmers can apply (AI) deep-learning technology to solve environment problems to influence their plant food grow. If the whole year seasonal change is very good and it is suitable for any plant food to grow in farming land easily, e.g. rain is enough and soil is enough for any plant food to grow in the farm lands. Then, fruit, rice, vegetable etc. agriculture businesses will have much beneficial attribution to global farmers.

The question is how to use deep-learning technologies in the environmental field to predict the status of pro-environmental consumption. We predicted the pro-environmental consumption index based on Google search query data, using a recurrent neural network ( RNN model). To certify the accuracy of the index, we compared the prediction accuracy of the RNN model with that of the ordinary least square and artificial necessary network models.

For example, the RNN model predicts the pro-environmental consumption index better than any other model. we expect the RNN model to perform still better in a big data environment because the deep-learning technologies would be increasingly as the volume of data grows. So, deep-learning technologies could be useful in environmental forecasting to prevent damage caused by climate change to influence any rice, vegetable, tomato, potato, fruit etc. different plant food grow in any countries' farming land easily.

For South Korea example, over 800 government agencies spent 2.2 trillion Korea won on eco-products in 2014 year. However, green products are rarely purchased outside these agencies. This phenomenon occurs because there is a gap between consumer attitudes and behavior , that is environmental attitude is a major factor in decision making vis-a-vis the consumption of " green" food and services ( Jorea Ministry of Environment, 2015).

Therefore, it is necessary to understand those consumer attitude, that will lead to sustainability-conductive behavior and consumption. (AI) Deep learning system can be applied to attempt understand those traveler attitude to environment protection to fly to which country. For example, (AI) deep learning system can attempt to gather data concerns how many Hong Kong people concern air pollution challenge to influence their health, then it can attempt to predict how many Hong Kong travelers do not choose to go China travel, due to the air pollution challenge to influence their health.

Environmental travel consumption prediction

Recently, many researchers have studied pro-environmental consumption and household indexes as well as suicide rate predictions using messages posted by internet users on Google trend, Tweets etc. channel.

Whether can environmental consumption be predicted by (AI) deep-learning technological internet channel to influence how many travelers choose to go to the country to travel?

How can impact the pro-environmental consumption attitudes of green policies to influence how many travelers choose to go to the country to travel?

For example, Korea scientists estimated pro-environmental attitudes using search query data provided by Google trend and confirmed through regression analysis, that pro-environmental attitude has a positive correlation with the pro-environmental attitude index. They also explained that environment-friendly attitude of residents plan an important role in policy making. In the past, most household consumption indexed were calculated through surveys, but (AI) deep-learning technological tool " big data" have recently gained research attention ( Lee et al. 2016). So, (AI) deep learning technology can attempt to gather whether how many Korea residents who concern environment pollution to influence their eating green food attitude then to judge whether how many Korea residents hope to leave their country to travel anywhere either high risk environment pollution countries to travel or low risk environment pollution countries to travel in the future.

It seems that (AI) deep-learning technology can help agricultural export countries‘ farmers , e.g. US, UK, Canada, New Zealand, Australia, Japan, China, India etc. they can predict environmental behavioral consumption to any rice, tomato, potato , fruit, vegetable etc. plant food consumers. The beneficial advantages to them include as below:

(a) Assuming they know their countries' weather, when it has less rain to cause drought or when it has more rain in any seasonal time in the year.

They can choose not to grow any kinds of above these plant food to avoid loss.

(b) They can make any kinds of above these plant food price raising after their prediction of these bad seasonal time to cause their plant food shortage supply challenge. Because these plant food consumers‘ demand number is more, but the supply of these above plant food supply number is less. However, due to they had predicted when the bad seasonal time can not allow them to grow these above plant food before. So, they have enough time to grow many these above plant food number in predictive good seasonal time to prepare to supply to their plant food import countries' plant food consumers to eat. Thus, these predictive environmental consumption plant food export countries can raise their plant food price to sell to them. When, the other non-pre-predictive environmental consumption plant food export countries can not supply any one of those plant food to them to eat, due to the bad climate to cause them can't grow any one of these plant food to export to sell.

Thus, (AI) deep-learning technology can be applied to predict how to raise the plant food supply number in order to raise price to the import plant food countries consumers to eat, due to they feel difficult to buy these plant food to eat in the bad climate seasonal time in whole year.

(c) (AI) deep-learning technology can help climate scientists to find what reasons cause their countries; rain sudden increases or cause their countries‘ rain sudden decreases. After its gathering data analysis, it can assist climate scientists to find solution methods to attempt to control the rain level can be right falling down level to let agricultural export farmers who can grow their plant food to sell to agricultural import countries in whole year.

(d) The agricultural export countries' farmers can apply (AI) deep-learning technology to help them to choose whether growing which kinds of plant food in that whether climate time to earn more plant food consumption number more easily.

Due to the agricultural countries climate will often change, for example, tomato, potato, rice, fruit etc. plant food can be adapt to grow in more rain time, but vegetable can not be adapt to grow in more rain time. If farmers can apply this technology to predict when it will have move rain or when it will have less rain to fall down in their countries. Then, they can choose to grow which kinds of plant food number more, in the suitable seasonal climate time in order to raise plant food growing number productivities to supply to sell to satisfy any agricultural food import countries‘ demand effectively.

(e) (AI) deep-learning technology can help agricultural import countries to solve agricultural food shortage challenge in long term. When this technology can be popular to base applied by the agricultural plant food export countries. It will solve global agricultural food shortage challenge. For example, when one agricultural export countries' farmers can popular accept to apply this technology to predict when to grow which kinds of plant food more to rise number productivities to sell. e.g. vegetable, fruit, rice Besides another agricultural export countries‘ farmers can also accept to apply this technology to predict when to grow plant food, e.g. potato, tomato to raise number productivities to sell. Then, they can concentrate on growing the specific kinds of plant food in order to raise the specific plant food number productivities in every seasonal change time every month. Then, global agricultural plant food supply must be raised, due to these predictive environmental change farmers can know who ought grow which kinds of plant food to sell to raise number productivities.

Consequently, (AI) deep learning can gather where countries will have high risk environment pollution to influence health food supply. Then, it can give opinions to travelling businesses when these high risk environment pollution countries will encounter the traveler number to be decreased, due to the environment pollution serious challenge will occur.

What methods can predict future travel behavioral consumption ?

How to use qualitative of travel behavioral method to predict future travel consumption from (AI) big data ?

I also suggest to use qualitative of travel behavioral method to predict future travel consumption. Methods such as focus groups interviews and participant observer techniques can be used with quantitative approaches on their own to fill the gaps left by quantitative techniques. These insights have contributed to the development of increasingly sophisticated models to forecast travel behavior and predict changes in behavior in response to change in the transportation system. I shall indicate the weaknesses of human travelling investigation methods as below:

First, survey methods restrict not only the question frame but the answer frame as well, anticipating the important issues and questions and the responses. However, these surveys methods are not well suited to exploratory areas of research where issues remain unidentified and the researched seek to answer the question "why?".

Second, data collection methods using traditional travel diaries or telephone recruitment can under represent certain segments of the population, particularly the older persons with little education, minorities and the poor. Before the survey, focus group for example can be used to identify what socio-demographic variables to include in the survey, how best to structure the diary, even what incentives will be most effective in increasing the response rate.

After the survey, focus, focus groups can be used to build explanations for the survey results to identify the "why" of the results as well as the implications. One Asia Pacific survey research result was made by tourism market investigation before. It indicated the travel in Asia Pacific market in the past, had often been undertaken in large groups through leisure package sold in bulk, or in large organized business groups, future travelers will be in smaller groups or alone, and for a much wider range of reasons.

Significant new traveler segments, such as female business traveler. The small business traveler and the senior traveler, all of which have different aspirations and requirements from the travel experience.

Moreover, Asia tourism market will start to exist behaviors in the adoption of newer technologies, a giving the traveler new ways to manage the travel experience, creating new behaviors. This with provide new opportunities for travel providers. The use of mobile devices, smartphones, tablets etc. and social media are the obvious findings to become an integral part of the travel experience. Thus, quality method can attempt to predict Asia Pacific tourism market development in the future. It is such as (AI) big data gathering tool can give traveler quality opinions to any travelling businesses to make the more accurate where will be the popular travel destination choice next month or next half year or next year.

However, improving the predictive power of travel behavior models and to increase understanding travel behavior which lies in the use of panel data( repeated measures from the same individuals). Whereas, cross-sectional data only reveal inter-individual differences at one moment in time, panel data can reveal intra-individual changes over time. In effect, panel data are generally better suited to understand and predict ( changes in ) travel behavior. However, a substantial proportion was also observed to transition between very different activity/travel patterns over time, indicating that from one year to the next, many people renegotiated their activity/travel patterns.

How to apply advanced traveler information systems (ATIS) to predict future travelling behavior?

Nowadays, information can impact on traveler behavior and network performance. For example, when steadily growing levels of vehicle ownership and vehicle miles traveled information has been identified as a potential strategy towards man aging travel demand, optimizing transportation networks and better utilizing available capacity. Toward, this goal to predict further tourist behavioral consumption. Many countries, government tourism development institutes has applied advanced traveler information systems (ATIS) which travel behavior models and high-fidelity network performance models made increasingly feasible through the rapid advances in computer power. Crucial components of this problem domain are the modeling of individual tourist drivers' response to travel information and the development accurate guidance of relevance to real would trip makers. So, this advanced traveler information systems (ATIS) can assist the tourist who like to rent travelling car tools to travel in any countries own free traveler information systems service conveniently. Also, this travel information system can be intended to assist travelers to make better travel choices. e.g. this system can improve the decision making of individual traveler rather than improvements of network performance overall. So, we need to understand how tourists make their travel plans. Also, understanding decision process that lead to booking of the trip is equally important, as it allows of a potential behavior.

How can online tourism sale channel influence traveling consumption of behavior?

Nowadays, internet is popular, it seems that booking air ticket behavior of using internet is predicted to influence overall tourism air tickets payment method. Tourism industry has grown in the previous several decades. Despite its global impact, questions related to better understanding of tourists and whose habits. Using online travel air ticket booking benefits include booking electronic air tickets can be made from entering any electronic travel agents websites in the short time and electronic travel ticket payers do not need leave home, who can pay visa card to pre booking any electronic travel ticket from online channel conveniently.

How can analyze activity based travel demand ?

Nowadays, human are concerning the traffic congestion and air quality deterioration, the supply oriented focus of transportation planning has expanded to include how to manage travel demand within the available transportation supply. Consequently, there has been an increasing interest in travel demand management strategies, such as congestion pricing that attempts to change aggregate travel demand. The prediction aggregate level, long term travel demand to understanding disaggregate level ( i.e. individual levels ) behavioral responses to short term demand policies, such as ride sharing incentives, congestion pricing and employer based demand management schemes, alternate work schedules, telecommuting limitation of travel agent traditionally work nature shall influence oriented trip based travel modelling passenger travel demand indirectly.

Finally, online travel purchase will be popular to influence the number of travel behavioral consumption nowadays. Any travel package products can be sold from websites to attract travelers to choose to pre-book air ticket for any trips conveniently. In the past ten years, the internet has become the predominant carrier of all types of information and transactions. Regarding travel decisions, internet has also become an important sales channels for the travel industry, because it is associated with comparably lower distribution and sales costs, but also because it adapts to high supply and demand dynamics in this industry. Consequently, the travel and tourism industry tries to increase the internet sale specific share of sales volumes. So, internet sale channel has changed travel consumption behavioral pattern and characteristics and travel experience. For example, Switzerland has one of the highest population-to-computer ratio in Europe. It is also one of the most highly internet penetrated countries in terms of use of the WWW on a day-to-day basis, with more than 75 percent of the population older than 14 years using the WWW daily ( ICT, 2005).

The reason of booking online tourism may include: convenience, fast transaction, finding traveling package choice easily, more airline seats available. So, online booking tourism will influence the traditional tourism agents visiting of sales and air tickets and travelling package numbers to be decreased. Finally, the online booking tourism market shares will be expanded to more than traditional tourism agents visits sale market in the future one day. So, the travel agents who still use the traditional tourism visiting sale channel which ought raise whose features to compare to differ to online tourism sale channel if these traditional tourism agents want to keep competitive ability in tourism industry for long term.

What is actively based patterns of urban population of travel behavioral prediction method?

Actively based patterns of urban population. It is a method of motivational framework means in which societal constraints and inherent individual motivations interact to shape activity participation patterns. It can be used to predict one city or urban the numbers of travel demand in the year. It has two elements: First, capability constraints refer to constraints are imposed by biological needs, such as eating and sleeping and/or resources, such as income, availability of cars etc. to undertake the urban or city's family activities in the year. Second, coupling constraints define where, when and the duration of planning activities that are to be pursued with other individuals. So, this method needs to gather information ( data) to get the relationship between activities, travel and spending work time and space time to evaluate whether there are how many families who have real needs to spend time to go to travel in the year.

What is trip based versus activity based approaches?

What is trip based versus activity based approaches? The fundamental difference between the trip-based and activity based approaches is that the former approach directly focuses on trips without explicit recognition of the motivation or reason for the trips and travel. The activity based approach , on the other hand, views travel as a demand derived from the need to pursue travel activities. So, it is better understand the individual or family behavior basis for individual or family travelling decision regarding participation in travelling activities in certain places or cities or countries at given times and hence the resulting travel needs. This behavioral basis includes all the factors that influence the why, how, when and where of performed activities and resulting individuals and household, the cultural/ social norms of the community and the travel surrounding environment.

Another difference between the two approaches is in the way travel is represented. The trip based approach represents travel as a collection of trips. Each trip is considered as independent of other trips, without considering the inter-relationship in the choice attributes , such as time, destination and mode of different trips. As tours are chains of trips beginning and ending at a same location , say home or work. The tour based representation helps maintain the consistency across and capture the interdependency and consistency of the modeled choice attributed among the trips of the same tour.

In addition to the tour based representation of travel, the activity based approach focuses on sequences or patterns of activity participation and travel behavior, using the whole day or longer periods of time is the unit of analysis. Such as approach can address travel demand management issues through an examination of how people modify their activity participation, for example, will individuals substitute more out-of-home activities for in home activities in the evening of who arrived early form work due-to a work schedule change?

The major difference between trip based and the activity based approaches is in the way, the time dimension of activities and travel is considered. In the trip based approach, time is reduced to being simply a cost making a trip and a day's viewed as a combination, defined peak and off peak time periods. On the other hand, activity based approach views individuals' activity travel patterns are a result of their time use decisions with a continuous time domain. As individuals have 24 hours in a day or multiples of 24 hours for longer periods of time and decide how to use that travel among or allocate that time to activities and travel and with who, subject to their socio-demographic, transportation system and other and scheduling of trips. So, determining the impact of travel demand management policies on time use behavior is an important step to assessing the impact of such policies on individual travel behavior. The final major difference between this two approaches relates to the level of aggregation. In the trip based approach, most aspect of travel, e.g. number of trips etc. are analyzed at an aggregate level.

Consequently, trip based methods accommodate the effect of socio-demographic attributes of households and individuals in a very limited fashion, which limits the activity of the method to evaluate travel impacts of long term socio-demographic characteristics of the individuals who actually make the activity travel choices and the travel service characteristics of the surrounding environment. So, the activity based models are better equipped to forecast the longer term changes in travel demand in response composition and the travel environment of urban areas. Also, using activity based models, the impact of policies can be assessed by predicting individual level behavioral responses instead of employing trip based statistical averages that are aggregated over defined demographic segments.

Can apply (AI) big data gathering method predict senior age will be main travelling target?

In the past, Germany government had established tourism survey analysis to analyze survey data in order to arrive at reliable conclusions on future trends in travel behavior. To aim to find how demographic change will influence the tourism market and how the industry can adapt to those changes. The travel analysis provided data on tourism consumer behavior, including attitudes, motives and intentions. Since, 1970 year, it is based on a random sample, representative for the population in private households aged 14 years or older. Then, a continuous high scientific standard combined with a national and international users makes the travel analysis a useful tool and reliable source for tourism industry and policy decisions. It aimed to gather statistical data. e.g. on the age structure and on demographic trends, quantitative and qualitative analysis with time series data from the travel analysis. It shows e.g. not only the future volume , quite different from today's seniors, or how who will travel of family holidays will change, e.g. single parents of low, but grandparents of growing significance for tourism.

Demographic change is said to be one of the important drivers for new trends in consumer traveling change behavior in most European countries ( e.g. Lind 2001). Because the growing number of senior citizens in the European Union and other industrialized countries, such as the USA and Japan, looks to become one of the major marketing challenges for the tourism industry. United Nations statistics predict that the share of people being 60 age or older will grow dramatically in the coming future, and is expected to rise from 10 percent of the world population in 2000 year to more than 20 percent in 2050 year ( United Nations Population Division, 2001). From its statistic, some data showed that travel propensity increased throughout life until the age of about 50 years of age and was then kept stable until very late in life 75 age. The most important results is that the travel propensity when getting older is not going down between 65 and 75 age of course, the overall development of this variable is influenced by a lot of other factors which are responsible for quite a variation over time. It is now possible to suggest that the general pattern of travel propensity is one of the key indicators for holiday life cycle travel behavior, includes three stages. The growth stage tends to increase from early adult hood until 45 age old or when reaching some 80%. The next stage is stabilization from the ages of around 50 age, until 75 age old, starting with a lower increase.

Finally, the decrease stage is a slight decrease occurs once people reach the more advanced age of 75 age to 85 age old ( Lohmann & Danielsson 2001).

So, it seems Germany government tourism prediction to future travelers' behavior indicated these findings, such as on how future senior generations will travel, who had used survey data to examine the patterns of travel behavior of a generation getting older and applied the findings to draw conclusions on the future. Also, it predicted that on the future of family trips, family segmentation will be the travel behavior patterns in the future. These findings together with the statistical data on demographic change allowed for a better understanding of the coming tends in family holidays. It's aim developed in consumer behavior related to demographic change and predicted what will happen future of tourism one had to consider other influences and drivers as well, for example, trends on the supply side. e.g. low cost airlines or in travelling consumption behavior in general whether how the past may provide a key to predict travel patterns of senior citizens to the future.

Given the projected growth of the senior citizens market, designing specific marketing strategies to meet the prospective needs of elderly tourists will become increasingly important. It has been an implicit assumption that it will be a close relationship between the travel behavior of today's senior citizens and the those of future ones. The growing number of senior citizens in the world. e.g. China, Hong Kong, Japan, USA etc. countries. Global senior citizen tourism market will be based solely on demographic predictions about the future of the population's age structure. However, many of these seniors won't only live longer but will be fitter and more active until later in life. Many of the will also have plenty in life. Many of them will also have plenty of time and money to spend on travel. So, will these new seniors behave like today's senior citizens? Will they adopt the same travel behavior as the previous generation or become a new market of oldies for the leisure and tourism industry? However, to determine the actual number of senior citizens who will be travelling and to sought to evaluate and specify certain difficult to predict the actual numbers of senior citizen to any country. However, they can be based on the implicit assumption that there is a close relationship between the travel behavior of past, present and future seniors. But is this a valid assumption? As the revise- analysis travel analysis survey, which was conducted in Germany every year, offered some interesting data possibilities. It was designed to monitor the holiday travel behavior, opinions and attitudes of Germans and has been carried out since 1970 year, questions in the questionnaire. Data are based on face to face interviews, with a representative sample of more than 7,500 respondents, the interviews being carried out in January each year. All results refer to the average for the defined generated, which ranges generally over ten years. The group of people then at the age of 60 to 69 age is described. This corresponds to the same generation ten years ago, when they had an age of 50 to 59 age. When this methodological approach is not necessarily very sophisticated, it does have the important advantages of being cost effective.

IS (AI) big data gathering method a better psychological method to compare human marketing research method predict travel behavioral consumption?

On the psychological view point, I think individual traveler's character will have those kind of personal characteristics. First, simplicity searchers value above everything ease not transparency in their travel planning and holiday making, and are willing to avoid having to go through extensive research. Second, cultural purists use their travel as an opportunity to immerse themselves in an unfamiliar looking to break themselves entirely from their home lives and engage. Sincerely with a different way of living. Third, social capital seekers understand that to be well travelled is a personal quality, and their choices are shaped by their desire to take maximum of social reward from their travel. They will exploit the potential of digital media to enrich and inform their experiences, and structure their adventures always keeping in mind they are being watched by online audiences. Finally, reward hunters seek a return on the investment who make in their busy , high-achieving lives. Linked in part to the growing trend of wellness, including both physical and mental self-improvement who seek truly extraordinary and often indulgent or luxurious' must have experiences.

Why needs to know the personal character of individual traveler's characteristics? Because if travel agents could feel which kinds of individual traveler's character, then who can predict which kind of travel package to design to them more easily. For example, how to determine future travel behavior from past travel experience and perceptions of risk and safety? We need to concern that the influences of past international travel experience, types of risk associated with international travel and the overall degree of safety feeling during international travel on individual's travelling experiences likelihood of travelling to various geographic regions on their next international vacation trip or avoidance of those regions, due to perceived risk. Because individual traveler's experience of safety risk degree to the countries, it will influence who chooses to go to the countries/ country to travel again.

Why travelers avoid certain destinations are as relevant decision making as why who choose to go to the country(countries) to travel. Perceptions of risk and safety and travel experiences are likely to influence travel decisions; efforts to predict future travel behavior can benefit to individual tourist's decision making.

As Weber & Bottorn (1989) defined risky decision is as "choices among alternatives that can be described by probability distributions over possible outcomes" (p.114). Some psychologists judge subjective perceptions of physical reality, i.e. image of a particular tourist destination, whereas value judgement refers to the way individual rank destinations according to whose attributes. i.e. attractiveness, safety, risk etc. factors to form on overall image. So, if the individual traveler had unhappy and worried and unsafe experiences to go to where the place(country) to travel during whose vacation time before. Then, this negative travel experience will influence who is afraid to go to the place ( country) to travel again. Risk of place, country, destination or region means the danger is relatively high to the place, i.e. increasing in airplane accidents, crime or terrorist activity targeting citizens of potential traveler's nationality or the probability of occurrence is great , i.e. recent occurrences involving travel regions/ destinations under consideration or effective actions to control consequences exist. i.e. selecting safe regions and destinations, taking extra precautions when traveling to risky destinations. These risk factors will influence the individual traveler who chooses to cancel travel plan to go to the country again.

Another interesting research, how to predict behavioral intention of choosing a travel destination, which has focus of tourism research for years, but the complex decision making process leading to the choice of a travel destination has not been well researched. The planned behavior model using its core constructs, attitude, subjective norm and perceived behavioral control, with the addition of the past behavioral variable on behavioral intention of choosing a travel destination.

Understanding why people travel and what factors influence their behavioral intention of choosing a travel destination is beneficial to tourism planning and marketing. Understanding travel motivation is the push and pull model. The idea of the push and pull model is the decomposition of an individual's choice of a travel destination into two forces. The first force is the push factor that pushes an individual away home and attempts to develop a general desire to go somewhere else, without specifying where that may be. The second force is the pull factor, that pulls on individual toward a destination, due to a region specific travel location or perceived attractiveness of a destination. The respective push and pull factors illustrate that people travel because who are pushed by their internal motives and pulled by external forces of a destination. Nevertheless, how push and pull factors guide people's attitude and how these attributes lead to behavioral intentions of choosing a travel destination have rarely been investigated. The decision making process leading to the choice of a travel destination is a very complex process. The planned behavior model is as a research framework to predict the behavioral intention of choosing a travel destination. The model based on the three constructs of attitude, subjective norm, and perceived behavioral control ( Fishbein & Ajzen, 1975).

In conclusion, the factors can influence travelers who decide to choose to travel the country, which include personal safety was perceived to the highest motivation factors among the important factors which include, scenic beauty, cultural interests, friendliness of local people, price of trip, services in hotels and restaurants, quality and variety of food and shopping facilities and services. The factors include both push and pull. Push factors include knowledge, prestige, and enhancement of human relationship etc., whereas, the most significant pull factors include high technologic image, expenditure and accessibility etc. For example, Japanese travelers visiting Hong Kong. Push factors are such as exploration dream fulfillment and pull factors are such as benefits sought, attractions and good climate city. It will be the factor of future travel patterns and motivations of sub-cultural and ethic groups for Japanese choice to go to Hong Kong travelling.

How can apply (AI) digital channel ( big data gathering method) predict travelling consumer behaviors?

(AI) big data digital channel can be applied to help travelling businesses to evaluate whether how much the e-ticket price and travelling package price is the most attractive or reasonable to persuade travelling consumers feel it is the most reasonable price to choose to buy the airline's e-tickets or the travel agent's travelling package product from internet channel . It helps travelling consumers to feel which airlines or travelling agents which ought change their e-ticket and/or travelling package price to let travelling consumers to choose to buy the airline e-ticket or the travelling agent's travelling package products from internet channel. It can be applied to predict whether how many travelling consumer numbers can be increased or decreased when the airline e-ticket price is variable or the travelling agent travelling package price is variable . It aims to give opinions to help any online airlines or travelling agents to judge whether which e-ticket or travelling package price is the most reasonable to let travelling consumers to accept to choose to buy which airline's e-tickets or traveling agent's package products more attractive.

Thus, (AI) e-ticket or e-travelling package price measurement technology can be preference to be applied online communication ecommerce and mobile phone internet platform aspect. As traveling businesses can enter their past e-ticket or travelling package prices data and past travelling customer number data into computer or mobile. Then, (AI) price measurement technology can gather these data to analyze these e-ticket or travelling package product prices and past travelling customer number to compare their e-ticket and/or travelling package prices variable changing range level to find their e-ticket and /or travelling package price variable difference to measure to make conclusion about every travelling package or/and e-ticket product's price variable changing will influence how many travelling customer number increase or decrease changing to choose to sell their different kinds of travelling package or e-ticket products more accurate. Then, (AI) price measurement software will help them to analyze all past e-ticket and/or travelling package price variable changing data to compare whether which e-ticket and/or travelling package price range can let travelling customers to feel it is more reasonable and attractive to influence them to choose to buy their e-ticket or travelling package product among different airlines and travel agent choices. Because any e-ticket or travelling package product's price is one important factor to influence travelling consumers to choose to buy the airline's e-tickets or travelling agent's travelling package products.

For example, Amazon publish has applied (AI) price measurement technology to help authors to decide how much every different topic of e-book or paper book price, it can attract the largest number of readers to buy. Any one author only needs to type whose book name to Amazon publish author himself/herself Amazon website. Amazon publish (AI) price measurement learning machine will help them to auto-calculate and judge how much e-book or paper book price is the most attractive and the most reasonable in order to increase reader number to buy their e-books or paper books to read. So, (AI) online price measurement machine will gather past similar book names and past every similar book readers' reading times and the number of readers to give opinions to let every author to judge whether his/her very new e-book or paper book ought charge how much price to the e-book or paper book which can attract many readers to choose to buy. Although, it is not ensure that the e-book or paper book price must let readers to feel it is the most reasonable price to choose to buy in reader's view point. However, it has other factors to influence readers‘ choice to buy the e-book or paper book, e.g. whether the book content is attractive to public, the author's familiarity, the book's page is enough or not to satisfy readers to read etc. factors. But, instead of all these extra factors to influence readers to choose to buy the book to read. (AI) price measurement learning machine can real give opinions to every author to let them to judge the e-book or paper book different price range whether is too high to influence readers to choose to buy to read or tool low to influence readers feel it is possible poor content book to compare other similar content books. Thus, (AI) price measurement machine can help authors to predict every reader's reading behaviors or reading experience and reading habit from online channel in short time easily. The author only enter the book name to let Amazon publish price measurement machine to check, it will follow past reader's reading habit and reading experience to judge whether the similar all book topic sale record to judge how much price is the reasonable price to attract many readers to buy the book.

Hence, (AI) can be applied to digital channel to help travelling businesses to predict travelling consumer behavior in the future. In the future, mobile/ smartphone, laptop, desktop will be most frequent used ecommerce channels to develop online business. So, (AI) can be also applied to these platforms to gather data to make analysis to help travelling businesses to predict travelling consumer purchase behaviors popularly. Due to , ecommerce is popular to global, so digital online and instore channels can be one good channel to let (AI) learning machine to make platform to gather past every online travelling consumer purchase ( buying) experience data to help travelling businesses to build airline or travelling agent brand personality and having a responsible, positive impact on society.

To apply (AI) learning machine technology to understand travelling customer online purchase behavior, it will raise business e-commerce

successful chance: For example, (AI) learning machine can help travelling businesses to gather data to analyze to determine whether short-term or long-term signals in the online travelling consumer behavior that indicate higher purchase intents to let every online travelling business to know. (AI) learning machine can find that online users with long-term purchasing intent tend to save and click through on more content.
However, as online travelling users approach the time of purchase their activity becomes more topically focused and actions shift from saves to searches from online travelling consumption channel. Then, (AI) learning machine will further find that the brand airline and/or travelling agent purchase signals in online travelling consumption behavior can exist weakness before an online travelling purchase is made and can also be traced across different online travelling purchase categories. Finally, (AI) learning machine synthesize these insights in predictive models of online travelling user purchasing intent to the brand of airline or/and travelling agent travelling package product. Taken together, it's work identifies a set of general principles and signals that can be used to model online travelling user e-ticket and/or travelling package purchasing intent across many online content discovery applications. Thus, (AI) learning machine can help online travelling businesses to gather any online travelling users' click online travelling behaviors data to judge whether there are how many online travelling users will choose to find their online travelling business websites to make final decisions to buy their travelling package or/and e-ticket products from online channels. Then, it will give opinions to help the online travelling businesses to let it to judge whether what are the important website factors will help its online travelling business to attract many online travelling consumers, e.g. designing unattractive travelling website issue, online unattractive scene photos issue, unclear website travelling photo color issue, unclear website travelling advertisement message, contents and words impressions issue, lacking image movement frequent attractive seeing issue etc. different website factors. Thus, online digital channel will be one good choice to apply (AI) learning machine to help travelling businesses to predict travelling consumer behaviors.

Thus, (AI) big data technology can also assist travelling consumers to gather different manufacturers' data to compare what their advantages and disadvantages of their travelling package products are. Then, travelling consumers can make comparison to choose which airline or travelling agent is the suitable to whom to buy e-ticket or pre-booking travelling package in online travelling consumption market.

.

Thus, I believe that artificial intelligent "big data" gathering method can be suggested to be applied to attempt to predict travelling consumer behavioral changes in global online travelling business environment, the reasons are as below:

On the travelling consumer's beneficial hand, travelling consumers can apply this (AI) big data gathering method to attempt to gather any global airline e-tickets and/or travelling agent's package product data to be analyzed by this artificial intelligent learning system to compare human general marketing research method, e.g. survey, questionnaire, marketing plan etc. different human judgement methods to predict traveler consumption behavioral change model. Then, it analyzed all the different data to compare what are the range of the most reasonable e-ticket and/ or travelling package online purchase history and sale in order to make more accurate prediction to future traveler change traveling consumption behavioral model in next month, or next half year or next year short term period traveling consumption change prediction. Thus, it seems that future AI tool can be attempted to apply to predict any industries price behavior, e.g. deciding what level of price is the attractive level to attract consumer in these industries, e.g. fuel, education, tourism, health, entertainment, etc. different product purchase. It can give more absolute price suggestion to any merchants to set their price change predict in order to increase many customer numbers to buy their products in every year, or every quarter every month, or month week, even every day etc. different sale period.

Reference

Backman and others "motivation is conceptually viewed as " a state of need, a condition that services as a driving force to display different kind of behavior toward certain types of activities, developing preferences, arriving at some expected satisfactory outcome.", 1995, p.15.

Fishbein & Ajzen, "The model based on the three constructs of attitude, subjective norm, and perceived behavioral control". 1975.

Hsu et al. "A tourist behavior model has been developed, called the expectation, motivation and attitude " ( EMA) model ,2010.

ICT,WWW . "Switzerland has one of the highest population-to-computer ratio in Europe." Switzerland, 2005.

Jorea Ministry of Environment, " For South Korea environmental attitude is a major factor in decision making vis-a-vis the consumption of " green" food and services", Korea, 2015.

Korea Ministry Of Environment. Public Organizations spend 2.2 Trillon Korean Won To
Purchase green Products in 2014; Ministry Of Environment: Sejoung, Korea, 2015.

Lind , Lohmann & Danielsson , United Nations Population Division, "Demographic change is said to be one of the important drivers for new trends in consumer traveling change behavior in most European countries". 2001.

Mayne, Lonnie. " Evolve of die in the age of the consumer". Entrepreneur, N.P. , 16 Apr. 2014. web of Oct. 2016.

Lee, D.; Kim, M. ; Lee, J. adoption of green electricity policies: Investigating the role of environmental attitudes via big data-driven search-queries. Energy policy 2016. 90, 187-201.

Lee, Terrence, " Tech in Asia-connecting Asia's startup system " Tech. in Asia- connecting Asia's startup ecosystem, N.p.,4 July 2016.

Weber & Bottorn "risky decision is as choices among alternatives that can be described by probability distributions over possible outcomes" , 1989, p.114.

What factors can influence travel behavioural consumption

Prediction travel behavioral consumption from traditional human's mind of tourism market research method

How to predict travel consumption? It is one question to any travel agents concern to use what methods which can predict how many numbers of travelers where who will choose to go to travel more accurately. I think that who can consider how to predict travel behavioral consumption from psychology view and computer science view both.

On the psychology view, It has evidence to support the relationship between self-identify threat and resistance to change travel behavior to any travelers, controlling for whose past travelling behavior, resistance to change if a psychological phenomenon of long standing interest in many applied branches of psychology. Past travelling behavior has been acknowledged as a predictor of future action. Such as travelling behavior that is experienced as successful is likely to be repeated and may lead to habitual patterns. Some psychologists differentiate habit between two concepts, such as goal oriented and automatic oriented both. Although repeated past travelling behavior is addition goal oriented and automatic oriented. Further non-deliberative nature of habit may make appeals to judge and to predict future individual traveler's behaviour accrately. However, repeated travelling behavior without a necessary constraint of goal orientation and automatic oriented both. So, it seems that psychological factor can influence any individual traveler why and how who choose to decide whose travelling behaviour.

On the computer statistic view, structural equation modeling is an extremely flexible linear-in-parameters multivariate statistical modeling technique. It has been used in modeling travel behavior and values since about 1980 year. It is a software method to handle a large number of variables, as well as unobserved variables specified as linear combinations ( weighted averages) of the observed variable.

Whether climate change can influence travelling behaviours.

The flexibility of human travelling behavior is at least the result of one such mechanism, our ability to travel mentally in time and entertain potential future. Understanding of the impacts is holidays, particularly those involving travel. Using focus groups research to explores tourists' awareness of the impacts of travel own climate change, examines the extent to which climate change features in holiday travel decisions and identifies some of the barriers to the adoption of less carbon intensive tourism practices. The findings suggest many tourists don't consider climate change when planning their holidays. The failure of tourists to engage with the climate change to impact of holidays, combined with significant barriers to behavioral change, presents a considerable challenge in the tourism industry.

Tourism is a highly energy intensive industry and has only recently attracted attention as an important contributions to climate change through greenhouse gas emissions. It has been estimated that tourism contributes 5% of global carbon dioxide emissions. There have been a number of potential changes proposed for reducing the impact of air travel on climate change. These include technological changes, market based changes and behavioral changes. However, the role that climate change plays in the holiday and travel decisions of global tourists. How the global tourists of the impacts travel has on climate change to establish the extent to which climate change, considerations features in holiday travel decision making processes and to investigate the major barriers to global tourists adopting less carbon intensive travel practices. Whether tourists will aware the impacts that their holidays and travel have on climate changes.

When, it comes to understand indvidual traveler's behavioral change, wide range of conceptual theories have been developed, utilizing various social, psychological, subjective and objective variables in order to model travel consumption behavior. These theories of travel behavioral change operate at a number of different levels, including the individual level, the interpersonal level and community level. Whether pro-environmental behavior can be used to predict travel consumption behavior in a climate change. However, the question of what determines pro-environmental behavior in such a complex one that it can not be visualized through one single framework or diagram.

Despite the potentially high risk scenario for the tourism industry and the global environment, the tourism and climate change ought have close relationship. Whether what are the important factors and variables which can limit tourism? e.g. money, time, family problem, extreme hot or cold weather change, air ticket price, journey attraction etc. variable factors. Mention of holidays and travel were deliberately avoided in the recruitment process, so as not to create a connection factor to influence traveler's individual mind. However, the dismissal of alternative transportation modes can be conceived as either a structural barrier, in the sense that flying is perhaps the only realistic option to reach long-haul holiday destination, or a perceived behavioral control barriers in that an individual perceives flying as the only option open to whom. The transportation tool factor will be depend to extent on the distance to the destination. This can also be interpreted in a social perspective as an intention with the resources available where much international tourism is structured around flying. To increase the availability of different transportation modes, tourists could choose holiday destination closer to home.

Finally, also how to predict future travel behavioural consumption. I feel that travel agents need to predict whether any country's random daily variation of weather factor is also important to influence travel behaviour. e.g. in weather, temperature, rainfall adn snowfall with traffic accidents factors will have relationship to cause travel demand. Some scientists estimate suggest that when warmed temperatures and reduced snowfall are associated with a moderate decline in non-fatal accidents, they are also associated with a significant increase in fatal accidents. Thus increase in fatalities and temperature. Half of the estimated effect of temperature on fatalities is due to changes in the exposure to pedestrians, bicyclists and motorcyclists as temperature increase. So, if any countries have rainfall, snowfall and low temperature to cause traffic accidents, whether this accident occurrence will influence the travelers who liking climb snow hills, riding bicycle, running sports who will avoid to travel to these countries' bad weather after occurs. So, why I feel that this natural climate factor will also be one serious factor to influence travel behavioral consumption.

Market method predicts future travel consumption behavior

Whether individual habitual behaviour can influence travelling behaviour : e.g. renting travel transportation tools

Whether habit can be intended to predict of future travel behavior to people are creatures of habits. Many of human's everyday goal-directed behaviors are performed in a habitual fashion, the transportation made and route one takes to work, one's choice of breakfast. Habits are formed when using the some behavior frequently and a similar consistency in a similar context for the some purpose whether the individual past travel consumption model will be caused a habit to whom. e.g. choosing whom travel agent to buy air ticket or traveling package; choosing the same or similar countries' destinations to go to travel ; choosing the business class or normal (general) class of quality airlines to catch planes. Does habitual rent traveling car tools use not lead to more resistance to change of travel mode? It has been argued that past behavior is the best predictor of future behavior to travel consumption. If individual traveler's past consumption behavior was always reasoned, then frequency of prior travel consumption behavior should only have an indirect link to the individual traveler's behavior. It seems that renting travel car tools to use is a habit example. So, a strong rent traveling car tools useful habit makes traveling mode choice. People with a strong renting of traveling car tools of habit should have low motivation to attend to gather any information about public transportation in their choice of travelling country for individual or family or friends members during their traveling journeys.

Even when persuasive communication changes the traveler whose attitudes and intention, in the case of individual traveler or family travelers with a strong renting travel car tools habit. It is difficult to change whose travel behaviors to choose to catch public transportation in whose any trips in any countries. However, understanding of travel behavior and the reasons for choosing one mode of transportation over another. The arguments for rent traveling car tools to use, including convenience, speed, comfort and individual freedom and well known. Increasingly, psychological factors include such as, perceptions, identity, social norms and habit are being used to understand travel mode choice. Whether how many travel consumers will choose to rent traveling car tools during their trips in any countries. It is difficult to estimate the numbers. As the average level of renting travel car tools of dependence or attitudes to certain travel package policies from travel agents. Instead different people must be treated in different ways because who are motivated in different ways and who are motivated by different travel package policies ways from travel agents.

In conclusion, the factors influence whose traveler's individual behavior either who chooses to rent traveling car tools or who chooses to catch public transportation when who individual goes to travel in alone trip or family trip. It include influence mode choice factors, such as social psychology factor and marketing on segmentation factor both to influence whose transportation choice of behavior in whose trip.

How to determine future travel behavior from past travel experience and perceptions of risk and safety for the benefits to travel consumers?

How to determine future travel behavior from past travel experience and perceptions of risk and safety for the benefits to travel consumers? Why does individual traveler avoid certain destination(s) is(are) as relevant to tourist decision making as why who chooses to travel to others. Perceptions of risk and safety and travel experience are likely to influence travel decisions. If travel agents had efforts to predict future travel behavior to guess whether travelers will feel where is(are) risk and unsafe to cause who does not choose to go to the country to travel. Then, the travel agents will avoid to choose to spend much time to design the different traveling package to attract their potential travel consumers to choose to travel. The reason is because in the case of individual traveler's tourism experience, the traveler whose past disappointment travel experience ( psychological risk) will be a serious threat to the traveler's health or life ( health, physical or terrorism risk). The past safety or unhealthy risk to the country(countries) will influence the traveler decides to choose not to go to the countries(country) to travel again in the future.

What is push and pull factors to influence any
traveler who chooses where is whose preferable travelling destination

How to predict individual traveler's behavioral intention of choosing a travel destination. Understanding why people travel and what factors influence their behavioral intention of choosing a travel destination is beneficial to tourism planning and marketing. In general, an individual's choice of a travel destination into two forces. The first force is the push factor that pushes an individual away from home and attempt to develop a general desire to go somewhere, without specifying where that may be. The other force is the pull factor that pull an individual toward in destination, due to a region-specific or perceived attractiveness of a destination. The respective push and pull factors illustrate that people travel because who are pushed by whose internal motives and pulled by external forced of a destination. However, the decision making process leading to the choice of a travel destination is a very complex process. For example, a Taiwanese traveler who might either choose new travel destination of Hong Kong or another old travel Asia destinations again or who also might choose any one of Western country, as a new travel destination. The travel agents can predict where who will have intention to choose to travel from whose past behavior and attitude, subjective and perceived behavioral control model.

The factors influence where is the traveler choice, include personal safety, scenic beauty, cultural interest, climate changing, transportation tools, friendliness of local people, price of trip, trip package service in hotels and restaurants, quality and variety of food and shopping facilities and services etc. needs. So, whose factors will influence where is the individual travel's choice. It seems every traveler whose choice of travel process, will include past behavior. e.g. travelling experience, travelling habit, then to choose the best seasoned travelling action to satisfy whose travel needs. This process is the individual traveler's psychological choice process, who must need time to gather information to compare concerning of different travel packages, destination scene, climate change, transportation tools available to the destination, air ticket price etc. these factors, then to judge where is the best right destination to travel in the right time.

Why expectation, motivation and attitude factor can influence travelling behaviour.

Social psychology is concerned with gaining insight into the psychological of socially relevant behaviors and the processes. For instance, on a global level bad influence to global warming, it influences some countries extreme cold or hot bad climate changing occurrence, then it ought influence some travelers' behavioral decision to change their mind to choose some countries to go to travel at the moment which do not occur extreme hot or cold climate ( temperature). e.g. above than 40 degree in summer or below than 0 degree in winter. Due to the extreme climate changing environment in the countries, it will cause them to feel uncomfortable to play during their trips. So, the global warming causes to climate changing factor will influence the numbers of travel consumption to be reduced possibly. This is global climate changing environment factor influences to bad or uncomfortable social psychological feeling to global travelers' mind of traveling decision. What is individual traveler expectation, motivation and attitude? Tourism sector includes inbound (domestic) tourism and outbound (overseas) tourism both incomes to any countries. According to recent article, a tourist behavior model has been developed, called the expectation, motivation and attitude ( EMA) model ( Hsu et al., 2010).

This model focuses on the pre-visit stage of tourists by modeling the behavioral process by incorporating expectation, motivation and attitude. Travel motivation is considered as an essential component of the behavioral process, which has been increasing attention from the travel; industry. The economic approach defines "tourism" is an identifiable nationally important industry. It includes the component activities of transportation, accommodation, recreation, food and related service. So, tourism behavioral consumption is concerned the individual tourist's usual habituate of the industry which responds to whose needs, and of the impacts that both the tourist and the tourism industry have on the socio-cultural, economic and physical environment.

However, travel motivation means how to understand and predict factors that influence travel decision making. According to Backman and others (1995, p.15), motivation is conceptually viewed as " a state of need, a condition that services as a driving force to display different kind of behavior toward certain types of activities, developing preferences, arriving at some expected satisfactory outcome." So, motivation and expectancy which has close relationship to any tourist before who decided to do any tourism of behavior. Some economists confirmed motivation and expectancy which has relations, such as expectation of visiting an outbound destination has a direct effect on motivation to visit the destination;

motivation has a direct effect on attitude toward visiting the destination; expectation of visiting the outbound destination has a direct affect on attitude toward visiting the destination and motivation has a mediating effect on the relationship in between expectation and attitude.

What methods can predict future travel behavioural consumption

How to use qualitative of travel behavioural method to predict future travel consumption?

I also suggest to use qualitative of travel behavioural method to predict future travel consumption. Methods such as focus groups interviews and participant observer techniques can be used with quantitative approaches on their own to fill the gaps left by quantitative techniques. These insights have contributed to the development of increasingly sophisticated models to forecast travel behavior and predict changes in behavior in response to change in the transportation system. First, survey methods restrict not only the question frame but the answer frame as well, anticipating the important issues and questions and the responses. However, these surveys methods are not well suited to exploratory areas of research where issues remain unidentified and the researched seek to answer the question "why?". Second, data collection methods using traditional travel diaries or telephone recruitment can under represent certain segments of the population, particularly the older persons with little education, minorities and the poor. Before the survey, focus group for example can be used to identify what socio-demographic variables to include in the survey, how best to structure the diary, even what incentives will be most effective in increasing the response rate. After the survey, focus, focus groups can be used to build explanations for the survey results to identify the "why" of the results as well as the implications. One Asia Pacific survey research result was made by tourism market investigation before. It indicated the travel in Asia Pacific market in the past, had often been undertaken in large groups through leisure package sold in bulk, or in large organized business groups, future travelers will be in smaller groups or alone, and for a much wider range of reasons. Significant new traveler segments, such as female business traveler. The small business traveler and the senior traveler, all of which have different aspirations and requirements from the travel experience.
Moreover, Asia tourism market will start to exist behaviors in the adoption of newer technologies, a giving the traveler new ways to manage the travel experience, creating new behaviors. This with provide new opportunities for travel providers. The use of mobile devices, smartphones, tablets etc.

and social media are the obvious findings to become an integral part of the travel experience. Thus, quality method can attempt to predict Asia Pacific tourism market development in the future.

However, improving the predictive power of travel behavior models and to increase understanding travel behavior which lies in the use of panel data( repeated measures from the same individuals). Whereas, cross-sectional data only reveal inter-individual differences at one moment in time, panel data can reveal intra-individual changes over time. In effect, panel data are generally better suited to understand and predict ( changes in ) travel behavior. However, a substantial proportion was also observed to transition between very different activity/travel patterns over time, indicating that from one year to the next, many people renegotiated their activity/travel patterns.

How to apply advanced traveler information systems (ATIS) to predict future travelling behaviour?

Nowadays, information can impact on traveler behavior and network performance. For example, when steadily growing levels of vehicle ownership and vehicle miles traveled information has been identified as a potential strategy towards man aging travel demand, optimizing transportation networks and better utilizing available capacity. Toward, this goal to predict further tourist behavioral consumption. Many countries, government tourism development institutes has applied advanced traveler information systems (ATIS) which travel behavior models and high-fidelity network performance models made increasingly feasible through the rapid advances in computer power. Crucial components of this problem domain are the modeling of individual tourist drivers' response to travel information and the development accurate guidance of relevance to real would trip makers. So, this advanced traveler information systems (ATIS) can assist the tourist who like to rent travelling car tools to travel in any countries own free traveler information systems service conveniently. Also, this travel information system can be intended to assist travelers to make better travel choices. e.g. this system can improve the decision making of individual traveler rather than improvements of network performance overall. So, we need to understand how tourists make their travel plans. Also, understanding decision process that lead to booking of the trip is equally important, as it allows of a potential behavior.

How does online tourism sale channel can influence traveling consumption of behaviour?

Nowadays, internet is popular, it seems that booking air ticket behavior of using internet is predicted to influence overall tourism air tickets payment method. Tourism industry has grown in the previous several decades. Despite its global impact, questions related to better understanding of tourists and whose habits. Using online travel air ticket booking benefits include booking electronic air tickets can be made from entering any electronic travel agents websites in the short time and electronic travel ticket payers do not need leave home, who can pay visa card to pre booking any electronic travel ticket from online channel conveniently.

How to analyze activity based travel demand ? Nowadays, human are concerning the traffic congestion and air quality deterioration, the supply oriented focus of transportation planning has expanded to include how to manage travel demand within the available transportation supply. Consequently, there has been an increasing interest in travel demand management strategies, such as congestion pricing that attempts to change aggregate travel demand. The prediction aggregate level, long term travel demand to understanding disaggregate level ( i.e. individual levels ) behavioral responses to short term demand policies, such as ride sharing incentives, congestion pricing and employer based demand management schemes, alternate work schedules, telecommuting limitation of travel agent traditionally work nature shall influence oriented trip based travel modelling passenger travel demand indirectly.

Finally, online travel purchase will be popular to influence the number of travel behavioural consumption nowadays. Any travel package products can be sold from websites to attract travellers to choose to prebook air ticket for any trips conveniently. In the past ten years, the internet has become the predominant carrier of all types of information and transactions. Regarding travel decisions, internet has also become an important sales channels for the travel industry, because it is associated with comparably lower distribution and sales costs, but also because ir adapts to hign supply and demand dynamics in this industry. Consequently, the travel and tourism industry tries to increase the internet sale specific share of sales volumes. So, internet sale channel has changed travel consumption behavioural pattern and characteristics and travel experience. For example, Switzerland has one of the highest population-to-computer ratio in Europe. It is also one of the most highly internet penetrated countries in terms of use of the WWW on a day-to-day basis, with more than 75 percent of the population older than 14 years using the WWW daily ( ICT, 2005).

The reason of booking online tourism may include: convenience, fast transaction, finding traveling package choice easily, more airline seats available. So, online booking tourism will influence the traditional tourism agents visiting of sales and air tickets and travelling package numbers to be decreased. Finally, the online booking tourism market shares will be expanded to more than traditional tourism agents visits sale market in the future one day. So, the travel agents who still use the traditional tourism visiting sale channel which ought raise whose features to compare to differ to online tourism sale channel if these traditional touriam agents want to keep competitive ability in tourism industry for long term.

Actively based patterns of urban population of travel behavioural prediction method.

Actively based patterns of urban population. It is a method of motivational framework means in which societal constraints and inherent individual motivations interact to shape activity participation patterns. It can be used to predict one city or urban the numbers of travel demand in the year. It has two elements: First, capability constraints refer to constraints are imposed by biological needs, such as eating and sleeping and/or resources, such as income, availability of cars etc. to undertake the urban or city's family activities in the year. Second, coupling constraints define where, when and the duration of planning activities that are to be pursued with other individuals. So, this method needs to gather information ( data) to get the relationship between activities, travel and spending work time and space time to evaluate whether there are how many families who have real needs to spend time to go to travel in the year.

What is trip based versus activity based approaches?

What is trip based versus activity based approaches? The fundamental difference between the trip-based and activity based approaches is that the former approach directly focuses on trips without explicit recognition of the motivation or reason for the trips and travel. The activity based approach , on the other hand, views travel as a demand derived from the need to pursue travel activities. So, it is better understand the individual or family behavior basis for individual or family travelling decision regarding participation in travelling activities in certain places or cities or countries at given times and hence the resulting travel needs. This behavioral basis includes all the factors that influence the why, how, when and where of performed activities and resulting individuals and household, the cultural/ social norms of the community and the travel surrounding environment.

Another difference between the two approaches is in the way travel is represented. The trip based approach represents travel as a collection of trips. Each trip is considered as independent of other trips, without considering the inter-relationship in the choice attributes , such as time, destination and mode of different trips. As tours are chains of trips beginning and ending at a same location , say home or work. The tour based representation helps maintain the consistency across and capture the interdependency and consistency of the modeled choice attributed among the trips of the same tour.

In addition to the tour based representation of travel, the activity based approach focuses on sequences or patterns of activity participation and travel behavior, using the whole day or longer periods of time is the unit of analysis. Such as approach can address travel demand management issues through an examination of how people modify their activity participation, for example, will individuals substitute more out-of-home activities for in home activities in the evening of who arrived early form work due-to a work schedule change?

The major difference between trip based and the activity based approaches is in the way, the time dimension of activities and travel is considered. In the trip based approach, time is reduced to being simply a cost making a trip and a day's viewed as a combination, defined peak and off peak time periods. On the other hand, activity based approach views individuals' activity travel patterns are a result of their time use decisions with a continuous time domain. As individuals have 24 hours in a day or multiples of 24 hours for longer periods of time and decide how to use that travel among or allocate that time to activities and travel and with who, subject to their socio-demographic, transportation system and other and scheduling of trips. So, determining the impact of travel demand management policies on time use behavior is an important step to assessing the impact of such policies on individual travel behavior. The final major difference between this two approaches relates to the level of aggregation. In the trip based approach, most aspect of travel, e.g. number of trips etc. are analyzed at an aggregate level.

Consequently, trip based methods accommodate the effect of socio-demographic attributes of households and individuals in a very limited fashion, which limits the activity of the method to evaluate travel impacts of long term socio-demographic characteristics of the individuals who actually make the activity travel choices and the travel service characteristics of the surrounding environment. So, the activity based models are better equipped to forecast the longer term changes in travel demand in response composition and the travel environment of urban areas. Also, using activity based models, the impact of policies can be assessed by predicting individual level behavioral responses instead of employing trip based statistical averages that are aggregated over defined demographic segments.

Why senior age will be main travelling target?

In the past, Germany government had established tourism survey analysis to analyze survey data in order to arrive at reliable conclusions on future trends in travel behavior. To aim to find how demographic change will influence the tourism market and how the industry can adapt to those changes. The travel analysis provided data on tourism consumer behavior, including attitudes, motives and intentions. Since, 1970 year, it is based on a random sample, representative for the population in private households aged 14 years or older. Then, a continuous high scientific standard combined with a national and international users makes the travel analysis a useful tool and reliable source for tourism industry and policy decisions. It aimed to gather statistical data. e.g. on the age structure and on demographic trends, quantitative and qualitative analysis with time series data from the travel analysis. It shows e.g. not only the future volume , quite different from today's seniors, or how who will travel of family holidays will change, e.g. single parents of low, but grandparents of growing significance for tourism.

Demographic change is said to be one of the important drivers for new trends in consumer traveling change behavior in most European countries ( e.g. Lind 2001). Because the growing number of senior citizens in the European Union and other industralised countries, such as the USA and Japan, looks to become one of the major marketing challenges for the tourism industry. United Nations statistics predict that the share of people being 60 age or older will grow dramatically in the coming future, and is expected to rise from 10 percent of the world population in 2000 year to more than 20 percent in 2050 year ( United Nations Population Division, 2001). From its statistic, some data showed that travel propensity increased throughout life until the age of about 50 years of age and was then kept stable until very late in life 75 age. The most important results is that the travel propensity when getting older is not going down between 65 and 75 age of course, the overall development of this variable is influenced by a lot of other factors which are rsponsible for quite a variation over time. It is now possible to suggest that the general pattern of travel propensity is one of the key indicators for holiday life cycle travel behaviour, includes three stages. The growth stage tends to increase from early aduithood until 45 age old or when reaching some 80%. The next stage is stabilisation from the ages of around 50 age,until 75 age old, starting with a lower increase. Finally, the decrease stage is a slight decrease occurs once people reach the more advanced age of 75 age to 85 age old ( Lohmann & Danielsson 2001).

So, it seems Germany government tourism prediction to future travellers' behaviour indicated these findings, such as on how future senior generations will travel, who had used survey data to examine the patterns of travel behaviour of a generation getting older and applied the findings to draw conclusions on the future. Also, it predicted that on the future of family trips, family semgmentation will be the travel behaviour patterns in the future. These findings together with the statistical data on demographic change allowed for a better understanding of the coming tends in family holidays. It's aim developed in consumer behaviour related to demographic change and predicted what will happen future of tourism one had to consider other influences and drivers as well, for example, trends on the supply side. e.g. low cost airlines or in travelling consumption behaviour in general whether how the past may provide a key to predict travel patterns of senior sitizens to the future.

Given the projected growth of the senior citizens market, designing specific marketing strategies to meet the prospective needs of elderly tourists will become increasingly important. It has been an implict assumption that it will be a close relationship between the travel behaviour of today's senior citizens and the those of future ones. The growing number of senior citizens in the world. e.g. China, Hong Kong, Japan, USA etc. countries. Global senior citizen tourism market will be based solely on demographic predictions about the future of the population's age structure. However, many of these seniors won't only live longer but will be fitter and more active until later in life. Many of the will also have plenty in life. Many of them will also have plenty of time and money to spend on travel. So, will these new seniors behave like today's senior citizens? Will they adopt the same travel behaviour as the previous generation or become a new market of oldies for the leisure and tourism indudtry? However, to determine the actual number of senior citizens who will be travelling and to sought to evaluate and specify certain difficult to predict the actual numbers of senior citizen to any country. However, they can be based on the implicit assumption that there is a close relationship between the travel behaviour of past, present and future seniors. But is this a valid assumption? As the reiseanalyse travel analysis survey, which was conducted in Germany every year, offered some interesting data possibiltieis. It was designed to monitor the holiday travel behaviour, opinions and attitudes of Germans and has been carried out since 1970 year, questions in the questionnaire. Data are based on face to face interviews, with a representative sample of more than 7,500 repondents, the interviews being carried out in January each year. All results refer to the average for the defined generated, which ranges generally over ten years. The group of people then at the age of 60 to 69 age is described. This corresponds to the same generation ten years ago, when they had an age of 50 to 59 age. When this methodological approach is not necessarily very sophisticated, it does have the important advantages of being cost effective.

Psychological method to predict travel behavioural consumption.

On the psychological view point, I think individual traveler's character will have those kind of personal characteristics. First, simplicity searchers value above everything ease not transparency in their travel planning and holiday making, and are willing to avoid having to go through extensive research. Second, cultural purists use their travel as an opportunity to immerse themselves in an unfamiliar looking to break themselves entirely from their home lives and engage. Sincerely with a different way of living. Third, social capital seekers understand that to be well travelled is a personal quality, and their choices are shaped by their desire to take maximum of social reward from their travel. They will exploit the potential of digital media to enrich and inform their experiences, and structure their adventures always keeping in mind they are being watched by online audiences. Finally, reward hunters seek a return on the investment who make in their busy , high-achieving lives. Linked in part to the growing trend of wellness, including both physical and mental self improvement who seek truly extraordinary and often indulgent or luxurious‘ must have experiences.

Why needs to know the personal character of individual traveler's characteristics? Because if travel agents could feel which kinds of individual traveler's character, then who can predict which kind of travel package to design to them more easily. For example, how to determine future travel behaviour from past travel experience and perceptions of risk and safety? We need to concern that the influences of past international travel experience, types of risk associated with international travel and the overall degree of safety feeling during international travel on individual's travelling experiences likelihood of travelling to various geographic regions on their next international vacation trip or avoidance of those regions, due to perceived risk. Because individual traveler's experience of safety risk degree to the countries, it will influence who chooses to go to the countries/ country to travel again.

Why do travellers avoid certain destinations are as relevant decision making? Why do they choose to go to the country(countries) to travel? Perceptions of risk and safety and travel experiences are likely to influence travel decisions; efforts to predict future travel behaviour can benefit to individual tourist's decision making. As Weber & Bottorn (1989) defined risky decision is as "choices among alternatives that can be described by prodability distributions over possible outcomes" (p.114). Some psychologists judge subjective perceptions of physical reality, i.e. image of a particular tourist destination, whereas value judgement refers to the way individual rank destinations according to whose attributes. i.e. attractiveness, safety, risk etc. factors to form on overall image. So, if the individual traveler had unhappy and worried and unsafe experiences to go to where the place(country) to travel during whose vacation time before. Then, this negative travel experience will influence who is afraid to go to the place ( country) to travel again. Risk of place, country, destination or region means the danger is relatively high to the place, ie. increasing in airplane accidents, crime or terrorist activity targeting citizens of potential traveler's nationality or the probability of occurrence is great , ie. recent occurrences involving travel regions/destinations under consideration or effective actions to control consequences exist. i.e. selecting safe regions and destinations, taking extra precautions when traveling to risky destinations. These risk factors will influence the individual traveler who chooses to cancel travel plan to go to the country again.

Another interesting research, how to predict behavioural intention of choosing a travel destination, which has focus of toursm research for years, but the complex decision making process leading to the choice of a travel destination has not been well researched. The planned behaviour model using its core constructs, attitude, subjective norm and perceived behavioural control, with the addition of the past behavioural variable on behavioural intention of choosing a travel destination.

Understanding why people travel and what factors influence their behavioural intention of choosing a travel destination is beneficial to tourism planning and marketing. Understanding travel motivation is the push and pull model. The idea of the push and pull model is the decomposition of an individual's choice of a travel destination into two forces. The first force is the push factor that pushes an indvidual away home and attempts to develop a general desire to go somewhere else, without specifying where that may be. The second force is the pull factor, that pulls on individual toward a destination, due to a region specific travel location or perceived attractiveness of a destination. The respective push and pull factors illustrate that people travel because who are pushed by their internal motives and pulled by external forces of a destination. Nevertheless, how push and pull factors guide people's attitude and how these attributes lead to behavioural intentions of choosing a travel destination have rarely been investigated. The decision making process leading to the choice of a travel destination is a very complex process. The planned behaviour model is as a research framework to predict the behavioural intention of choosing a travel destination. The model based on the three constructs of attitude, subjective norm, and perceived behavioural control ( Fishbein & Ajzen, 1975).

In conclusion, the factors can influence travelers who decide to choose to travel the country, which include personal safety was perceived to the highest motivation factors among the important factors which include, scenic beauty, cultural interests, friendliness of local people, price of trip, services in hotels and restaurants, quality and variety of food and shopping facilities and services. The factors include both push and pull. Push factors include knowledge, prestige, and enhancement of human relationship etc., whereas, the most significant pull factors include high technologic image, expenditure and accessibility etc. For example, Japanese travelers visiting Hong Kong. Push factors are such as exploration dream fulfillment and pull factors are such as benefits sought, attractions and good climate city. It will be the factor of future travel patterns and motivations of sub-cultural and ethic groups for Japanese choice to go to Hong Kong travelling.

Bibliography

Backman, K., Backman, S., Uysal, M. And Sunshine, K. (1995). Event Tourism : An Examination Of Motivations And Activities. Festival Management And Event Tourism, 3(1), 15-24.

Fishbein, M., & Ajzen, Z. (1975). Belief, Attitude, Intention And Behaviour: An Introduction To Theory And Research, Boston: Addison Wesley.

Hsu, C.H.C., Cai , L.A., Li, M(2010). Expectation, Motivation And Attitude: A Tourist Behavioral Model. Journal Of Travel Research, 49(3), 282-296. http://dx.doi, org/10.1177/004728750 9349266.

ICT Information And Communication Technology Switzerland, 2005. ICT Fakten (ICT facts).
Available from http://www.ictswitzerland.ch/de/ict%2fakten/ factsfigures.asp(retrieved Dec.12, 2005) in German.

Lind, (2001): Befolkningen, Familjen, Livscykeln- Och Ekonomisk Tillvaxt. Institutet For Tillvaxtpo-litiska studier/Vinnova/Nutek.

Lohmann, Martin (2001): The 31 st. Reiseanalyse-RA 2001. Tourism: vol. 49, no.1/2001;pp.65-67, Zagreb.

United Nations Population Division (2001). World Population Prospects: The 2000 year Revision, New York.

Weber E.U., & W, P.Bottom (1989). "Axiomatic Measures Of Perceived Risk: Some Tests And extensions." journal of behavioral decision making, 2 (2): 113-31.

However, green or nature tourism strategy may include these elements : Quality, tourism should have an impact on the quality of life for all members of the tourist process, exploitation of nature resources should be optimal and ensure their generation, balance, distribution of benefits among participants in the tourist process must be fair. So, future any kinds of green or nature tourism will need have these features in order to attract many travelers to visit any countries' green lands, e.g. they may rent cars to travel to green lands. So, developing attractive green lands will be one kind new travelling trend for green tourism in global future travel market.

There are two types of models that contribute to the better understanding of future tourism industry development, explanatory model refer to factors that cause development growth. For example, whether the travelers feel necessary to travel to different destinations, very often nice landscapes and sightseeing, pescriptive modes ( e.g. life clcle explanations, physical models) examines tourism from what appears on ground e.g. large hotels facilities etc. Hence, any kinds of tourism leisure must need build these both models in order to attract travelers to choose to buy the tourism package from the travel agent more easily. It is important tourism leisure element to any one travel agent's tourism service package if it hopes to develop its tourism service success. So, the expansion of the tourist region over the natural boundaries of the city centre that occured in the first place as a result of the growth of tourism demand, is the end causing this very expansion to continue.

Butler (1980) involves a six stage evoluation of tourism, namely explanation, involvement, development, consolidation, stagnation, and post-stagnation. The last stage is further characterized by a period of decline, rejuvenation or stabilization. The applicability of the model to a given area has been assessed and judged of a tourist destination's development matched the six phases conceptually described by Butler

reference

Butler, R.W. (1980). the concept of a tourist area cycle of evolution: Implications for management of resources. Canadian Geographer, 24, 5-12.

Hence, our tourism industry is facing decline life cycle stage because COVD 19 human mouth disease has influenced many travelers feel fear to catch airplanes to travel, even they also feel to contact the potential COVD 19 human mouth disease people when they arrive the country , they feel that they may contact these sick people, instead of airplanes. So, this kind disease had influenced many travel agents reduce tourism service package number , due to many travelers' tourism leisure activities will reduce, due to travelers number reduces, they only carry cargos to transport to replace travelers COVD 19 disease influence our tourism industry is experiencing decline life cycle stage nowadays. Unless, COVD 19 human mouth attacking to lung disease can be treated by new medicine invention . Otherwise, tourism industry can not re-grow to mature life cycle stage easily.

The most used framework for examing stagnation and possible decline in tourism destinations has been tourist area life cycle model ( Butler, 1980). The model has been operationalized frequently in the tourism lierature. It includes series of stages in tourism development, leadning eventually to the stagnation and post-stagnation stages. When a nature destination can either decline, however, it does not offer a systematic explanation of hoe tourism destination might avoid decline . Such as COVD 19 human mouth disease may influence travelers feel fear to catch air planes. So, even the country has beautiful nature scene to attract people to travel, althoug it is a nature attractive destination, but due to COVD19 disease occurs, it may influence this country's this nature attractive destination to enter decline life cycle stage at this moment.

Hence, tourism industry's life cycle stage , sometime it can be influenced by non predicted factor, such as COVD19 disease factor, it can influence travelers' travelling desire to be reduced suddenly from 2019 , due to they feel afraid to catch air planes to avoid to get this kind COVD 19 human mouth disease to bring lung disease when they are sitting in closed window inside air plane environment. So, COVD 19 human counth disease causes global tourism industry is facing serious decline life cycle stage. The question is that any one does not know when this kind COVD 19 disease will be treated by new medicine invention, so if this kind COVD 19 disease still can not be killed by new medicine invention, then it will continue to influence global tourism development to be improved , even any nature attractive scenes, they can not persuade any travelers to catch air planes to visit any countries to travel easily. But, however, we still need to keep our natural environment to prepare future COVD 19 diease disappears , e.g. parks are important places for the protection of ecological systems and natural resources as well as for the provision ot recreational and tourism opportunities for the public. Then, nature or green tourism can be continue to develop to attract many travelers to travel after COVD 19 disease disappears in the future.

● What are the characteristics of birth life cycle stage to tourism industry ?

Butler , R.W. (1980)'s model begins with a discovery and exploration or birth stage in which a location is discovered by a small, select group of people as a place with desirable assets often, this discovery is nature population who may see the perceived assets. As just ordinary aspects of their environment or local culture. The early tourists have very little support in the form of amenities, and typically, this is preferred and is part of a location's of being undiscovered. The early tourists, therefore rely heavily on and interact frequently with the residents of the region. This small group of early tourists is largely in dependent and shares information about a destination by word of mouth or by select affinity groups. Over time, as more people are introduced to the destination, the number of visitors begins to increase. So " word of mouth" will be traveler information to persuade them to make travelling destination choices in the tourism industry beginning. It is tourism industry's birth life cycle stage characteristics . However, internet invention can let any one see any countries' scene photos, so it is one kind of good advertisement method to introduce any countries' scene, instead of travelling magazine in tourism growth and maturity life cucle both stages.

Moreover, space tourism is at the birth life cycle stage. It needs travelers feel interest to travel space, if this kind space tourism service providers hope to implement their any space journeys in success. These factors may influence its development succeeds. Nowadays, its target market is wealthy travelers group, wealthy individual are needed, as they serve as the main consumers for space tourism . For space tourism to succeed there must be enough demand from those who are able to afford to expensive ticket. To date there have only been seven commercial space travelers, or space tourists, although they prefer to be called space flight participant, as they see themselves as pioneers and adventers as opposed to ordinary tourists. So, any future space tourism that price must need to reduce to general public, e.g. ordinary income level people, they can spend, if space tourism hopes to reach from stage stage rapidly. So, space tourism is still far to mature stage.It depends on whether how long time its any space journey ticket price can be reduced to any one can pay. So, when its customer target is not only wealthy travelers, many ordinary or common income level people, they can pay to any one space jounrney. It may mean to reach growth life cycle stage.

- What characteristics to space tourism growth stage?

When human space tourism of commericalization of activities in outer space can bring these feeling to let any one space traveler feels then, it may mean that it can reach growth stage, such as they may feel their any space journeys may bring positive impacts that outer. Space recreation can produce, in order to come up with space tourism, exploring and untravelling the hidden anystories of the space are needed. Also they can feel need drastically broadens and enrichs human's technical awareness and constructive knowledge need from any one space tourism journey package. When space tourism reachs mature life cycle stage? What its characteristics are? When any one space travelers can feel that not only earth based attractions that simulate the space experience , they must need to catch airships to experience this different tourism experience, such as space theme parks, space training camps, virtual reality facilities , space hotels ( skotel), multimedia interactive games and tele robotic moon rovers controlled from earth, but also parabolic flights, lasting up to three days or week long stay at floating space hotel, including participatory educational ,as well as sports competitions ( i.e. space olympics). Hence, above these will be nay space tourism development. It can reach mature life cycle stage characteristics when any one can feel the real travelling mouth to compare to travel our earth anywhere, they can not find that they feel space tourism may be same to our earth's holiday ( need to rela) or cultural ( know different places or specialized tourism, e.g. expectations of adventures , even space scientists discover new experiences to expectations of adventure or get more information, scientific interest feeling. Then, at this moment, we can call space tourism has reached the mature stage. However, I believe that to develop space tourism in success. We must need to control space tourism ticket price to be reduced to general low income people. They may spend budget level. So, ticket price may be one major factor to influence future space tourism growth when it can reach mature stage. Also, it mean that whether space tourism may become another kind of popular tourism lesiure activities to use. It depends on ticket price factor, instead of its any space tourism trip arrangement factor. So, any one space tourism service provider must need long time to spend in order to implement its different strategies, e.g. ticket price, space trip arrangemet to achieve its their space tourism to achieve its their space tourism different destination package in success if they hope their future space tourism business can grow up in short time.

Airport service life cycle stage improvement strategy

Any organizations will have life cycle stage from birth, growth , mature to decline. In airport service organizations have theis life cycle stages in service aspect. Airports organizatins aim to provide safe, comfortable , even shopping environment to let passengers to stay and to wait to transfer another air planes to visit another destination or arrive the country's airport to check out or check in to enter the airport to leave. If airports have life cycle stages, what the characteristics to every stage? How to improve airport service in order to reach mature life cycle stage rapidly? How to implement airport service strategy in order to reach mature life cycle stage to the aorport organization rapidly?I shall explain as below:

Any airports need to be planned in order to raise excellent service to let passengers to let any travelers choose to travel the country whether the country can provide excellent service and facilities. It will bring indirect emotion impact to influence the travelers chooce to revisit the country to travel again. However, soft or hard element or ) staff service performance or airport facility), they will influence whether the different countries travelers to choose to travel to re-visit the country again. So, learning how to keep the mature or airport service life cycle stage to stay long time, it will be one important factor to influence any airport business in success.

In the birth life style stage to airport, airport organizations must maintain the capability to provide expert advice to airport owners an matters including operational safety, during construction, environmental compatibility, and airport development standards. No other private or public organization can be expected maintain this level of proficiency. These value-added services enhance public trust when assuring consistant application of standards for the nation's airport system. So, it seems that when the new airport is built if it hopes its passenger customers can consider themselves emotion need. So, it ought concentrate on nowadays airplane landing cunways or airport transfer free service transport etc. facilities can let them to feel safe when they were walking in any airport places. If they feel anywhere are dangerous when they are walking or staying in the ne sirport, then new airport non safe or dangerous factor may influence travelers to choose the country to travel again.

Any new airports will need have good new national airport plan in order to it might operate in the near future with respect to safety areas. The plan elements may include as below:

Achieving zero accidents aim, establish standard safety areas at all commercial service airports , achieving the most minimum 85% of all passenger flights operate on runways with safe feeling, increase measure to 100% of all passenger flight operating on runways with standard safety areas after three months. Within 5 years, 95% of all passenger flights begin and end on runways with standard safety areas.

On benefits aspect, aims to mobilize work force to improve safety area performance describes realistic investment benefits. So, in any new airports birth life cycle stage, they must need to consider safety and expenditure for repair aspect in order to keep its service performance to avoid passengers have dissatisfactory feeling when they are staying in their new airports.

When the country has many travelers travel to the country , then the country's new airport passengers number must increase. It is its the new airport growth life cycle stage. These are critical success factors influence the airport, whether it can improve service performance in order to excite different countries travelers visiting the country's airport desire or grow up the visitors number successfully. The critical success factors may include: Having necessary support from internal and externa stakeholders to implement and willing to share information and identify anywhere the total airport facilities of repair needs that are both reliable and feasible projections to let passengers to feel more safe feeling when they are staying in the airport, understand its future service vision and mission, set strategic direction and goals to process/product specific objectives and decision-making across and doen the organization, define, model and prioritize planning prcesses critical for mission performance, practice hand-on sernior management ownership of planning process and allow field, personnel flexiblity in performing jobs, adjust organizational structures , an essessment program to evaluate planning process and product management , e.g. national airport system performance, create organizational understanding of the value management to customer and stakeholder current and future expectations developing human resources management strategies to support new process that solves needs planners and engineers, building information resources strategies change, especially for entering data at the source and maintains data integrity and timeliness.,establish central support group to support reengineering efforts, outreach and training efforts across the organization, phase in short-and long-term results that achieve set goals and objectives over the next two years.

Thus, when one new airport begins to feel passengers number is increasing. It ought experience the growth life cycle stage to the new airport , if it hopes that it can reach mature life cycle stage rapidly as well as keeps its mature life cycle stage to stay in this stage long time or reachs the airport service performance to the most satisfactory level in this mature life cycle stage. It must need to attempt to plan these strategies to implement in order to avoid decline life cycle stage occurs in short time. So, it explains why some new airport can experience the development to mature life cycle stage from grow life cycle stage in short time,even when it reachs mature life cycle stage. It can keep to stay in this stage long time. The reason is that it had prepared effective strategies to achieve how to improve its airport service performance aim in order to satisfy passenger needs. When they are staying in the country's airport any time. Hence, every year revising service performance is needed to any airports.

Any airports must have development processes. The question is that whether the airport needs how long time to reach growth or mature life cycle stage from birth stage or decline life cycle stage will be delayed how long to occur. The development processes may mean that the airport development life cycle stages changes that had toard a particular result or even as a series of continuous actions or operations coducting to an end ( Merriam-Webster, 2013).

reference
Merriam-webster ( 2013). On line dictionary. Available at:
https://www.merriam-webster. com/( last accessed July , 8 2013).

Hence, any airport organizations with experience development pricess. When the new airport is built, it must be in the birth life cycle stage. Its passengers number can not increase rapidly. It needs time to grow their number. But, when the new airport operates a period, many different countries begin feel this new airport is existence in the country. They will attempt to catch airplance to visit this country airport to catch airplane to visit tis country airport to travel. If they feel this country airport service performance can satisfy their short time staying feeling or its passengers or airports visitors number may increase rapidly. It meand that this airport is experiencing growth life cycle stage. So, if the airport can attract many visitors in short time. It will reduce time to growth life cycle stage from birth life cycke stage.

So , service performance may be one important factor to inflow the airport grows. When the airport develops to the period, passengers number can not increase rapidly, it may be the airport's mature life cycle stage. Due to it's passengers number can not grow rapidly, its passengers number also may reduce. When its passengers number has significant decrease, if its reduction number is increasing more. It implies that the airport is experiencing decline life cycle stage. All any country's airport may experience whole life cycle stages. If the country's airport can not implement successful strategies, it may experience birht life cycle stage in long time because it can not grow its passengers number significantly. So, any airports need to learn how to help them to change growth life cycle stage, even mature life cycle stage can stay in long time easily. If they hope to attract many different countries passengers to visit their airports or travel themselves countries or enjoy to stay short time in themselves airports in order to grow themselves airline industry development.

● How can processes improvement management strategy influence airport service performance?

Overall processes in an airport may involve passengers, luggage, cargo, aircraft movements, ground handling, and crews . All of these operations can be systematised into processes at airport terminal. Three main types of processes can be established departing , arrival and transfer . Departure consists in catching a flight to a final or intermediate destination, arrival consists in landing and leaving the airport, and transfer consists in landing at the airport only to catch another flight to a final or an intermediate destination. Airports also deal with cargo. It involves in the movement of cargo by air, cargo fies from the shopper to the consignee through one or more airlines. However, when the airport can let them freight forwarder, being familiar with the necessary procedures how permits the airline to concentrate on the provision of air transport and to avoid time consuming details of the facilitation and landside distribution system. It will raise efficiency and improve service performance. The services product by the ground handling are crucial to the success and efficiency of the airport operations.

These services are usually provided by specialised companies. Briefly, it includes the luggage treatment, passengers carrying from plan to terminal when needed and aircraft assistance. Also, focusing on crew, there are two majoe processes, one for departures and the other for arrivals. The crew members also have to pass the security and passport controls. However, they have special channels for this. Once they reach the aircraft, the similarities with the passengers‘ procedure stop. Hence, they have to perform a set of activities , such as check the aircraft load sheets and help passengers to name a few. Also airport terminal operations processes for passengers and luggage, typically for departures , passengers do the check on the airline area, pass security controls, proceed to the general lounge and lastly to the gate holding area. arriving passengers are able to immediately go from the luggage claim area, but the non-passengers have to pass the passport control at first. After this passengers have to decide if they need to declare goods or not as the paths are different . Hence, if the airport can reduce all of this service processes are less complex as immigration check in-out service, liggage claim can be efficient to carry when passengers need to find themselves luggage. Then, it will reduce waste time and let they satisfy airport service absolutely. So, reducing service process time amy also help the airport to increase customers number significantly. When airport role is the middleman between airlines , cargo transport service providers and passengers, e.g. short time transport cargo service and reducing passengers check in or check out service time. then, it will let them to feel more satisfactory service to the airport.

Hence, airport capacity is as a multifactor function leaves open the exact relationship between the factors but stresses that all factors are relevant to assess airport capacity . So , understanding airport capacity and what drives the capacity usage at airports may provide an insight in the set of instructments available to optimise the use of capacity. All of these factors may influence any capacity of an airport, they may include as below:

For example, technical constraints, e.g. ATM per hour service in a runway in a combined arrival and departure fashion, when many passengers are staying at the airport, they can withdraw money from ATM easily. So, ATM number facilities service supply number and location choice to the airport factors will infuence passengers ' satisfactory level, another factor is environmental constraints, it can directly offer the wellbeing of the communities surrounding the negative emotion to passengers and communities surrounding the airprt. For this factor, the change in technology and/or operational procedures can provide more capacity in the system.

Airline business models factor, it can affect the capacity spoke model when other under a point-point one ,these models directly affect the peak hour operational capacity, particularly in big international hubs. Airlines often compete with high frequencies between destinations, thus increasing the number of movements. In addition, conncectivity also has downsides for this model: the delays in one airport might be exported and sometimes in another, due to the connectivity influencing the real capacity. This factor has been setting economic incentives or pricing models. Furthermore, expanding information systems, from one airport to multiple airports gate-to-gate concept, and the use of larger airport to redcuce frequencies.

Hence, above these factors may influence whether the airport needs how long time to reach maturiry life cycle stage when it is staying the growth life cycle stage. It depends on how its strategies implementation and how environment influence its implementation , if it hopes to achieve to reach the maturity life cycle stage in success in short time.

Finally, I shall explain life cycle cst analysis to any country pavement strategy will bring what significant influential benefits to any airports continue to develop in order to avoid to reach decline life cycle stage time in short time easily , when they are staying in the mature life cycle stage. In the construction or rehabilitation investments of highway's pavements, it is already common to perform a life-cycle analysis or life cycle cost analysis for different alternatives to airport pavements. Becauae when any airport pavements are using for a long time, every day has many airplanes need to fly to land on the pavement. It can bring significant repace influence when the airport has many airplanes are needed to land on the pavements every day in the maturity life cycle stages.

Hence, how to evaluate the repair cost expenditure budget in order to satisfy every day air planes land on the airport pavement need. In the calculations are different cost factors ( including direct and indirect cost)to any airport itself pavement. Direct costs are related to the critical construction cost landing on pavement activities and are calculated with information from the airport agency and constructors that work for them. The indirect costs are related with the loss of daily revenue of the airport during work activities, such as landing on the airport pavement.

Runways are the most critical pavements area of airport , so it is critical to ensure the quality of these pavement to let airplanes to land on the airport safety, e.g. they need to be constructed with sufficient strength to carry the moving airport and have a high resistance to skidding and aquaplaining. It is most of the time accomplished with reconstructions or deep rehabilitation. Hence, predicting how much will spend on airport pavement facilities expenditure must need in every day.

However, the life cycle assessment (LCA) is a mult step procedure for calculating the life time environmental impact of a product or service is needed to any airport organizations, when they reachs maturity life cycelt stage . The complex process includes goal and cope definition in inventory analysis impact assessment. The process is vaturally iteractive as quality and completeness of information is constantly being testes. When the definition of the aim and scope of the study is done the next step is the development of an inventory, in which all significant environmental burdens during the lifetime of the product,, such as airport pavements or process , such as airplanes landing on the pavement or airplanes leaving from the pavement in the airport.

( Araujo, Oliveria & Silve ) 2014 explained that life cycle snslysis of pavements are focused on the activities of extraction, production, transportation application of materials, concisely the construction of the road. Because its difficult to obtain other relevant data knowing that the use phase of the pavement is predominant with repect to energy consumption and also to gas emissions related to the atmosphere. One of the main factors for the use phase is the rolling resistance, this depends on the surface and structural characteristics of the different pavements.

reference

Araujo, J.P.C. Oliveria, J.R.M. & Silva H.M.R.D. ( 2011) . the importance of the use phase on the LCA of environmentally friendly solutions for asphalt road pavements. transportation research part D: trasport and environment, 32(0), 97-110. Retrieved in March 2015 from:// dx. doi.org/10.1016/j.trd.2014.07.006.

Hence, , if the airport can have good repairment or renew skills to help its pavement to improve. Then, it may bring long time benefit, such as reducing airplanes energy consumption and also to avoid gas emissions or reduce gas emissions accident occurrene, even air plane landing on pavement accident occurrence chance can reduce to the zero. so, defining the expected pavement performance time improvement strategy can influence whether the airport pavement can satisfy all airplane users how long time landing on or leaving on the airport pavement. Also it is the major factor to influence airport main function success for any airplanes arriving to the country's airport pavement or leaving from the country's airport pavement. Hence, calculating any airport pavement life cycle costs factor. It is necessary to analysis and interpret carefully the results to identfy the most economic pavement strategy in any airport's whole life cycle development stages.

Why tourism and airline industries have close relationship to influence their profitability between of them.

In my study, I suppose terrorism, profitability and the price of petroleum which had properties of distinct and interrelated close relationship. Moreover, these variables ( terrorism, profitability and the price of petroleum) displayed differentiation, self replication, efficiency and hierarchy which can cause risk events to airline industry. However, I also think the other internal and external threat factors of airline industry, such as inflation, bank interest rate, business model, service quality, airline fuel or plane engine technology, air ticket pricing, brand loyalty, airline strategic management, government policy and fuel hedging of these factors which can also raise the risks to threaten any airlines existence in airline industry.

There are two basic business models in airline industry. They are network ( full service) and low cost ( discount) carriers. The network carrier model employs diversification strategy by increased domestic destinations, serving international routes, providing diverse seating arrangements ( business, economy and first class), maintaining a complex system of offering high quality service. Otherwise, low cost ( discount) airlines focus on lower air fares. To keep operating costs down, discount airlines offer shorter routes and provide point-to-point destinations rather than through sophisticated flights are primarily in domestic destinations. So, discount airlines operate a common model aircraft fleet, offer a single seating arrangement and cheaper flight services offered to compare network airlines. However, these two basic business models have their unique competitive abilities to provide any airlines existence in airline industry nowadays.

In fact, natural resource of oil is decreasing in our earth. But as the same time, human demand is increasing and oil supply is decreasing, so it also causes the oil fuel price is increasing to supply to airline industry. It influences not only to airline industry, it also impacts of higher oil fuel price to tourism, such as expansion of airports are made based on expected demand increase.

Tourism has been proven to many adverse events, including terrorism, flight disruptions. Beside, the bad natural climate change influences, such as the volcanic ash cloud event occurred in April 2010 year. So, airline industry need to concern climate change because it will cause high fuel prices indirectly. For example, the event occurred the extreme increase in operating costs for airlines in 2008 year, due to unprecedented prices for aviation fuel also meant, that despite the introduction of fuel charges, so this event causes the global airline industry recorded losses seriously. Even if alternative fuels become commercially available for airlines which are still likely to be more expensive than present aviation fuel. Thus, it seems that poor tourism will influence poor travel consumption and low airline tickets sale.

Higher airfares in the future are likely to lead to reduction in travel and cause tourists to shift from more distant to closer destination. When some of the economic responses to higher oil prices are obvious assessing the overall economic impacts on tourism is difficult. However, long term changes in global oil price rises will be similar to global changes in other commodity prices, exchange rates and income. It is therefore important to consider the impact of high oil prices on tourism from a general equilibrium perspective rather than relying only on bottom partial equilibrium. However, I believe tourism and airline industries have close relationship, such as tourism and airline industries are likely to suffer in an environment of high oil prices. Given that tourism destinations receive tourists from a range of origins, it would be useful to understand of some countries are increasing oil prices than others. Such as the net oil importing countries are selling higher oil prices than oil exporting countries generally. For example, New Zealand is an oil import country to provide planes for international visitor arrivals, so its oil fuel price is usually higher to charge to NZ airlines because any NZ airlines need to pay to foreign countries to buy any oil more expensive price. So, NZ airlines usually charge higher airfares to its visitors to compare the other exporting oil countries' airlines.

In economic theory, on income effects indicate negative impacts on tourism demand, the exact effects of higher oil fuel prices for specific destinations are far from clear. However, airline industry's different market segments show different sensitivities to air ticket fares changes. On the first hand, if the visitors are long destinations generally wealthier than average and therefore potentially less affected, as energy costs would be a smaller proportion of their income compared will be those from less wealthy groups. On the second hand, oil prices don't translate into higher transport costs especially not on air routes that are highly competitive and that are maintained for strategic reasons. On the third hand, many other factors shape tourists' decision making, including emotion drivers or those related to images, fashions and perceptions.

Increasing environmental protection awareness of tourists could also be an important factor to influence tourism consumption, instead of oil fuel price raising causes air ticket fares raising factor to reduce traveler numbers. However, oil price raising reason causes also due to high use of cars, vans and domestic air transport in some countries, e.g. Hong Kong, China countries, there are many people like to buy cars to drive. So, the private driver numbers are increasing demand to cause these countries' oil fuel prices raise in the short time suddenly. It will influence HK and China air tickets prices need to be risen , due to there are many cars, vans and domestic air transport tools need to use oil to supply energy to cause oil import numbers will increase to HK and China and HK and China airlines need to pay higher price to buy oil to use. In the result, HK and China airlines air ticket prices will also need to rise and it will influence HK and China travel consumption desire.

Fuel raising price solve methods

● Why oil fuel raising price factor can cause risk to airline.

In long run, implications of changes to supply and demand side conditions of oil fuel energy may differ qualitatively. For example, due to investment responses of producers, consumers and governments in alternative energy sources and more energy efficient plants, vehicles are supplied in order to achieve oil fuel price can't be risen seriously.

However, I believe oil fuel rising charge will be an important factor to influence global airline ticket fares to be also increased. Firstly, on the bank interest changing factor, e.g. bank interest rate rising which only attract more bank saving. But it can not influence the bank savers who choose to reduce relax time to go to other countries travelling. Otherwise, when the bank savers can save more money to earn higher interest in banks, who will prefer to choose to use their saving to consume travelling. Due to who can earn higher interest rate after a period of saving time. So, I believe whose behavioral travelling consumption will be raised when the banks will raise interest rate, then the bank savers won't choose to save more money in banks. So it is possible that who will withdraw more money to consume to go to travelling from their bank saving. It seems bank interest rate changing won't influence bank savers' behavioral travelling consumption to be reduced. Secondly, on the exchange rate changing factor, although any country's exchange changing will cause other countries' money value to be fallen down or risen up. However, it won't influence any travelers' behavioral consumption to be reduced seriously. Although, it is possible that the traveler won't spend too much to go to shopping when who travel to the another country and arrive the country. But, it is not possible to influence the traveler decides to reduce consumption to buy any air ticket to go to travelling. Thirdly, any country inflation also can not reduce travelers' travelling consumption easily because inflation can influence consumers who choose to buy cheaper foods and clothing and reduce entertainments in their every day life. But, one country's inflation can not influence it's citizen do not spend much travelling expenditure because travelers only spend one time or two times of travelling every year usually. So, the travelling expenditure rate of any households is not too much to compare daily essential expenditure. So, it seems that bank interest rate and exchange rate changing and inflation factors won't influence any travelers' travelling consumption of decisions to be reduced easily. Otherwise, if the oil fuel price raises too much, then global airlines' cost will be raised. So, the airlines only choose to increase their air fare prices to aim to avoid loss possibly. It seems that oil fuel price has direct influence airline income.

● Methods to solve rising air fare prices demand.

I. Why will biofuels energy be demanded ?

I suggest these methods how to avoid the oil raising price factor to cause airline air fare prices to be risen to lead the risk of traveler numbers to be reduced.

The first method: Whether aviation fuel markets will have what benefits from biofuels supply to planes. I shall refer the scope includes trends in jet fuel price, airline response to fuel price, increases and volatility and environmental goals for aviation. The aviation fuel supply industry includes production, distribution and consumption of aviation fuel and it outlines players in the aviation fuel supply chain. For example, at each airport, fuel supply chain organization and fuel sourcing could differ with regard to the role of oil companies, airlines, airport owners and operators and airport service companies. However, major jet fuel purchasers are airlines, general aviation operators, corporate aviation and the military, with most of the jet fuel in global different countries demanders being used for domestic commercial and civilian flights carrying passengers, cargos or both. Commercial aviation fuel efficiency has improved dramatically over time, largely due to aircraft and engine upgrades and operational and air traffic control improvements. So, it seems that fuel supply factor can influence airline fare prices majorly.

However, jet fuel prices generally correlate with prices of crude oil and other refined petroleum products, such as diesel. So, increasing prices and the persistent price volatility of jet fuel markets import airline industry finances in any countries. However, airlines use various strategies to manage aviation fuel price certainty, including financial hedges, increased vertical integration and adjustments in aircraft utilization and size to avoid the jet fuel raising price risk. Investments in alternative aviation fuel could be a mechanism to diversity expose to the price of petroleum. It seems the use of alternative aviation fuel would serve to diversify the fuel mix to reduce the risk of jet fuel monopoly raising price threat. If a diversified fuel mix were to avoid either fuel raising price in short term or to avoid fuel raising price in long term. Potential benefits include reduced actual fuel costs from only choice of jet fuel supply increased price certainty and lessened fuel costs. This diversify could allow airlines to become more consistently profitable and to make other investments in their businesses.

So, biofuels have potential to meet aviation industry needs, possibly including managing risks of upward fuel price trends and fuel price volatility and avoid risks with greenhouse gas emissions. So, the aviation fuels market could use biofuels to reduce greenhouse gas emission and mitigate long-term upward price trends, fuel price volatility or both.

What are the challenges of high priced oil for aviation? In fact, nowadays not the resources of oil as such, but much more the insecurity of supply, due to geopolitical instability in combination with a tight oil market makes a scenario with much higher oil prices than the world is currently experiencing not unlikely. Aviation is completely dependent upon oil as its fuel source. Since no practical energy substitute is readily available for commercial aviation, a scarcity of petroleum relative to demand will present a major aviation policy. In addition, efficiency gains, due to operational measures and new aircraft medium term. In particular, it has been demonstrated that the annual reduction rate in fuel consumption traffic unit is not a constant, but is itself also falling, in contrast to past estimates.

So, a high-priced oil scenario will have severe consequences for demand, airline revenues, the competitive position of airports and eventually airline networks, strategies and fleet development. In particular, transfer demand, short-haul and leisure traffic can be expected to be heavily affected by high oil prices, due to their relative high price sensitivity. So, different countries' governments or/and airlines are valuable to research another new and potential biofuel energy to substitute oil energy to supply our planes to reduce the threat of oil monopoly supply to influence the cause of air fare raising prices. Because the elasticity is very high to travelers, when the travelers feel air fares are rising high or even low level to influence travelers who will choose not to buy the air tickets to go to travel easily.

Will the fuel (oil based inputs) risk be higher to compare other costs to cause air ticket prices to be increased?, e.g. engineering maintenance, employees salaries, general cleaning, security office expenses etc. expenditures to airlines? If the probability-weighted upside effect on firm value when a risk is resolved favorably is greater the risk than the probability-weighted downside effect if the risk is resolved badly, then expected value work not be enhanced by hedging. So, the risk will be resolved badly to any commercial airlines. Airlines are an interesting case because the direct effect of source of risk resides squarely within the no offset in revenue functions ( unlike for oil producers, for example), so value effects from costs feed directly into equity value. Most directly, the risk source is fuel costs to commercial airlines. Jet fuel is of course, a mix product of crude oil, so airlines indirectly face oil price risk. There are reasons to expect that airlines' fuel costs might to convex in oil price (i.e. absent any hedging). For example, oil prices, being generally pro-cyclical in recent times, tend to be highest when airline demand is strong. Airlines are therefore apt to use more high priced fuel than low-priced fuel over time. Airlines can raise air fare benefit is limited by the elasticity of demand. Also, cost functions could be influenced from fuel cost corresponds to upturns in economic activity overall ( due to demand pressures on oil related prices), so it causes that airline's capacity delivers their services given their level of fixed capital. The essence of airlines basis risk in the case of jet fuel is essentially the time profile of the refining margin between crude and jet fuel, or the time profile of the price differential between other refined distillates and jet fuel. Thus, it is far from clear that risk management with oil is sure to add value to any airlines. It seems the impact of airline energy and any countries' domestic or foreign airline passenger travel numbers which have direct close relationship.

II. Whether the relationship between terrorism and oil prices has close relationship.

Whether the relationship between terrorism and oil prices has close relationship. It needs to judge to determine if a combination of terrorism and the price of petroleum significantly predicted airline profitability and which variable whether the further period was the most significant between the terrorism occurrence and the price of petroleum influence. So, different countries' governments or airlines need to collect samples of financial records from which country's any airline commercial passengers and cargo airlines on costs of fuel and any airline profitability. Also, gathering the terrorism data were comparison of terrorist attacks on petroleum in oil-producing nations, and incidents of high jacking aboard any country's aircraft. When any countries' airlines or governments can judge whether the impact of airline energy and terrorism risk level is high or middle or low level. Then, which can use this sample data to measure how to do positive social change to whether to increase or reduce employment in commercial aviation industry, or ought need to invest other higher commercial activity in tourist and other travel related service businesses and when is the most right time to adopt of green technologies by the civil aviation manufacturing industry after the terrorism attacks occurrence to any country. It seems that any countries' governments or airlines which ought concern that the event of when the terrorism attacks will occur and gather past sample data to predict when the next time terrorism attacks event will be occurred and the risk will be high or middle or low level to influence global airline industry development.

III. What factors will influence airline industry's price elasticity of supply and demand?

In fact, the airline industry is largely dependent on the supply of the oil industry. Otherwise, the oil industry is inelastic. However, the increase or decrease of the price of airfare is directly related to the increase or decrease of the oil's price to fuel the aircrafts because there has no any new energy which can be substituted to oil fuel to airline industry. So, it seems oil fuel producers are monopolies to control its sale price to be raised easily.

Another factor that can affect airline industry to be directly targeted by a tragedy brought about by terrorism. The past four years, from 2001 year to 2005 year, there had been at least $40 billion worth of losses in the airline industry because of the September 11 date terrorism attacks in 2000 year. There had been an expected and significant decrease in the demand for the airline industry services because of the attacks that involved planes hijacking and crashing into key locations like the World Trade Center and the Pentagon in USA. Although, terrorism attacks can bring risk to influence fuel price rising in airline industry. However, this risk occurrence to airline industry is only that after the terrorism attacks occurred. It is possible that terrorism attacks won't occur again in the future.

Otherwise, our concerning ought be the greenhouse emissions and how it affects global warming. The air quality would be better once this new regulations are adopted. However, it would affect large airlines. So, it would increase the price of airfares because of economic fees that airline companies have to cover. Air pollution can give a negative impact on the domestic or oversea owned airline companies for long term. If airlines' planes can use clean fuel to fly, e.g. biofuel, then it will bring benefits to global airlines for long term. On the positive side, the environment would be healthier as the earth's temperature would rise, and greenhouse effect would be dramatically reduced. This positive effect can come at a cost that is greater than most people perceive. So, the environment protection travellers who will reduce travelling times to avoid air pollution is caused to influence human health. It seems that airlines need to concern to apply psychological method to predict whose travelling consumption of behavior which is more suitable than behavioral economy method.

On the psychology view point on travelers, who will be more preferable to catch planes to go to different countries to travel, due to the chance of air pollution and global environmental warm issues will be reduced to low risk to influence our health if planes can use biofuel to be energy to fly in the future one day. It seems that spending expenditure to research other non polluted biofuel new energy is one solvable method to global airline industry in the future. To solve, any airlines or countries' governments or oil producers ought choose to spend more time to research new biofuel. Otherwise, the predicting when terrorism attacks event will be occurred, it is more difficult to predict the time more than researching to produce new biofuel energy method in the future.

So, I recommend that researching the new biofuel energy or other kinds of energy to substitute the oil energy and air pollution risk these two factors are the urgent behavioral economy method is used to solve this challenge which the airlines or oil producers or different countries' governments which need to concern nowadays. Because these two negative environment factors are the most influential to cause traveller individual travelling consumption desire to be fallen among of other negative environment factors.

The difference between online and offline travel agents

The main cost related factors to offline or online travel agents

Nowadays,many online or offline travel agents have interest to find what the main factors that can affect their strategies to reduce airline costs. The main factors include route structure, type and characteristics of the aircracft, cost of labor and management quality, which will influence whether which airline routes are the most suitable to let online travel agents or offline travel agents to help them to sell paper air tickets or electronic air tickets to attract travel consumption more easily.

Thus, a cost-related strategy is the main important factors to influence travel consumption choice between online or offline travel agents. For example, considering that advantages in costs is an important strategy for carriers to remain in travel transportation market.

The deregulation process of travel markets and increasing opportunities for competition have created excess capacity in many markets that causes lower rates, even with its rising costs. Thus, the travel strategic costs management as well as travel consumers that their behavior under different influences can bring competitive advantages over travel players.

Cost reduction in the travel market -based industry is a very important way of being competitive between offline and online travel agents, when facing travel air ticket prices decreasing for every trip. So reduce to total travel cost, e.g. fuel, maintenance, labor etc. is relevant, but the influence of each component on every total trip cost depends on factors that are related or not to airline operation. For example, some airline can adopt the lowest cost model to sell air tickets from offline or online travel agents which compete for travel passengers with traditional modes as self driving road transport trip in large areas of countries domestic travel market, such as US, UK domestic travel market.

However, the decision about the relevance of one cost is not a simple matter. The effectiveness of reduction of each item that comprises the total cost of airline can change over time, depending on both the business model and the scope of the airline company or online /offline travel agent company as well as external factors.

However, there are three types of competition advantage between online and offline travel market: They are such as agility, differentiation cost and the differentiation may be related to a product of superior quality, higher value f the brand or the company's positive reputation. Such as the online travel agent's providing the different airline cheap air ticket price and kind of trips to provide to travel consumer consumer comparison or the offline travel agent's famous brand or positive reputation to let travel consumers feel travel agents can provide many actual trip package to let them to compare by oral clearly. Thus, the online travel agent's weakness is lack of travel agent individual exploration to let every travel consumer to understand every trip package more clearly.

But online travel agent's strength is it can provdide one website to let travel consumer attempt to compare different trip air ticket and/or hotel price to make personal travel pre-booking decision at home. The another advantage is related to techniques that reduce production cost, making it is possible to offer cheaper air ticket, or hotel room rents, or cheap trip package, than the competition. Such as online travel agent can sell more cheape electronic air ticket price to compare traditional offline travel agent's paper air ticket price.

Finally, agility refers to the speed which the company responds to market demands. For example, if the online travel agent can make statistics to analyze how many online travel consumers to choose to buy which airlines' electronic or paper air tickets, e.g. which airline trip destinations and trips and hotels choices are the most popular attraction to them. Then, the online airline has possible to respond to provide to the most popular airline trips choices, electronic air ticket price comparison choices and hotel rooms prices choices to attract many online travel consumers to enter their online travel websites to choose different airline electronic tickets to buy or pre-book hotel rooms from travel agent websites. Also, if the traditional offline travel agents can attempt to gather every travel consumer's destination trips, hotels , airline paper or electronic ticket prices enquires to make statistics to make which travel trip journeys or destinations and airline paper travel ticket prices are the most popular. Then, it is possible that they can respond to every travel consumer individual demand more to attract whose travel agent choice more easily.

Airline travel agency AirAsia in the domestic airline low cost strategy

There are three major characteristics of the airline industry namely is product nature, its expenditure structure and its market entry conditions. Airline agent's product is homogeneous or undifferentiated , causing significant competition in airline domestic travel or foreign travel both markets, which are free from regulations and economic barriers. However, high capital and operating expenditure is another important characteristic of the airline industry. Aircrafts, airlines' major capital expenditure are very costly to acquire . For operating expenditures, aviation fuel and labor make up the two major costs in the industry.

Another important characteristic of the airline industry is the conditions for market entry, which differs between international and domestic airline markets . In the international travel market, airline travel agency entry is very difficult as international flights and routes are the results of regotiations between governments . On the other hand, in the domestic and regional travel market, travel agency entry depends on the level of deregulation or liberalisation.

More and more countries, however are opening up their domestic travel markets for more competition. In addition, government plays an important role to regulate the travel markets and existing players may significant influence over now travel agent entrants.

In fact, the mjor factors influence to international or domestic travel consumption increasing numbers are the global economy and safety issues, instead of other different economic factors, such as travel destination choice, electronic air ticket or paper air ticket price, hotel price , the country's political change, e.g. war occurrence, bad weather , e.g. very cold or very hot etc. different factors infuence. Because generally , the world or any region of it is in an economic crisis or depression , the demand for airline services will fall. The late 1990 year Asian financial crisis for example, resulted in minimal increase in the number of worldwide airline passengers incrased only minimally from 1997 to 1998 year. Another factor of influencing the travel passenger number to be decreased, it concerns safety issues are also an important driver of the travel industry, which is subject to very safety standards to influence travel passengers' travel choice to the country. In addition, they are also unexpected safety related events, such as the 11 Sept. 2001 year tragedy in the US, which caused reduction in passengers . The increasing popularity of low cost airlines is the newest trend in the airline industry if which hope many passengers choose to buy whose electronic air ticket or paper air ticket to catch which planes to fly from online travel agent or offline travel agent channels.

The rise of low cost airlines, such as AmericaWest, JetBlue and Airtran in US, Ryanair and EasyJet in Europe and Vigin Blue in Australia. The share of low cost airline strategy is popular in the US and European airline market. For example, the Southwest airline low cost strategy is the basis of most low cost airlines operations. The key of the strategy is to reduce costs when at the same time offering low prices to passengers. History showed that the low cost airline strategy is easy to replicate , but difficult to implement successfully.

However, I suggest airlines need to know what functions which can attract passengers to chose to catch their planes to fly if they expect to rise passenger numbers. For example, the critical function of the Malaysia airline travel is to connect the major towns and remote interior areas within East Malaysia, which has poor road systems and limited availability of other significant means of transportation . In contrast, West Malaysia has more developed and extensive rod and railway systems.

Therefore, airline travel is not the main mode of long distance transportation. It implies Malaysis airline ought concentrate on focusing short distance transportation strategy for passenger beneficial choice function. For example, a new small Malaysia airline serving one or two routes may enter easily. Otherwise, a larger airline servicing multiple routes may be harder to enter Malaysis airline market. It also means access to capital and labor are the major obstacles for new airline entrants to Malaysia airline market. Thus, small airlines into a larger airline is probably more likely to be successful as in Air Asia's case to Malaysia airline market.

Thus, the airline low cost strategy competition positions include very low or minimal pressive from other airline similar service substitute products, low or medium power of airline similar input suppliers. In conclusion, low cost airline strategy is a god method to be attempted to win competitors in airline market.

How consumers select travel service between online and offline mode in travel industry

Nowadays, the travel industry is operating through two different modes, online and offline respectively. It involves the identification of the competitive strategies adopted by the tour operators. For example, it was found that e-retil travel is platform that is bringing two market forced the demand and supply tour operators and the customers together, and both parties and more inclined towards online mode in near future. Tour operators are gaining by operating at low cost and increasing their business reach when customers get what they desire as per their convenience. For example, many tour operators had promoted tourism destination through website that allow user to use interface for booking transporttion, foreign exchange etc. However, the role of travel operators ( agents) should be assisted any airlines to promote their travel package service by internet more easily , such as tourism destination , arrangement of hospitality, restaurants, transportation tools during their trips.

The reasons why consumers choose online travel service include:

Firstly, it is online researching hospitality service. Online travel websites can provide many different accommodation furniture, such as seeking hotel locations, rooms prices comparison, prepaid hotel rooms by visa card payment transaction method, range from luxury five stars deluxe category hotels to small guest houses. The primary need of tourist is to find a place for residing in foreign country or domestic country to ensure whose safety and relaxing needs. Online travel website channel can help whom to find a place , according to his/her needs and paying capacity in the most shorten times.

Secondly, it is online restaurant ( food and beverages researching ) service. Full service restaurants are divided into two categories, fine dining and casual dining restaurants . Fine dining restaurants are usually located in the premises of luxury hotels, provide high quality food at premium price with good ambience and highly trained professionals. Thus, travel consumers can also compare the different restaurant food price and seek where is the restaurant and find.

What food taste of food supply from the travel agency or travel operator website easily 250 + tour operators are registered with the ministry of tourism ( website of tourism ministry) , and the major players in the industry are dealing online and are dominating the travel industry. The major online travel players are Thomas cook, Cox and Kings, make any trips, clear trip, gatra.com and Expedia.

The tour operators whether online or offline offers a large number of services to the tourists including customized package where the customer selects each element of the tour package, specialized tourism package and complete tour guide package.

Nowadays, the tour operational travel ( agents) are working through two different modes: offline online . Big brands with luge investment are dealing online and enjoying low cost benefits and huge profit margins. When the small tour operators have their market niche and managing have their market niche and managing their profits by dealing offline.

It is generally prefer offline mode that is the opportunity for small capital investment or employee number for tour operators. But the large scenario is changing as with the usage of internet by the tour operations have given convenience to the customers and now the customers of modern age have started developing preference for online modern. Thus, internet technology change any countries' travel agents or tour operators' air ticket sale method. So, it brings electronic ticket sale method is more popular to compare to traditional travel paper air ticket sale method.

However, online electronic ticket sale method has its disadvantages such as online transaction is unsafe, if the consumer 's name and address and visa card number is stolen to let any internet users to know to be used to buy any products from internet channel easily. Otherwise, traditional walk in offline travel paper ticket sale method is more safe, because the travel consumers can pay cash to the travel agents directly.

However, offline travel agent disadvantages include that the research identified that information communication and technology has very crucial role for tourism industry. Tourist can access any kind of information about tourism destination and tourism products from any part of the world. Tourism comprehends with social media. For example, it was found that (ICT) is bosting up tourism industry. (ICT) helps in searching the location, search for information on tourism products, and e-booking of airline tickets and hotel reservation.

The online travel sale service attraction is that the recent development in the field of information communication and technology and its practical application in tourism and hospitality industry. Generally , online travel sale service must have consumer side and the supplier side.

The decision making prcess of consumer was analyzed and it was found that travel information search and traveller individual electronic ticker pre paid to prebook any plane seat, hotel rooms and restaurants prices comparison to prebook service of traveler individual purchase behavior are corresponding with the usae of (ICT).

What is the online travel sale service strategy?

The two most important things for travel operators ( agents) are online travel marketing and strategic management. Former can enhance business operations. Use of (ICT) develops financial capabilities , however, it depends on management choice, financial condition and position. Some researchers recommended that the usage of IT should not be restricted at operational level, however it should be extended up to senior level and should be used for decision making. Social media is regarded as a platform where the tourists and travel operators/agents ( suppliers) of tourism industry cross each other. Thus, the role of social media has been directed for future research in tourism industry. Hence, it seems online travel sale service has these features to attract travel consumers to choose to use this online mode to buy electronic air ticket. Such as, airline electronic air ticket price comparison, pre-booking plan seats to avoid full seats flights to delay consumer individual trip plan, pre-booking hotel rooms and prices comparison as well as prebooking restaurant seats and food price and taste comparison, travel destination easy search. Otherwise, these features to attract travel consumers to choose to walk in to travel agents to buy paper air ticket directly. They include: safe cash or visa card payment to avoid personal information is stolen by website payment channel, e.g. via card number, address, name , birth date personal information. Also the travel consumer can enquire any questions from the travel agent and gets individual feedback from the travel agent by oral before who ensure to choose to buy which kind of travel package for whose travel destination. In special, when the travel consumer has much time to spend to enquire any travel trip question, walk in travel agent is the best enquire methods to let the travel consumer to know the trip information clearly.

● Online/offline travel operators
(agents) maketing strategies

Offline walk in travel unique segment service strategy

Nowadays, online and offlce travel operators competitions are serious. In fact, tourism marketing , there will be more need for online travel operators in the future, due to online travel sale service is popular to be accepted by online travel consumers. Thus, I recommend walk in offline travel agents need to concentrate on focusing some unique travel service to attract new or old travel consumers if who hope to survive.

I recommend that they can focus on specific specialized services, such as travel consultation ( specialization) hypothesizing that systematic differences exist between the usage of travel agents for different travel contexts and travel agents can survive if they focus on specific segments of the market, such as older travelers ( segmentation; hypothesizing that systematic differences exist between the usage of travel agents depending on the personal characteristics of travellers). The unique travel needs include: specific services related to package holidays, transport services, beach on city holidays, as well as destinations travellers are not familiar with.

I shall give my opinions to provide insight into alternative strategies for travel agencies in a matured travel market with a high internet penetration as below:

The internet online travel sale service is a reality of popular to let travel consumers to feel convenient to pre-book air seat, hotel rooms , air electronic ticket prices comparison. In order to make final purchase decision very easily in the shortest time. Consequently , it has penetrated the decision making process of travel to attract them to choose to buy electronic air ticket, prebooking hotel rooms or restaurant seats from online travel agent channel more than walk in offline travel agent channel. This is especially true in the tourism business where consumption to consume ( booking) and the purchase-related information search ( Bieger & Lasesser 2004; Crotts 1998).

In fact , apply website to provide travel sale method has these good consequence. From travel operator ( agent) supplier's perspective, the success potential derived from operating a website consist of lower distribution costs, higher revenues and a larger potential market share ( due to the ubiquitous access). From traverler's perspective, the internet allows direct communication with tourism suppliers facilitatinf requests for information and allowing services and travel related products, e.g.

prebooking hotel rooms, restaurant seats , electronic or paper air tickets, travel trip arrangement package products to be purchased at any time and any place from online travel agents /operators conveniently.

Offline / online travel agency ( operator) business depends on earn commissions on behalf of airlines. Thus, offline walk in travel agency ( operator) business model that would extend existence as a booking agency ( thus focusing on consultation and interpersonal contact) strategy.

As a matter of fact, commission -cutting , which began in the US well ahed of Europe, has had a profound effect specially on business travel agents . Consequently , many of them have re-invented themselves as " travel managers", instead of selling tickets and making arrangements, they charge consultancy fees for reducing the amounts client companies spend on travel ( Daneshku, 1999).

- Systematic differences strategy applies to offline walk in travel agent

Thus, I recommend systematic differences strategy can be applied offline walk in travel agent ( operator). It means that walk in travel agents could reorient their offline walk in travel agent business to focus on contexts that are less substitutable by other channels and media . Factors hypothetically attributing to the delineation of travel contexts include: helping travellers to choose best travel destinations, helping travellers to attempt to find the number of previous trips ( indicating the familiarity with a destination) for their travel reference, helping them to find the cheapest, the most convenient and the most close transportation to ctch during their trips, helping them to find the different types of accommodation and rooms price comparison , nature/type of the trip comparison , arrangement of time of booking ( as indicator of spontneous / planned travel) nd helping them to budget overall travel expenditure .

Systematic differences in travel agent use exist in dependence of personal ( characteristics with with tourists. Walk in offline travel agents could benefit from a travelling client segmentation strategy and customize and target their services to those travellers that are most likely to be and remain their customers.

Factors hypotheticlly attributing to the traveller segment include: travel expenditure per day, useful travel information as indicator for perceived risk and socio-demographic ( age, gender, highest completed and education, professional positions) . Generally, the role of walk in offline travel agent with regard to the travel infrormation search and booking behavior have take an incoming perspective. Such as looking at visitors from different travel markets at a similar destinations. The comparison of central importance in determining whether specialization of travel contexts or market segments is the more promising strategy for walk in offline travel agents.

However, travel package tours strategy must b offline walk in travel attraction . Due to some walk in travellers target segmentation market has still needs. Generally, this travel package tours of travel segmentation consumer who like to enquire the travel agents to concern what the hotel rooms price are the cheapest to provide to them to live, what transportation tools the travel agent can arrange to them to catch anywhere the country destination, the travel agent can provide them to visit during their tour journey. Thus, the travel trip package service is still popular need to offline walk in travel agent ( operator). This market is only belonged to offline walk in travel agents ( operators) nowadays.

Service fees and commission cuts strategy

The reduction or removal of airline commission continues to challenge travel agencies' profitability It is crucial to understand what trends travel agencies need to be aware of to ensure how to profitability and increase travel agencies' revenues with service-fee models.

Service fees are not only a way to compensate for the loss of airline commission but also a way to generate new revenue sources for travel agencies that guarantee their long term profitability. Many travel agencies are expanding their service fee models, both in terms of the mounts changed and the number of service to airline.

However, if travel agent charge too much service fee to exceed the general airline travel market service fee reasonable or standard level. It will influence many airlines do not choose to find the travel agent to help them to sell air tickets. Travel agents apply fees most often for airline related services. They charge differentiated fees depending on the destination, type of reservation ( e.g. frequent flyer), number of tickets sold or type of airline ( e.g. full service versus).

However, service fee increases can raise customer loyalty and satisfaction. It won't reduce client numbers or result in a lose in clients.. The reason is that service fees can be tailored to suit individual customer. This helps travel agencies target their clients, with tailored services based on their past purchasing patterns and identity services for which clients' willingness to pay is greater , such as trip planning identity service for which pay , such as hotel only or special promotion.

To revenue mix for travel agencies is increasingly shifting to service fes as airlines have lowered or cut commissions. Successful travel agencies in many European countries are fast adopting, and constantly upgrading , their service fee schemes. Thus, it seems reasonable service fee level is one important factor to influence travel agents and airlines good relationship. In fact, even travel agents raise service fee, it won't influence travel consumer number to be reduced , even they raise air ticket price. It they can provide the informations concerning the reasonable hotel rooms prices and food quality comparison to satisfy travel consumers' living arrangement or helping them to find the reasonable restaurants' food prices and where are their location arrangement or providing the reasonable airlines' electronic air tickets or paper air tickets sale service, even arrangement any high entertainment quality of travel destination trips to let travel consumers to feel satisfactory.

However, I believe the raise air ticket price factor won't influence the travel consumer number to be decreased. Any offline or online travel agents will encounter this crisis. By cutting travel agents' commission. Airlines decreased their dependence on travel agencies as a distribution channel. In fact, three key variable factors will influence travel agents' commission income to be decreased. They include below:

- The unsustainable or no change financial losses by airlines , due to the growth of low cost carriers, leading to an increase in the number of bankruptcies.
- No negative consequences from previous commission cuts: airline had progressively lowed the commission payments.
- No effective resource for travel agencies to satisfy airlines needs.
- The appearance of now airlines and air routes to provide to travel agencies to fall down air ticket price to attract consumers' choices, due to who don't feel to spend much money to go to this new air routes or catch new airline plans , whether these new air routes are excite to entertainment or whether they are safe planes to catch.
- An increase in the number of bankruptcies to cause travel comsumption desire to be reduced.
- New competition forced down air fares.
- The necessity to cut production costs, especially with low cost meaning low production costs and low fares, even if the two are closely linked.

What an e-commerce strategy is used by internet travel websites?

Nowadays, the commercial use of electronic travel ticket travel is common, the most purchased online products include, for example, the name brands in online travel Epedia.travel .com and cheap tickets have been or are being integrated in large online travel firms.

Generally, online travel websites apply these strategies to attract travel consumers as below:

Firstly, shopping mall strategy, means to conduct a comprehensive factors for e-commerce. The online service provider needs to organize catalogs of services, take orders through their websites, accept payments securely, send service or related document, such as airline tickets to consumers and manage client data , such as client profiles.

Secondly, portal strategy, portal websites , such as yahoo give visitors the chance to find almost everything , they are working for in one place. Websites , such as Altavista.com and yahoo.com provide users with a shopping page that links them to many sites carrying a variety of products. Once a client is familiar with a website, who will be more likely to use the online service.

Thirdly, pricing strategy, low price is as a major competitive weapon. It includes a comparison pricing on discount price or price negotiation to let online travel consumers to get the best electronic travel ticket price choice to buy any airline tickets.

Travel agents vs online booking: Tackling the shortcomings and strengths

Consequently, however, one travel consumer who chooses either online booking sale service or traditional walk in offline travel agent to enquire travel service. These both of travel sale methods have shortcomings also. Such as it is possible that online electronic travel ticket purchase has personal data ,e.g. visa card, name, birth data, address, which will be stolen by online crime internet users more easily, who can not enquire any travel questions to get clear travel information concern whose travel destination package service choice or hotel room choice or transportation tool or restaurant choice and airline choice by travel agent. Also, it is possible that walk in travel agent paper travel ticket purchase shortcomings include that the travel consumer can not check any airlines' seat and pre book hotel room or transport tool or restaurant in the shorten time if who needs to fly immediately. Thus, it seems that online travel agent's client group is business travel intention, who does not need to enquire travel agent and has desire to per book airline seat in the short time. Otherwise, the offline walk in agent's client group is entertainment intention , who need to walk in to travel agent to enquire whose travel package and has no desire to pre book airline seat in the short time. Thus, online travel agent ought concentrate on design good travel package for the business travel consumers. Otherwise, offline travel agent ought concentrate on design good travel package for the entertainment travel consumers. Thus, they can have themselves unique travel target package to adopt to their different travel need. Such as business travel consumers need to live cheap and comfortable hotels, catching cheap and fast transportation tools in their business trips, eating in cheap and good taste food in restaurant and spending the less time to catch the airline plan to arrive the destination and cheap and comfortable business class plan seat. Such as entertainment travel consumers need the travel agent can help them to design cheap and enjoyable travel package, includes living comfortable hotel room, exciting and enjoyable trip, good taste food and railway, travel bus, cruise and plane provision in trip.

In conclusion, In fact, tourism is a quite unique area of business in a sense that is a travel sale service product and it can't be observed or manipulated through direct experience prior to purchase . Instead clients have to purely rely on indirect or virtual experience. Thus, every online or offline travel agent ought attempt to design different travel package to attract every business traveler or entertainment traveller trip need because every traveler will have personal unique trip need in this competitive travel sale service market in the future.

Reference

Bieger. Th., and Ch. Laesser ( 2004). " Information sources for travel decisions: Toward a source process model," Journal of travel reserch, 42(4): 357-371.

Daneshku, S. (1999). " Unwived travel agents unworried bi internet, " Financial Times , London. June 16, 1999:10.

Foucault, B. Lery, N. Rifkin, A. & Silfies , 2000.
" Comparision of textbook prices by retailer and by college" working paper. Cornell University, Ithaca, Ney.

CHAPTER FOUR

# Can technology improves oil sale

● Reasons cause oil industry experiences recession

Nowadays, global oil industry is experiencing decline cycle stage. From 1950 oil energy product is at the birth cycle stage. When cars , human walking replace tool is invented, human began to drive cars to go to anywhere in habit daily. Because human is often to drive cars to go to offices, or leisure places, so cars can cause gas need increases. Before, 1970, oil energy product is at the growth cycle stage, becuse cars are accepted to Western people more than Asia people only. But, after 1970, in Asia many countries, e.g. China, Japan, Singapore etc. people began to accept cars to replace catching public transport tools, so gas need had been increasing . Till to 1990. oil industy had been experiencing mature life cycle stage, because global car manufacture number had increased, global every family may have at least one car when the parent has children. So, global cars need number increases, it may be one factor to bring gas need increases. Also global travelers number increases, it will cause many airplanes need to fly to different countries frequently. So, it also bring gas need increases. Because global drivers and travelers number increases, this factor may cause gas need increases significantly because driving activities and flying activities are frequently occurence. However, nowadays oil industry is experiencing decline cycle life stage. Because COVID-19 human mouth disease influences many travelers feel fear to catch air planes when they need to sit in closed window airplanes , if one passenger has COVID 19 disease, he/she will bring other passengers to get this kind of lung disease by air contact. So, global travelers number decreases, it can influence airplanes need to fly frequently, so gas need is also influenced to reduce. Also, since electronic vehicle invention, because electronic vehicle is charged battery for its energy, so gas does not absolute need. If global many drivers have environmental protection awareness, they choose to buy electronic vehicles to replace traditional gas vehicles, then gas need must be influenced to decrease. So, these two main factors may influence global oil industry need decrease. The question is that: How gas manufacturers raise gas users need from decline life cycle stage to re-grow life cycle stage? I shall indicate the methods as below:

- How to raise global gas users need desire ?

Future of sustainable resources
scarcity economic and social loss to oil industry

In economic theory, it indicates two major factors are responsible for the emergence of economic problems. They are (i) the existence of unlimited human wants and (ii) the scarcity of available resources, such as limited numbers of food and natural resource shortage. I feel that human need to solve these two problems before 2050 years. How to balance an optimization approach for human and ecological flow needs ? How to solve climate change environment problem and welfare is for the centrality of human need? Because natural environment factor and natural resource and food shortage and our social economic growth which will have close connection relationship. If natural environment is bad, it will influence a lot of crops numbers can't be grown in farms. The reason of crops shortage will be caused, due to numbers of crops supply to be reduced because bad weather can not grow much crops and overpopulation numbers will increase largely at the same time before 2050 year. It will cause the numbers of demand is more than supply seriously. The result of the prices of foods will be increased by overpopulation and food shortage, so that it will cause every country inflation will be risen, it will occur in developing countries urban areas due to which have , such as India , China, Africa etc. countries have no many farms to provide to farmers to grow foods because air and water pollution and factories are built on farm land , so which need to pay higher price to import crops and foods to provide whose overpopulation to eat from overseas developed countries. Experience of developing countries that have succeeded in the reducing hunger and malnutrition shows that economic growth doesn't automatically ensure success, the source of growth matters too. This isn't surprising since 75% of the poor in developing countries live in rural areas and their incomes are directly or indirectly linked to agriculture. Many countries will continue depending on international trade to ensure their food security. It is estimated that by 2050 year developing countries net import of rice will were than double from 135 million tones in 2008/2009 to 300 million in 2050 year. It seems overpopulation will cause developing countries foods shortages in 2050 years.

Climate change and increased biofuel production represent major risks for long term food security. Studies estimate that the aggregate negative impact of climate change on African agricultural output up to 2080 year to 2100 year could be between 15% and 30%. Agriculture will have to adapt to climate change, but it can also help mitigate the effects of climate change. A recent study estimates that continued rapid expansion of biofuel production up to 2050 year would lead to the number of pre-school children in Africa and South Asia being 3 and 1.7 million higher. Thus, policies promoting the use of food based biofuels need to be reconsidered with the aim of reducing the competition between food and fuel for scare resources. The sharp increases in food price that occurred in global and national markets in recent years, and the resulting increases in the number of hungry have sharpened the awareness of policy makers and of the general public. Hence, different countries governments need to concern safe agricultural system to avoid any foods shortage to supply after 2050 year.

The perspective for 2050 year raises a number of important questions. Are current public and private investments sufficient to ensure adequate agricultural production potential, sustainable use of natural resources, information and communication research for technological breakthroughs to avoid foods shortage for the future? What needs to be undertaken to help agricultural meet the challenges of climate change and growing energy scarcity? What can be done to ensure food security in Africa, India , China etc. developing countries. The facing highest population growth rates,. The severest impacts from climate change and the heaviest burden of HIV/AIDS etc. diseases threats.

Finally, on the changing socio-economic environment hand, the main socio-economic factors that drive increasing food demand are population growth, increasing urbanization and rising incomes. In 2007 year, the USA dept. of Economic and Social affairs indicated that in fact, the developed countries population growth is slower than developing countries. However, all of the growth in the world's population will take place in urban areas. By 2050 year, more than 70% of the world's population is expected to be urban. Thus, scientists need to concern to predict developing countries urban area people foods demand and supply both numbers whether global foods can provide enough supply to urban area people in developing countries after 2050 year. On the other side, human will concern whether there be enough natural resource base of land, water and genetic diversity to meet developing countries needs after 2050 year.

What factors cause the resources scarcity and why human need to solve the resources scarcity before 2050 year

In comparison to the past 50 years, the rate at which pressure are building up on natural resources-land, water, bio-diversity will be increasing during the coming 50 years. An expanded use of agricultural feedstock for biofuels and ongoing environment degradation would work in the opposite direction. Much of the natural resource base already in use worldwide shows degradation . These include capture fisheries and water supply . In addition, actions to other ecosystem services, such as the ecosystem service, food production often cause the degradation of others, soil nutrient depletion, erosion, desertification, deflection of freshwater reserves, loss of tropical forest and biodiversity are clear indicators.

Whether natural resource base should be adequate to meet the future demand at global level. Whether any developing countries should still limit commercial natural resource import capacity to let rural area population to use to protect whose domestic natural industry development when rural area population will be increasing seriously in 2050 year. Biodiversity, another essential resource for agricultural and food production is threatened by urbanization , deforestation, pollution and the conversion of wetlands. As a result of agricultural modernization, changes in diets and population density, humankind increasingly depends on a reduced amount to agricultural biological diversity for its food supplies.Thus major reforms and investments are needed in all regions to cope with rising scarcity and degradation of land, water and biodiversity and with the added pressures resulting form rising incomes, climate change and energy demands.

There is a need to establish the right incentives to protect agriculture's environmental services to protect biodiversity and to ensure food production using new agricultural technologies before 2050 year. For the developing countries, in order to ensure that resources are available in the required quantity and quality and in the urban locations where they are needed, large additional investments need to be made in order to avoid rural people of hunger coincides with resource scarcity before 2050 year.

Increased investment incentives and provided stable production growth incentives : land, water and biodiversity of three natural resources. The aim should be to stop over-exploitation, degradation and pollution, promote efficiency gains and expand overall capacities as appropriate . To provide the rural population engaging in ecosystem services with win-win solution to improve the sustainability of ecosystems, mitigate climate change and improve rural incomes. Whether and under what conditions the estimated future food demand can be met and how food security can be achieved. Hence, every country needs to have an effective economy system to attempt to solve the basic economic problems. The function of the economy is to allocate scarce resources among unlimited wants. Moreover, every country needs to have effective economic system to study of its citizen behavior in relation to how scarce resources to allocated and how choices are made between alternative uses of the country government's limited expenditure. Due to our earth has scarce resources, it implies human will scarce natural resources to provide us to use. Our governments need to predict whether what our earth's limited natural resources will be all used in order to solve our natural resources to be used in the short time quickly as well as our governments need to apply effective economic system to design soluble methods to avoid our earth will be not to provide any natural resources to satisfy our daily essential needs in one day.

The average U.S. resident , in a year, consumes 275 pounds of meats, uses 635 pounds of paper and uses energy equivalent to 7.8 metric tons of oil. Before, long years ago, the average American ate 197 pounds of meat, used 366 pounds of paper and used energy equivalent to 5.5 metric tons of oil. In the U.S. there is about one passenger car for every two people. Otherwise, Europeans have about one passenger car for every 3.1 people. On the other side, Developing countries have on average, about one passenger car for every 49 people. What does economics have to tell us about these differences in consumption?

Consume sovereignty means the idea that consumer's needs and wants determine the shape of all economic activities. Is this belief valid? That is are the final goals of economic activity all to be found in the act of consumption. Hence, if one day, our earth scarce any kinds of natural resources to be caused shortage, e.g. water, air, oil, land , gas, solar, gas , unclear , wind energy resources as well as foods e.g. vegetables and meats etc. eating resources. Due to human numbers are increasing, such as China, India and Africa etc. developing countries' people numbers are increasing much than the USA, UK etc. developed countries 's people numbers every year. But, our earth's vegetables and pigs, cows, sheet etc. meats foods numbers are decreasing every year. I believe that our foods and vegetables and natural energy resources prices will be influenced to be rose too much due to human demands (wants) are excessive to compare to our earth natural energy resources and meats and vegetables foods supply numbers. On the other side ,if every country's inflation will be increasing , but our salaries will be decreasing, or our salaries will be kept to stable and no changing, even employers will decide to dismiss employees to cause unemployment ratio rising. In result, global consumers' shopping ability will be falling down and crime numbers will be rising by poor, such as developing countries, e.g. Africa, China, India etc. will have many people feel hungry, or who feel diseases , even who will be sick to die from diseases or will be kill to die by crimes. Also , these other factors include foods scarcity, foods and natural energy prices rising, working and home environment pollution etc. factors , these factors can then cause global economic poor , serious inflation ,unbalance incomes reallocation between rich and poor people, discrimination and unfair threat will be caused between countries, even , the war between countries will be caused. Hence, our governments need to concern how to solve our earth natural energy resources and foods and vegetables scarcity challenge , due to which will be caused shortage to supply to human to consume to use or eat in the future on day occurrence. Thus, above reasons can be concluded that as below:

Nowadays, the numbers of human ( every country people) are increasing more than just the increasing numbers of consumers' consumption activities , such as our daily essential consumption include meats and vegetables etc. foods and natural energy resources, such as lands, water, gas, oil, wind, water, nuclear, electricity etc. energy . Moreover, natural resources and foods numbers are decreasing due to overpopulation are increasing in developing countries and the numbers of emigration are rising to developing countries, such as UK, USA, France, Germany poor people numbers are increasing due to war or poor issues occur in the developing countries. Moreover, due to the provision consumption activities are most directly address living standard ( or lifestyle) goals, which have to do with satisfying basic needs and getting pleasure through the use of natural resources energy provision service demand and vegetables and foods tasty demand by the developed countries' people needs . Also, these poor issues will occur in the developing countries possibly in the future. Due to these factors, I predict our essential consumption , such as foods, vegetables and natural energy resources service provision price will be increasing in global competitive market due to foods and vegetables and energy shortage will be caused by the overpopulation demands rising up and foods and natural energy resources supply numbers falling down factors. Hence, our governments must need to find methods to solve the problem of our essential natural resources shortage and foods scarcity issues occurrence in the future.

Suggestions to solve resources scarcity methods

- Estimation of growth of rural population and income and expected changes of natural resources supply numbers

I recommend developing countries need to estimate growth of rural population and incomes numbers and expected changes numbers in consumption patterns . Taking into account developing countries‘ known resource capacities and projected development of yields, input use and technologies and making assumptions about their future trading capacity, estimates are also make of future food production level, land use and natural resource numbers import trade demand of developing countries estimation before 2050 year.

Estimation of water natural resources, such as water scarcity agreement on key definitions, the conceptualization of water scarcity in ways that are meaningful for policy development and decision making, the quantification of water scarcity, policy and technical response options available to ensure food security in conditions of water scarcity, criteria and principles that should be used to establish priorities for action to response to water scarcity in agriculture and ensure effective and efficient water scarcity copying strategies. Thus, developing countries will concern to reduce water resources shortage risk. Why is predict water supply important?

During the twentieth century, large multi-purpose dams have served the needs of agriculture, energy and growing cities, and helped protect population from flood hazards. On farm water conservation, particularly the adoption of agricultural practices that reduce runoff to increase the infiltration and storage of water in the soil in rained agriculture is the most relevant local supply enhancement option that farmers have to increase foods production by increasing water availability and decentralized water harvesting conveniently in rural areas for farmers needs. For example, ground water exploitation has grown or in scale. Ground water's capability to provide flexible, on demand water in support of irrigation has been as a major advantage by farmers in rural areas. Thus, farmers need to learn how to reduce water losses increase water productivity and water re-allocation to avoid natural resource of water shortage after 2050 year.

● Renewable natural resources and foods planting sustainability development

The concept of sustainability has become the current answer to absolving our earth of its environment and economic crises in the 21 ST. century. On the one side, the pessimists, usually ecologists and other scientists, who are convinced the earth can't forever support the different countries' demand of renewable and non renewable resources. On the other side, are the optimists, the economists, who are equally convinced that the earth, with market incentives, appropriate public policies, material substitution, recycling and new technology can satisfy the needs and improve the quality of human welfare. Both views are supporting arguments are explored used and sustainable development. Thus, renewable old energy natural resource can keep old energy natural resource to renew to use or research other new energy resource to substitute old natural resource, it will reduce the risk of energy resource shortage if the other new natural resource can be substituted to the old natural energy resource to use in our daily life , such as inventing one kind of new energy resource can be used to substitute gas to drive cars or drive boats or plans or the old gas can be renewed or cycled to use to drive cars or boats or the oil can be renewed or cycled to use to cook. Also, our earth foods, e.g. fruits, vegetables or meats etc. foods if which can be recopied to grow many numbers planting foods from any one kind food or many kinds of foods, such as one meat can be copied to manufacture two to three same kind tasty meats or unlimited same kind tasty meats. I believe the renewable natural resource energy or recopied foods can reduce our foods or energy shortage after 2050 year.

The application of sustainable strategy
between local and national and regional
of international countries

A redefined concept is of the society as whole system, made up of three concentric circles: the economy is found within the society, and both the economy and society exist within the environment. Sustainability indicators are therefore said to attempt to measure the extent to which these boundaries are respected.

I think sustainability measure as a whole concept environment, society and economy. At the bottom of the triangle is the environment or the ultimate means which represents natural resources as a precondition for decent human life. The economy ( which includes technology, politics and ethics) is on the next, is not independent but serves as a vehicle for achieving ultimate ends. At the top is equity or society or ultimate end which refers to the wellbeing of the human being.

According to Daly(1990) who indicated "that the economy therefore succeeds to the extent that it conserves and restores ultimate means the environment, and enables the achievement of ultimate ends society equity. This is the application of sustainable strategies to local, national and regional issues, as well as the role of international agencies in local /national strategies." Our earth occurs issues of overpopulation, diseases and political conflict, developed countries also have to deal with problems, such as pollution and unlimited urban expansion with limited resources. Sustainability is the process suggested to improve the quality of human life within the limitations of global environment. It involves solutions for improving human welfare that doesn't result in regarding the environment. We( human) need to concern living within certain limits of the earth's capacity to maintain life, understanding the interconnections among economy, society and environment and maintaining a fair distribution of foods and vegetables and natural energy resources and opportunity for this generation and the next. Thus, on the one side, our governments need to concern three categories: Social/ political, environmental and economic issues are interconnection. Social issues include poverty, consultation, empowerment and culture. Environmental issues include pollution, natural resources and biodiversity/ resilience and economic issues include efficiency, growth and stability. It seems our governments need to considerate social and environment and economic issues to reduce our natural energy resources and foods and vegetables to allocate to let every country people to use fairly.

Reducing global warming and biodiversity
issue occurrence

It seems that we need to know our society will influence our natural environment good or bad. If our society damaged our natural environment, then it will be possible to influence our foods supply of decreasing numbers.

e.g. fishes, pigs, cows, sheep and vegetables and fruits etc. foods . Due to bad climate and air and lands and ocean pollution can influence foods can not be grown easily and successfully in farms or fishes can not be lived healthy in ocean. Then, it will cause our meats, fruits and vegetables etc. foods supply shortage. Even, our gas , oil, water etc., natural resources will cause our oceans and lands pollution if human pollute our oceans and lands. In result, our natural resources used numbers will be reduced due to clean lands and oceans are polluted for long time. Finally, natural resources and meats and vegetables and fruits , rice etc. foods prices will be risen due to which are shortage to supply and developing countries‘ population numbers are increasing which will cause more demand.

Finally, it shall cause many developing countries' poor people who can't eat enough meats, fruits, rice vegetables etc. foods as well as who can't use enough natural resources to attempt to adapt whose past normal daily life, such as lacking enough oil to help them to cook foods to be heat to eat at home or lacked enough water to be boiled to drink. Even, whose health will be poor , then who get diseases to cause die easily when there is no enough oil to buy or enough water to drink. Hence, these developing countries governments need to concern foods and natural resource scarcity problems which will be occurred if who do not find methods to reduce this issue to be occurred after 2050 year.

As Erekson et. al.(1999) concerns about" loss of resources, such as biodiversity or global weather (climate) warming are pacified with the potential of new technology which will lead to greater investments to the future generations for alternative resources and welfare."

Hence, I recommend our governments need to concern global warming or biodiversity issue because of our foods and vegetables and natural resources, such as water, air will be possible polluted to be caused shortage quickly if our earth's global warming or biodiversity issue occurrence to cause our earth's large oceans or lands areas to be polluted. Our governments can attempt to control natural resources , such as oil, gas, water supply into the market and not though the political special conditions to keep them, without considering the political and social standings, which rule the control power and the use of those resources. Such as developed countries can be able to minimize the impact of foods or/and natural resources production and consumption over the natural resources, they are only mechanisms built within an economic rationality, which should be possible to control its people's demand of natural resources, e.g. oil, gas, water and supply of natural resources get more balance. Then these natural resources sale price won't be raised more every year. When there developed countries' people , such as American and Britain who can control to reduce to spend to use the excessive natural resources too much in any time and any place habitually. Then , I believe the developing countries' governments e.g. Africa, China, India, which can buy those developed countries governments' excessive natural resources to raise those developed countries' natural resources supply numbers to provide to whose people to use as well as the most important benefit is that developed countries can gain foreign income from excessive natural resources expectation. Then, these governments will raise GDP economic growth. Hence, if developed countries could control whose people consume natural resource numbers and they could also control to produce natural resource supply numbers . Then, they can gain more excessive natural resources export chance to achieve to raise GDP economic growth aim for long term. As Kirkby et al., (1995)explained "the complexity of sustainable development our natural environment. If our governments can let our earth natural environment gets creation to maintenance, then our natural environment will be reduced the time to degradation. In the long time result, our society rural and urban economy will be growth , then our different countries' global growth will be caused diversity." Hence, it seems different countries' governments need to concern sustainable development to our natural environment .

## How to apply agricultural green bio-economy concept to solve control sustainable food consumption and production in a resource-constrained world

Nowadays, challenges for the global food supply have never been so complex. Between now and 2050 year, it has been predicted that growth in the global population and changing diets in developing countries, special in India and China and Africa etc. developing countries which may lead to an increase of around 70% in food demand. At the same time, depletion of fossil hydrocarbons will increase the demand for biomass for biofuels and industrial materials. Hence, developed and developing countries' governments ought need to coordinated to reduce air and water pollution and approached to lands use planning and oceans use planning to supply enough farms to grow potatoes, vegetables, tomatoes, fruits and let cows, pigs, sheep etc. animals can have comfortable and clean farm to live to produce good tasty meats to provide human to eat as well as to reduce pollution to supply fresh and clean water to let fishes to be lived and provides to human to drink clean water. Due to overpopulation will be predicted by scientists after 2050 year, so it will be caused foods and energy shortage possibly. Hence, different countries' governments need have long term perspectives to prepare to have enough foods and energy supply to provide us to eat and use for our earth with resource constraints and environmental limits, and which includes guideline on agricultural research to achieve foods supply aim.

On the one hand, I believe the knowledge-based bio-economy can play in realizing there challenges in particular the balance demand between foods, feed and fuel and the strategic role new technologies can have upon developing a sustainable an green bio-economy. On the other hand, I also think production of the presently high resource dependence and to build more environmentally begin sustainable agriculture system able to feed 9 billion people by 2050 year. I recommend global governments need to concern all aspects of food security including the total food chain and impacts of other land-use and management as well as non food areas, research areas which can be closed to free resources for new priorities, research to manufacture more new unique natural resources, due to gas, oil etc. resources will be used all in one day. On the energy shortage aspect, Substitution of these oil, gas etc. natural resources are needed . For example, nuclear energy is a kind of new natural resource, it can be used to push machines of rockets to be moved in space. In the future, I hope that nuclear energy can be used to drive cars or ships or trains etc. transportation tools in land. Hence, new natural resource research is essential and valid investment to be improved by scientists in the future.

On the global food supply interconnected challenges hand, including climate changes, energy and water supply are further encountered by the financial and economic changes in an increasingly globalized world. As a result, it is unclear how the growing demand for food and bioenergy ( both biomass and biofuels) within a wider bio-economy can be met without further compromising ecosystem services on which all economic activities and social depend. I shall emphasizes the interaction of the economic, social and ecological components of our food systems at various levels, with feed backs increasingly the uncertainty and risks relating to future developments.

We need to face the food requirements of a growing world population have to be satisfied and we also need to the face of increasing resource scarcities, such as water, energy and land and foods etc. with the situation further exacerbated by climate change. Thus, we need to focus on our reducing demand through food consumption behavioral changes and structural changes in food systems and food chains change. Due to some developed countries people often to choose to buy these foods to eat excessively e.g. cow meat and pig meat and drink excessive soft drinks, e.g. man-made color juice. So, these developed countries consumers will feel these excessive foods and soft drinks can be rubbish if these developed countries consumers often drink these man-made color juice and eat pig and cow meats often excessively. It seems who ought to change their diet behavior and food consumption to avoid to spend too much money to buy excessive foods and drinks and who often shall not decide to eat and drink them when who feel not hungry habitually . Hence, changing human diet habit is one important psychology factor to reduce water and foods shortage, due to the meats and juices can be reduced to be rubbish if human can learn how to control their diet habit to reduce to consume excessive meats and vegetables and rice and soft drinks etc. kind of foods and drinks. Then, I believe that food and water drinking numbers will be reduced too much in the future. Hence, different countries‘ governments need to educate whose people to know that why who will face foods and water scarcity possibly and to let who to know how the issue can be avoided to cause by the changing of their diet habit and consumption behavior. Teaching includes, such as let who to learn why resources scarcities are expected to reduce and defining food security concept, the need is for a better understanding of complexity of vegetable systems, the need to improve the diversity and response capacity of food systems to enhance resilience, the need to address both food consumption and production, knowledge generation and innovation through cross-sector approaches is essential and the need for agricultural knowledge and innovation systems that are fit for farming purpose. After developed countries' people are educated to let who to know why who need to reduce to consume excessive foods and soft drinks habitually to aim to avoid the chance of foods and water supply shortage will be occurred after 2050 year.

On the other side, in the case of biodiversity, the loss of functional biodiversity destabilizes ecosystems and weakens their ability to deal with natural disasters or human induced stresses, such as pollution and climate change. Hence, scientists need to research how to reduce new diseases to cause foods and water pollution, even new diseases cause to influence human health. Due to unpredictable new diseases will be caused foods, fruits, vegetables etc. can't be grow easily , even cows, pigs, sheep etc. animals are not health to cause diseases to be died easily. Then, those new diseases will be decreases our foods supply numbers seriously.

Resources scarcities are expected to define future food security. The predominant form of agriculture, food processing and retailing relies heavily on cheap inputs and the potential impact on this of long term resource scarcity trends has been largely overlooked. Scarcities are either biophysical limits, such as resource supply and availability or environment limits relating to pollution and its impacts on ecosystems and the global climate system. Hence, every country's government ought to educate to let whose citizen to discuss how to protect future food security topic to avoid resource scarcities occurrence after 2050 year. We need to know we are facing pollution (e.g. land, water, energy) and related to environmental limits e.g. climate change, ocean acidification and biodiversity loss. They represent a real threat, not only to future food supplies, but also to global stability and prosperity, through increasing poverty to developing countries and impacts on international trade, finance and investments.

Hence, pollution and environmental limits will have direct relationship to influence every countries' foods supply numbers , then it will influence every country's gross domestic product income if the consumption is reduced by foods inflation. For example, the combined effect of climate change and bio-diversity which makes the food production systems poorly due to a reduced resilience to shocks and changes over the long term , such as the limited availability of ore resources, soil degradation to loss of biodiversity. Both of these require a long term strategic approach to research and an openness to new research directions. These will need to help provide solutions towards more sustainable food consumption and production, some of which will need to break with current farmers or food manufacturers way of producing food methods. For example, research into ecological approaches: foods nutrient and water clean management and replacement of energy intensive inputs are priorities. Research to support energy efficient technologies for use in the food chain is also needed. Industry should assist in tackling the forthcoming challenges with new business models that can support the decoupling of resource use and changing consumption excessive foods behaviors and improving health foods production methods. For instance, changing the foods supply chains ) e.g. more local purchasing) may have huge impacts on costs and also on creating closer links and confidence between producers and consumers.

In conclusion, different countries need find methods to solve foods and energy scarcity problem before 2050 year. I recommend that who can attempt to solve earth warm climate, innovate agricultural production and supply system, change human diet habit and food consumption of behavior, co-operate the trade of foods and energy demand and supply between countries fairly and reasonably, reduce food and natural resource waste, renew and recopy new kind of foods, research new natural resource substitution etc. different methods. However, if every country government can attempt to find any one or more of these methods to solve food scarcity to avoid to occur before 2050 year. I believe that the food scarcity challenge won't be occur after 2050 year in the future.

Reference

Erekson, O.H., Loucks, O.L. Strafford, N.C. 1999. The context of sustainability . In: Sustainability perspectives for resources and business USA, p. 3-21.

Daly, H.E. 1990, Towards some operational principles of sustainable development, ecological economics, 2(1), 1-6.

Kirkby, J; O' Keefe P., Timberlake, L. (eds.) 1995. The earthscan reader in sustainable development. Earthscan Publications Ltd., London, 1-14p.

4.1 Suggestions to solve resources scarcity methods to oil supply

I. Estimation of growth of rural population and income and expected changes of natural resources supply numbers

I recommend developing countries need to estimate growth of rural population and incomes numbers and expected changes numbers in consumption patterns . Taking into account developing countries' known resource capacities and projected development of yields, input use and technologies and making assumptions about their future trading capacity, estimates are also make of future food production level, land use and natural resource numbers import trade demand of developing countries estimation before 2050 year.

Estimation of water natural resources, such as water scarcity agreement on key definitions, the conceptualization of water scarcity in ways that are meaningful for policy development and decision making, the quantification of water scarcity, policy and technical response options available to ensure food security in conditions of water scarcity, criteria and principles that should be used to establish priorities for action to response to water scarcity in agriculture and ensure effective and efficient water scarcity copying strategies. Thus, developing countries will concern to reduce water resources shortage risk. Why is predict water supply important? During the twentieth century, large multi-purpose dams have served the needs of agriculture, energy and growing cities, and helped protect population from flood hazards. On farm water conservation, particularly the adoption of agricultural practices that reduce runoff to increase the infiltration and storage of water in the soil in rained agriculture is the most relevant local supply enhancement option that farmers have to increase foods production by increasing water availability and decentralized water harvesting conveniently in rural areas for farmers needs. For example, ground water exploitation has grown or in scale. Ground water's capability to provide flexible, on demand water in support of irrigation has been as a major advantage by farmers in rural areas. Thus, farmers need to learn how to reduce water losses increase water productivity and water re-allocation to avoid natural resource of water shortage after 2050 year.

II. Renewable natural resources and foods planting sustainability development

The concept of sustainability has become the current answer to absolving our earth of its environment and economic crises in the 21 ST. century. On the one side,
the pessimists, usually ecologists and other scientists, who are convinced the earth can't forever support the different countries' demand of renewable and non renewable resources. On the other side, are the optimists, the economists, who are equally convinced that the earth, with market incentives, appropriate public policies, material substitution, recycling and new technology can satisfy the needs and improve the quality of human welfare. Both views are supporting arguments are explored used and sustainable development. Thus, renewable old energy natural resource can keep old energy natural resource to renew to use or research other

new energy resource to substitute old natural resource, it will reduce the risk of energy resource shortage if the other new natural resource can be substituted to the old natural energy resource to use in our daily life , such as inventing one kind of new energy resource can be used to substitute gas to drive cars or drive boats or plans or the old gas can be renewed or cycled to use to drive cars or boats or the oil can be renewed or cycled to use to cook. Also, our earth foods, e.g. fruits, vegetables or meats etc. foods if which can be recopied to grow many numbers planting foods from any one kind food or many kinds of foods, such as one meat can be copied to manufacture two to three same kind tasty meats or unlimited same kind tasty meats. I believe the renewable natural resource energy or recopied foods can reduce our foods or energy shortage after 2050 year.

## III. The application of sustainable strategy between local and national and regional of international countries

A redefined concept is of the society as whole system, made up of three concentric circles: the economy is found within the society, and both the economy and society exist within the environment. Sustainability indicators are therefore said to attempt to measure the extent to which these boundaries are respected.

I think sustainability measure as a whole concept environment, society and economy. At the bottom of the triangle is the environment or the ultimate means which represents natural resources as a precondition for decent human life. The economy ( which includes technology, politics and ethics) is on the next, is not independent but serves as a vehicle for achieving ultimate ends. At the top is equity or society or ultimate end which refers to the wellbeing of the human being. According to Daly(1990) who indicated "that the economy therefore succeeds to the extent that it conserves and restores ultimate means the environment, and enables the achievement of ultimate ends society equity. This is the application of sustainable strategies to local, national and regional issues, as well as the role of international agencies in local /national strategies." Our earth occurs issues of overpopulation, diseases and political conflict, developed countries also have to deal with problems, such as pollution and unlimited urban expansion with limited resources. Sustainability is the process suggested to improve the quality of human life within the limitations of global environment. It involves solutions for improving human welfare that doesn't result in regarding the environment. We( human) need to concern living within certain limits of the earth's capacity to maintain life, understanding the interconnections among economy, society and environment and maintaining a fair distribution of foods and vegetables and natural energy resources and opportunity for this generation and the next. Thus, on the one side, our governments need to concern three categories: Social/ political, environmental and economic issues are interconnection. Social issues include poverty, consultation, empowerment and culture. Environmental issues include pollution, natural resources and biodiversity/ resilience and economic issues include efficiency, growth and stability. It seems our governments need to considerate social and environment and economic issues to reduce our natural energy resources and foods and vegetables to allocate to let every country people to use fairly.

IV. Reducing global warming and biodiversity
issue occurrence

It seems that we need to know our society will influence our natural environment good or bad. If our society damaged our natural environment, then it will be possible to influence our foods supply of decreasing numbers. e.g. fishes, pigs, cows, sheep and vegetables and fruits etc. foods . Due to bad climate and air and lands and ocean pollution can influence foods can not be grown easily and successfully in farms or fishes can not be lived healthy in ocean. Then, it will cause our meats, fruits and vegetables etc. foods supply shortage. Even, our gas , oil, water etc., natural resources will cause our oceans and lands pollution if human pollute our oceans and lands. In result, our natural resources used numbers will be reduced due to clean lands and oceans are polluted for long time. Finally, natural resources and meats and vegetables and fruits , rice etc. foods prices will be risen due to which are shortage to supply and developing countries' population numbers are increasing which will cause more demand. Finally, it shall cause many developing countries' poor people who can't eat enough meats, fruits, rice vegetables etc. foods as well as who can't use enough natural resources to attempt to adapt whose past normal daily life, such as lacking enough oil to help them to cook foods to be heat to eat at home or lacked enough water to be boiled to drink. Even, whose health will be poor , then who get diseases to cause die easily when there is no enough oil to buy or enough water to drink. Hence, these developing countries governments need to concern foods and natural resource scarcity problems which will be occurred if who do not find methods to reduce this issue to be occurred after 2050 year.

As Erekson et. al.(1999) concerns about" loss of resources, such as biodiversity or global weather (climate) warming are pacified with the potential of new technology which will lead to greater investments to the future generations for alternative resources and welfare." Hence, I recommend our governments need to concern global warming or biodiversity issue because of our foods and vegetables and natural resources, such as water, air will be possible polluted to be caused shortage quickly if our earth's global warming or biodiversity issue occurrence to cause our earth's large oceans or lands areas to be polluted. Our governments can attempt to control natural resources , such as oil, gas, water supply into the market and not though the political special conditions to keep them, without considering the political and social standings, which rule the control power and the use of those resources. Such as developed countries can be able to minimize the impact of foods or/and natural resources production and consumption over the natural resources, they are only mechanisms built within an economic rationality, which should be possible to control its people's demand of natural resources, e.g. oil, gas, water and supply of natural resources get more balance. Then these natural resources sale price won't be raised more every year. When there developed countries' people , such as American and Britain who can control to reduce to spend to use the excessive natural resources too much in any time and any place habitually. Then , I believe the developing countries' governments e.g. Africa, China, India, which can buy those developed countries governments' excessive natural resources to raise those developed countries' natural resources supply numbers to provide to whose people to use as well as the most important benefit is that developed countries can gain foreign income from excessive natural resources expectation. Then, these governments will raise GDP economic growth. Hence, if developed countries could control whose people consume natural resource numbers and they could also control to produce natural resource supply numbers . Then, they can gain more excessive natural resources export chance to achieve to raise GDP economic growth aim for long term. As Kirkby et al., (1995)explained "the complexity of sustainable development our natural environment. If our governments can let our earth natural environment gets creation to maintenance, then our natural environment will be reduced the time to degradation. In the long time result, our society rural and urban economy will be growth , then our different countries' global growth will be caused diversity." Hence, it seems different countries' governments need to concern sustainable development to our natural environment .

V. How to apply agricultural green bio-economy concept to solve control sustainable food consumption and production in a resource-constrained world

Nowadays, challenges for the global food supply have never been so complex. Between now and 2050 year, it has been predicted that growth in the global population and changing diets in developing countries, special in India and China and Africa etc. developing countries which may lead to an increase of around 70% in food demand. At the same time, depletion of fossil hydrocarbons will increase the demand for biomass for biofuels and industrial materials. Hence, developed and developing countries' governments ought need to coordinated to reduce air and water pollution and approached to lands use planning and oceans use planning to supply enough farms to grow potatoes, vegetables, tomatoes, fruits and let cows, pigs, sheep etc. animals can have comfortable and clean farm to live to produce good tasty meats to provide human to eat as well as to reduce pollution to supply fresh and clean water to let fishes to be lived and provides to human to drink clean water. Due to overpopulation will be predicted by scientists after 2050 year, so it will be caused foods and energy shortage possibly. Hence, different countries' governments need have long term perspectives to prepare to have enough foods and energy supply to provide us to eat and use for our earth with resource constraints and environmental limits, and which includes guideline on agricultural research to achieve foods supply aim.

On the one hand, I believe the knowledge-based bio-economy can play in realizing there challenges in particular the balance demand between foods, feed and fuel and the strategic role new technologies can have upon developing a sustainable an green bio-economy. On the other hand, I also think production of the presently high resource dependence and to build more environmentally begin sustainable agriculture system able to feed 9 billion people by 2050 year. I recommend global governments need to concern all aspects of food security including the total food chain and impacts of other land-use and management as well as non food areas, research areas which can be closed to free resources for new priorities, research to manufacture more new unique natural resources, due to gas, oil etc. resources will be used all in one day. On the energy shortage aspect,

Substitution of these oil, gas etc. natural resources are needed . For example, nuclear energy is a kind of new natural resource, it can be used to push machines of rockets to be moved in space. In the future, I hope that nuclear energy can be used to drive cars or ships or trains etc. transportation tools in land. Hence, new natural resource research is essential and valid investment to be improved by scientists in the future.

On the global food supply interconnected challenges hand, including climate changes, energy and water supply are further encountered by the financial and economic changes in an increasingly globalized world. As a result, it is unclear how the growing demand for food and bioenergy ( both biomass and biofuels) within a wider bio-economy can be met without further compromising ecosystem services on which all economic activities and social depend. I shall emphasizes the interaction of the economic, social and ecological components of our food systems at various levels, with feed backs increasingly the uncertainty and risks relating to future developments.

We need to face the food requirements of a growing world population have to be satisfied and we also need to the face of increasing resource scarcities, such as water, energy and land and foods etc. with the situation further exacerbated by climate change. Thus, we need to focus on our reducing demand through food consumption behavioral changes and structural changes in food systems and food chains change. Due to some developed countries people often to choose to buy these foods to eat excessively e.g. cow meat and pig meat and drink excessive soft drinks, e.g. man-made color juice. So, these developed countries consumers will feel these excessive foods and soft drinks can be rubbish if these developed countries consumers often drink these man-made color juice and eat pig and cow meats often excessively. It seems who ought to change their diet behavior and food consumption to avoid to spend too much money to buy excessive foods and drinks and who often shall not decide to eat and drink them when who feel not hungry habitually . Hence, changing human diet habit is one important psychology factor to reduce water and foods shortage, due to the meats and juices can be reduced to be rubbish if human can learn how to control their diet habit to reduce to consume excessive meats and vegetables and rice and soft drinks etc. kind of foods and drinks. Then, I believe that food and water drinking numbers will be reduced too much in the future. Hence, different countries‘ governments need to educate whose people to know that why who will face foods and water scarcity possibly and to let who to know how the issue can be avoided to cause by the changing of their diet habit and consumption behavior. Teaching includes, such as let who to learn why resources scarcities are expected to reduce and defining food security concept, the need is for a better understanding of complexity of vegetable systems, the need to improve the diversity and response capacity of food systems to enhance resilience, the need to address both food consumption and production, knowledge generation and innovation through cross-sector approaches is essential and the need for agricultural knowledge and innovation systems that are fit for farming purpose. After developed countries' people are educated to let who to know why who need to reduce to consume excessive foods and soft drinks habitually to aim to avoid the chance of foods and water supply shortage will be occurred after 2050 year. On the other side, in the case of biodiversity, the loss of functional biodiversity destabilizes ecosystems and weakens their ability to deal with natural disasters or human induced stresses, such as pollution and climate change. Hence, scientists need to research how to reduce new diseases to cause foods and water pollution, even new diseases cause to influence human health. Due to unpredictable new diseases will be caused foods, fruits, vegetables etc. can't be grow easily , even cows, pigs, sheep etc. animals are not health to cause diseases to be died easily. Then, those new diseases will be decreases our foods supply numbers seriously.

Resources scarcities are expected to define future food security. The predominant form of agriculture, food processing and retailing relies heavily on cheap inputs and the potential impact on this of long term resource scarcity trends has been largely overlooked. Scarcities are either biophysical limits, such as resource supply and availability or environment limits relating to pollution and its impacts on ecosystems and the global climate system. Hence, every country's government ought to educate to let whose citizen to discuss how to protect future food security topic to avoid resource scarcities occurrence after 2050 year. We need to know we are facing pollution (e.g. land, water, energy) and related to environmental limits e.g. climate change, ocean acidification and biodiversity loss. They represent a real threat, not only to future food supplies, but also to global stability and prosperity, through increasing poverty to developing countries and impacts on international trade, finance and investments. Hence, pollution and environmental limits will have direct relationship to influence every countries' foods supply numbers , then it will influence every country's gross domestic product income if the consumption is reduced by foods inflation.

For example, the combined effect of climate change and bio-diversity which makes the food production systems poorly due to a reduced resilience to shocks and changes over the long term , such as the limited availability of ore resources, soil degradation to loss of biodiversity. Both of these require a long term strategic approach to research and an openness to new research directions. These will need to help provide solutions towards more sustainable food consumption and production, some of which will need to break with current farmers or food manufacturers way of producing food methods. For example, research into ecological approaches: foods nutrient and water clean management and replacement of energy intensive inputs are priorities. Research to support energy efficient technologies for use in the food chain is also needed. Industry should assist in tackling the forthcoming challenges with new business models that can support the decoupling of resource use and changing consumption excessive foods behaviors and improving health foods production methods. For instance, changing the foods supply chains ) e.g. more local purchasing) may have huge impacts on costs and also on creating closer links and confidence between producers and consumers.

In conclusion, different countries need find methods to solve foods and energy scarcity problem before 2050 year. I recommend that who can attempt to solve earth warm climate, innovate agricultural production and supply system, change human diet habit and food consumption of behavior, co-operate the trade of foods and energy demand and supply between countries fairly and reasonably, reduce food and natural resource waste, renew and recopy new kind of foods, research new natural resource substitution etc. different methods. However, if every country government can attempt to find any one or more of these methods to solve food scarcity to avoid to occur before 2050 year. I believe that the food scarcity challenge won't be occur after 2050 year in the future.

Environment Economy-Pollution and illness influences oil consumer behavior

How the economic consequences of outdoor air pollution influences consumer behaviors ? Air pollution can increase number of respiratory and cardiovas cular diseases. How they can impact economic growth, e.g. on human health, mortality and morbidity and agriculture aspects ? Whether when this diseases are caused from outdoor air pollution, why it can influence consumer behavior or brings negative consumpton emotion?

The macroeconomic costs of these impacts of outdoor air pollution that are linked to economic activity, and it raises welfare costs related to activity morality and pain and suffering from illness to consumers. For example, market costs are those that are associated with biophysical impacts that directly affect economic activity, e.g. lower crop yields affect agricultural production . Non market costs may also include the monetised welfare costs of morality ( premature deaths) , and of the disutility of illness ( pain and suffering).

Raising emissions reflect the assumptions on economic growth with increasing GDP and energy demand, especially in fast growing economies, such as the high population countries, India and China. These large changes are due to the increase in the demand for agricultural products and energy ( include transport and power generation). For continuousing increase in energy demand to China and India car drivers, when they need to drive their cars to go to anywhere often. The higher emission will bring serious pollution. The environment protecting householders will decrease to use emissions from energy demand for, with reflects technology improvement in energy efficiency, the use of cleaner fuels, and biomass in open fire to cleaner energy sources including LPG, ethanol or enhanced cooking stoves. Hence, when many people get the diseases from air pollution. It will increase the medical ( healthcare) cost to governments or when government needs to give welfare assistance to patients.

The three different market impacts of air pollution may include: reduced labor productivity, increased health expenditures and crop yield losses. They may reduce the GDP pollution feedback on the economy. At the global level, the consequences of labor productivity and health expenditure may impact to market cost increases,because increases expenditure to labor productivity, health expenditure and value added generated in agriculture from low productivity changes in crop yields.

What is the welfare costs of mortality and illness ? It is possible to attribute a cost to non-market impacts, such as the premature deaths and the costs of pain and suffering from illness . The welfares cost of the premature deaths caused by air pollution are calculated using the value of a statistical life to any one. Large costs can also associated with the pain and suffering from illness. So, pollution causes diseases to bring welfare cost increases, they include hospital living day to every patient when he is caused illnesses from air pollution. Moreover, it will impact government pollution expenditure to raise welfare cost to assist the low income level pollution illness patients' hospital living welfacre cost when they need to live long days in hospitals.

How does air pollutin impact on consumer automobile choices ? Air pollution levels can bring negatively affect the sales of fuel inefficient cars to China or India car drivers. They will choose to buy electronic cars to drive to replace fuel cars, because electronic cars only need to charge battery and it can reduce air pollution. When China or India their big city people's income level is rising, they will have more money to buy electronic cars to drive to reduce air pollution. Moreover, they believe that electronic cars can have better car quality and reduced air pollution need to charge battery fuel efficiency to compare fuel cars, when they need to often drive cars on roads. Som electronic cars demand will be the preference choice battery fuel efficiency or green driving tools to compare general fuel cars to satisfy China and India car purchasers when they are living in serious air pollution environment cities.

When the high environment protection awareness car buyers number is increasing in the countries, environment protection awareness will influence their car choice decison on which car to buy , when they are living in more heavily polluted cities tend to buy less fuel-inefficient cars. So, the electronic cars number need will increase in China and India both car market, because these two countries have similar characteristics, they have high population and gardens and farms number is less and there are many people are living in cities and many people are high income level , they usually have one car at least. So, they must feel cities are serious polluted by their diving behaviors. So, their environment protection awareness are ususally higher to compare other countries , they have less cities. So high air pollution to cities can excite the environment protection awareness to China and India car purchasers as well as they will prefer to choose to buy electronic cars to replace fuel cars to drive in possible, because they do not hope to live a high car dirty cities to cause their poor health when they have high income level. Also, it implies that it has direct relationship between China and India cities have high income level people number increases and air pollution level increases and electronic car demand number increases and fuel car demand number decreases in China and India car market in micro economic China and India electronic car and fuel car demand and supply market.

I assume that each China and India car consumer makes a relatively fuel or electronic car choice among possible car transmissions, between the option of buying no car and buy car or between the option of buying electronic car and fuel car. However, air pollution will be one major factor to influence China and India car purchase demand number on electronic and fuel car supply number. If china and India's air pollution can reduce, then car purchase number will increase, as well as the fuel car demand number will also increase ,because China and India have many cities are polluted serious. It can influence car purchase buyers how to decide car choice to make car or no car purchase decision, even purchase either fuel car or electronic car decison.

- How consumer decisions are impacted on environment?

Environmental impacts may occur on households, when they need to buy food, mobility, house, household goods and appliances for home use in household consumer behavior view. It can bring direct impacts, that occue because of the use of householder products and services during householders are staying at home. When householders feel need to raise living quality, they will considerate how they use services and related household products. When minimizing the use of natural resources and toxic materials as well as the emissions of waste and pollutants over the life cycle of the service or household product, e.g. using electricity or fuel time at home, cooling time and bathing time at home activities. So, for on householder who has high environment protection awareness and energy protection awareness, he will reduce long time to use electricity or fuel use time for cooking, bathing, watching television, listening radio time activities at homes, because he does not hope energy waste and protect air fresh at homes.

So, consumption is concerned by environment factors, such as demographics, technology, income and prices, psychological, social , cultural environments, e.g. consumers economic behavior is influenced by habt, routines, conventions etc. different environment factors influence. So, economic assumptions of rational and regular behavior is based on long-established principles, such as utility maximization. For example, when one country is encountering serious air or water pollution, then consumers will spend long time to search any data ( marketing research activities) when they need to make purchase decision on pollution environment as well as pollution environment is dependent on ( e.g. attitude, intention to the consumers ).

Because when pollution environment will influence consumption behavior, such as behavioral and experimental economic to consumers. It implies on pollution environment's psychological assumptions on individual consumption motives, such as on the role of mental habits, loss confidence. So, consumers usually feel to spend long time to make purchase choice or decison on pollution environment, exaggerated optimism, expectatons, avoiding miscalculation,short-sightedness more enjoyment etc. psychological factors. When they need to make purchase decision on pollution environment, e.g. when one car consumer will need to make choice to buy one car, when he is living in China city, city is polluted serious. So, he will need to spend long time to gather any car model and brand and quality and fuel quality air polluted level to achieve to choose to buy the most clean fuel and the most least air polluton car to avoid to cause air polluton when he is driving the car in the China's city. So, air pollution way causes the China environment protection awareness car consumers to spend long time to gather any less use fuel car information to avoid to cause air pollution when he needs often to drive the car on the city roads in the China cities.

Hence , air pollution may cause the China car purchasers feel need to spend more time to gather car information in order to decide whether he ought to buy one car or no car purchase choice on the air pollution environment. So, the car must use less fuel to avoid air pollution easily when he drives the car on the China's cities' roads.

Reference

Erekson, O.H., Loucks, O.L. Strafford, N.C. 1999. The context of sustainability . In: Sustainability perspectives for resources and business USA, p. 3-21.

Daly, H.E. 1990, Towards some operational principles of sustainable development, ecological economics, 2(1), 1-6.

Kirkby, J; O' Keefe P., Timberlake, L. (eds.) 1995. The earthscan reader in sustainable development. Earthscan Publications Ltd., London, 1-14p.

How can positive or negativesocial environment influence airlines oil need

Nowaday, airline industry is entering global competition. So, any some less positive or negative social environment changing which will influence any airlines‘ passenger behavioral consumption change. For example, air ticket price rises or fuel price rises or the country’s season is bad or the global economy is bad or the country has terrible death threat etc. different negative social environment change fastors which will influence any country passenger individual travel consumption desires.
In Special, business class airline transportation demands are also increasing, due to many business travelers need to catch planes to go to any different countries to do business as well as many cargoes need to be carried from planes to transport to different countries to sell. So, business class traveler target group behavioral consumption is difficult to influence travelling consumotion desires from external environmental factors because business class traveler target group concerns to need to catch planes to go to another country to discuss business co-operation with the country’s businessmen. So, their business travel desires won’t easy to be influenced more than individual entertainment travel consumer’s desire.

It seems cargo and business aim of aviation transportation industry has less chance to be influenced to reduce businessmen traveler or cargo transportation numbers to compare to entertainment traveler numbers by external environment change influences, due to the business travelers and cargo transportation travelling desires is difficult to reduce travelling or transportation needs to reduce the " doing businesses to earn profit chance with another country’s businessmen". However, ignorance of internal or external market dynamics, catching entertainment travelers business can be detrimental to airline profitability more than carrying cargoes or business travelers business. Because the demands of travelling different countries’ travelers‘ consumption are still more than the demands of businessmen carrying cargoes in any countries every year. So, the global GDP of travelling income sector is still have the important position to any country nowadays.

How can positive or negative social environment change influence any airlines’ air ticket prices to be risen or fallen as well as how can these social environment change influence passenger consumption desires ? For example: What is the petroleum price change influence ?In fact, the increase in petroleum price can have chance to affect every airlines passenger has a negative manner to reduce travel consumption because increased oil prices have resulted in the reduction of airline services operations, the number of airline schedules flights, even airline bankruptcies. Whether global economic inflation or deflation, terrorism threats to the country, oil shortage or oil price rising or fallening, bank interest rate increasing or decreasing etc. external factors which have the most influential causes to bring the bad or good effects to cause airline industry share price reducing or increasing or increasing or reducing air ticket price. In result, these external environmental changes will influence the global traveler numbers to be increased or decreased at the time.

To support this hypotheses, this are my research first question, such as : Does a combination of terrorism and price of petroleum significantly influence airline profit changing mostly? The alternative hypothesis was my research second question, such as: Whether a significant relationship exists between terrorism, price of petroleum and airline profitability more than other factors, such as inflation, bank interest rate or air ticket price changing of these factors to influence passenger consumption desires change. I shall indicate that the first assumption was that terrorism has a negative effect on airline profitability and another assumption was that only external factors as oil prices or terrorism affect airline profitability. Finally, the terrorism and oil shortage and oil rising price factors can influence every passenger travel consumption desire to be reduced mainly.

Terrorism attack influences traveller need

However the effects of oil price and terrorism on airline profitability was limited to a regional perspective, so oil price and terrorism external environmental change will only influence some countries‘ airline traveler numbers to be decreased, e.g. the terrorism attack of plane crash event to USA on 11 Sept. After the terrorism attack happened on USA 11 Sept. incident of terrorism attack was restricted to events of skyjacking, attacks on oil production, refinery and distribution. Then, due oil shortage will be caused due to reducing oil production, refinery and distribution as well as it will influence oil price is risen and airline ticket price is also risen. It will reduce travel consumption desire to some countries if their airlines' ticket prices are also increasing. Other types of terrorist activities, such as attacks on financial targets or senior government officials could have an adverse effect on the petroleum and airline industry. I think the disruption of the production or distribution of petroleum because of incidents of terrorism was costly in terms of loss of business and the inflationary effect on fuel dependent products or services.

In fact, some airlines have adopted more fuel saving technology, so whose fuel consumption would not use more than other non fuel saving technology airlines. It seems fuel price increasing will not be the only factor to influence the airline industry's traveler numbers decreasing due, the owning more fuel saving technologic airlines which air tickets prices won't influence to be risen , due to reducing oil production and shortage influences . However, due to some airlines which have fuel saving technology, so which can avoid to use more fuel to provide planes to use and which fuel costs will be reduced, then which can provide cheaper air ticket fare prices to compare the non fuel saving technology airlines. The result will cause some not owning fuel saving technological airlines which will lose travelling customers in this global airline travelling market, also the not fuel saving technological airlines need to renew their fuel technology if which want to keep their competitive abilities to avoid to close down their businesses. So, what factors will influence the not owning fuel saving technological airlines profitability to be reduce if the oil shortage factor can not influence their planes energy supply to be reduced to cause air ticket prices to be increased? To answer this question, I shall indicate another financial risk factor how it influences airline industry behavioral change.

Also, I shall indicate the financial risk of airline industry evidence from Cathay Pacific airways and China airlines against key determinants of which include interest rate, exchange rate and fuel price risk for the period of January 1996 year to December 2011 year. During this period, these key external factors which were the most serious influence to cause these two airlines choose to change their strategic behaviors. Due to any these financial risks is difficult to predict and it was also changing often, these factors will also affect any airlines stock returns which arise from changing economic conditions, e.g. fuel price movements and fluctuations in exchange rates. These external unpredicted changing factors will attribute to the air tickets cyclical demand, capital investment, fixed costs of labor and landing rights to this global airline industry. Finally, it will cause some airlines need to rise air ticket prices to reduce expenditures increasing.

However, the relationship between fuel price and stock prices varies across economies which will influence travel passenger consumption of desires. For example, the effects of oil price changes in sub-sector indices, such as wood, paper and printing, insurance and electricity. In the past, on global stock exchange market was positively significant in 2011 year. Otherwise, with respect to the U.S.A. aviation industry, some economists suggested that global airlines stock returns were negatively to percentage change in fuel prices related to any airline firm value, e.g. Qantas and Air New Zealand were negatively share price growth to fuel price risk in the short term in the 2011 year. Thus, due to these two airlines share price went down, it will influence investors who loss confidence to buy their shares as well as it will influence travelling passengers who choose to buy other airlines' air tickets to go to travel because they will feel these two airlines have business challenges, e.g. bad service quality and food quality and uncomfortable airline seat environment and poor management style. etc different bad feeling. So, these two airlines' share prices went down, it will influence every travel passenger's confidence to choose to buy their air tickets to sit their planes to go to travel.

Airlines fuel manufacturing supply strategy

However, there are some airlines which are the characteristic of self organization . It means that they are present in that both of oil fuel production and providing flights service in airline industry. So, these self organization airlines can control the oil fuel price by themselves. However, any self supply airline organization is also evident in efforts by businesses acts of terrorism against economic targets by adopting proactive steps, such as airline and airport security. So, it seems any self suply airline organization can reduce the risk to avoid oil price raising and terrorism attacks in airline industry risk management sector because oil shortage won't influence their air ticket prices need to be raised. Beside, these self supply airline organizations which have high technology of fuel efficient aircrafts, the use of one aircraft model, the adoption of direct routes versus customer loyalty programs and other operational cost reductions are strategies for increased profitability.

To solve oil price, terrorism etc. external risk to airline industry. Instead of high technology of fuel efficient aircrafts and self supply airline organization methods can solve terrorism attacks and oil price rising risks. However, I believe that there are other risks will threaten to airline industry. This risks concern traveller individual psychological factors influence, so it means that any airlines can apply psychological methods to predict which airline passengers' travel consumption desires. The risks include such as (1) user factor, such as : the travel country culture and tradition difference will influence the traveler chooses to prefer to go to the country to travel , the traveler's education level is high , who will choose to go to developed countries to travel, e.g. USA, UK. Otherwise, if the traveler's education level is low, who will choose to go to developing countries to travel, e.g. China, India etc. (2) economic factor, such as air tickets and airline fuel costs, (3) human resources and macro economic factor, such as political stability, economic development, educational policy, health policy, environmental policy. However, these risks occurrences are resulting in the relationship of cause and effect events. These events are not directly observable.

Such as, the complexity of relationship between terrorism and airline profitability. Hence, if global airline industry can predict when those risks occur to do protective strategic behavior. It is possible that which can understand why these risk events will occur and their protective strategic behaviors also influence their outcomes to be positive to avoid any external risk threats on the long term. However, I think hierarchy, self supply airline organization efficiency methods which are as possible predictors of user preferences to avoid risk threat events to cause whose airline businesses failure occurrences in airline industry because it can reduce oil shortage factor which causes their air ticket prices need to be rised to keep their planes can have enough fuel supply.

●

● How the price of oil changes influences global tourism industry growth or recession?

In macro-economic view, sudden mid and long term oil price shock can influence global torusim industry growth or recession. For example, a oil price of US$180 per barrel was considered only a few years ago, now this has a realistic scenario to which all plaers in the T&T sector have to adapt. At such a high level, the price of oil will become even more critical to almost every part of the tourism value chain. Although, weak global demand, caused by global economic recesson, resulted in a steep oil price decline to US$45 per barrel by the fourth quarter of 2008 in the past low oil price occurrence history, this won't change the mid to long -term oil forecast.

In fact, the past oil price occurrence history of the dramatic structural had changed a high price imposed on airlines, travelers, and destination countries, all of which will have to navigate through times of shifting or even declining travel demand. I assume that a high oil price scenario is assumed in the long term in order to highlight the changes , such a senario would mean for consumer behavior and the competitiveness of several destinations.

Low oil price in the 1970 and early 1980 did not bring significant growth of international air travel, but its growth has been strongest between 1980 and 2004, a period with stable and relatively moderate oil prices. Also, the rapid development of the low-cost carrier business model in the 1990s further fueled air travel growth by capturing tourism leisure demand , such as weekend leisure travel to cities using mostly secondary airports in any big area countries, such as UK, US . However, the tourism growth is whole influenced by high oil prices, due to oil price had been continue rising in possible.

Basis of oil is shortage supply product, oil is assumed to be the main energy source for the aviation sector for the nest 30 years. Although, second-generation biofuels seem to be on the horizon, the economics as well as the production scalability and aviation biofuel shortage will be a main challenge to airline industry. So, I assume that oil price will continue rise up, if there have none any aviation biofuel can be reflected to oil to use for air plane energy.

Until 2004, the only factors to have affected air travel growth, negatively were in external shocks , such as 9/11, causes catching air plane crisis or US regional geopolitical conflicts. It brings some travelers feel fear to go to US travel, as well as until recently 2019, human mouth disease can influence air to have disease to anyone from mouth. So, global travelers number had been continue decreasing, because they are fear to get disease by air when many themselves every stranger travelers are sitting on the without windows air planes. Although, mouth human and air disease and US 9/11 air attack both matters may influence oil price falls effect, because air planes flying times will reduce. They won't need frequent to fly, to cause aviation oil energy need reduce. Consequently, oil price will decrease, due to travelers number reduces and air planes flying times are also influenced to reduce. ( oil demand decreases cause oil price decrease). Although, air lines ' cost will also be influenced reduce, but oil price decrease can not bring travelers number increase , when air ticket price reduce because global many leisure and business trip travelers feel fear to catch air planes frequently when human mouth air disease occured in 2019. So, oil price decreases can not grow up tourism industry growth or rise tourism income.

However, the obvious impact of a high oil price is an increase in the operating costs of airline. Moreover, fuel cost as a percentage of airline operating costs vary significantly based on the length of the flight. The longer the flight, the higher the fuel costs as a percentage of the airline operating cost. So, from an online's perspective, long -hauel flights represent the most criticial challenge to profitable operation because the share of fuel on these flights, compared with other cost items, is largest, because of the unfacorable fuel economics, due to fuel costs even at high-load factors. For example, Thai airways dropped its non-stop Bongkok to US flights in the summer of 2008 for commercial reasons, because fuel reached operating cost levels of 55 percent on this route, a cost burden that could not be passed on to their customers. So, the estimated price elacticity of passengers demand at this Bongkok to US flights route is high, if Thai Airways rises less air ticket price, it will influence many travelers to choose other airlines to catch air plan to fly. Hence, due to Thai Airways can not make decision to rise air ticket price, because it believes that it will lose many travelers, so it only chooses to drop this non-stop Bongkok to US flights to avoid fuel cost rising economic loss.

However, although micro and macro economic theories may also that oil price variable or change, it may influence global tourism income. But, recently, on 2019, human mouth and air diseases, it can influence global individual leisure and business trip travelers feel fear to catch air plans to avoid their bodies get this kind of death sickness when they sit in the no fresh air supplying air planes. They feel that they reduce leisure travelling flying times or business trip flying times with strange travelers to sit in crowd air planes together. Then, they must many avoid human moth and air disease to avoid death crisis. Hence, in this global human mouth and air diseases threat environment occurrence, even oil price sudden reduces to low price, it brings airline's cost reduces and air ticke price reduces. However, when air ticket price reduce to be very cheaper, it can not still attract global many leisure or business trip travelers to buy air tickets to fly frequently. Why does air ticket reduction, it can not attract many leisure or businee trip travelers to buy air ticket to fly ? The main reason is because human mouth and air disease influences global many travelers feel fear to catch air planes frequently. In psychological view, this kind of human mouth and air sickness will bring long time negative influence to global traveles do not want to catch air planes for business trips or travelling leisure frequently. So, it implies that oil price changing to influence air ticket price reduction factor ought not main factor to influence tourism income. It may include traveler individual negative emotion psychological factor, such as human mouth and air disease or 2019 9/11 attack both cases, they can influence global travelers feel fear to catch air planes to fly to avoid death threat. So, oil changing price ought not be only one absolute main factor to influence global tourism income significantly.

On conclusion, in economic view, it seems that oil chang price may have indirect or direct relationship to influence tourism income, instead of some unpredicted external environment factors influence, such as US 9/11 attack crisis and human mouth and air disease factors, they may be main factors to influence travellers number to reduce in non-economic external unpredicted environment view.

COVID 19 human disease how influences global airline fuel manufacturers to rapid reach decline life cycle stage

Recently, since 2019 end, COVID 19 human disease confirms that any one can be gotten this kind disease by the COVID 19 patient individual mouth or air, hand, even things contact. This kind disease may hurt the heath person individual lung to let him/her to feel difficult to breathe, even death. So, this kind disease had influenced many people feel fear to catch airplanes, because when many passengers are sitting in the airplane, if one or more is/are COV19 human disease patient, then the patient has possible to bring this disease to let the health passengers to get his/her COVID 19 human disease in the none window airplanes environment easily. SO, when this kind of human disease is threatening global travellers to avoid to catch air airplanes to fly to travel frequently. Then, airplanes won't need to fly often. When airplanes do not need often fly in sky. Then gas fuel demand will be influenced to reduce to airlines because airplanes won't need often catch many travellers to go to different countries, due to travellers number reduces as well as many different countries' travellers had begun to reduce travelling times frequently and their airports restrict any high body temperature people to enter their countries, because they will have possible to bring COVID 19 human disease when they arrive any airports. Consequently, airplanes do not need to buy and use any more gas fuel to provide them to fly any more since COVID 19 human disease occurs.

How COVID 19 human disease influences global gas fuel sale number? Because travellers number had been decreasing, airlines do not any airplanes often catch many passengers to fly to any countries again. Surely, gas fuel demand to airplanes may be also influenced to reduce and it can also influence whole tourism leisure industry development will experience to the decline cycle life stage absolutely. Before , due to global has many travellers feel need to travel leisure activity. So, global travellers increasing number impacted to global needs to have many airplanes to be provide to fly every day frequently. Before average per day had above 10,000 times of airplane flying times in our earth every day, so it implied that gas fuel need must be influenced to increase to airlines, because airlines must need to buy a lot gas fuel to provide their airplanes to fly to different countries every day , when any countries have many travellers need to fly to different countries to travel. It is sure that airline gas fuel product must reach the maturity life cycle stage in this airplane gas fuel manufacturing industry, because travelling leisure activities are accepted to be on kind of popular habit leisure to global travellers, when air ticket price had been decreasing, it can also attract many travellers accept to spend money to buy air tickets to go to different countries to travel frequently.

So, cheap air ticket price and popular tourism leisure activity factors may influence global travellers number increases. When global travellers number increases, it impacts to global airplanes need to increase flying times to fly frequently and air tickets also increases purchase number. Consequently, airlines also are influenced to need to buy a lot gas fuel to provide to airplanes to fly. SO, due to gas fuel demand increases, but gas fuel supply number is not enough, then gas price can be influenced to raise, when airlines demand gas fuel number is more than gas fuel supply number. It is based on economic theory, when demand to the product increases in the market, but the product has shortage to supply, then price may be influenced to bring sale price increasing chance. So, in this airline gas fuel demand and supply case, due to airplanes need to fly frequently, so global flying numbers had been influenced to rise and global airplanes need to buy many airplanes to catch passengers or travellers to fly to different countries. So, airlines must need to buy a lot gas fuel to provide airplanes to fly to different countries every day in this airline industry mature life stage. Thus, before 1029, it is gas fuel manufacturing industry and airlines travelling transport industry and tourism industry their maturity cycle stage period. Every day, global gas manufacturers need to attempt to find any lands have gas and explore any gas lands, than using technology to manufacture gas fuel in order to supply and satisfy any airlines' gas fuel needs every day. But, since COVID 19 human disease occurred in 2019 end, it influenced many airlines lose confidence the travellers number will increase, due to travellers number had been beginning to reduce every day and airplanes' flying times are also influenced to reduce , these both factors must influence gas fuel need reduces to any airlines their airplanes needs.

Hence, after 2019 end, it may be global tourism leisure industry decline life cycle stage, moreover, it may also be global airline transport flying service industry decline life stage both. So, global gas fuel need on airline sector must be influenced to reduce, when global airplanes did not often fly and global airplanes flying times had been influencing to reduce to per day 500 flying times, even less from the top level per day 10,000 flying times. SO, it can prove that they have relationship between tourism leisure industry and airlines' airplanes transport flying service industry and airline gas fuel product manufacturing industry. It means that when any unpredicted factors influence tourism leisure industry's life cycle stage changes, then the unpredicted factors may influence airline transport flying service industry and airline gas fuel product manufacturing industry life cycle service or gas fuel product stage change suddenly , such as this unpredicted COVID 19 human mouth disease, it can influence global tourism leisure industry and airline airplanes transport flying service industry and airline gas fuel product manufacturing industry had been beginning to experience the decline life cycle stage nowadays.

What COVID-19 human mouth disease can let airlines transport service providers and gas fuel manufacturers and tourism leisure service providers to learn? Airlines clearly have a lot on their airplanes at the moment, but since COVID-19 human mouth disease occurred in 2019 end. Many airlines had brought many airlines to prepare to catch global different countries travellers to go to different countries to travel, but nowadays, they do not need to be driven to fly to countries per day. These airplanes are staying on any countries' airports, but per day airlines need to pay high rent to the countries' airports when they are staying on the countries' airports. SO, their airport airplanes rent expenditure must be high, but their airplanes do not need to fly to different countries every day again , because COVID -19 human mouth disease influenced global travellers number had been reducing continue. With unpredicted consequences, many airlines will choose to sell their airplanes later, it none any one medicine can be invented to kill this kind of human mouth disease later, because if some airlines did not make decision to sell their airplanes, then they may nor regrow to growth life cycle stage from decline life cycle stage easily, due to passengers number reduces and it can influence their income reduces. But airline staffs still need to pay , e.g. pilots, airplane front line staffs and airports front line check in service staffs. Hence, sale of airplanes their assets may be the final strategic decision, when any airplanes can not continue to fly every day after 2020 year. Due to COVID 19 human disease can not be killed by any new medicine. If this kind of disease can not be filled for two or more years, then I believe that there are many airlines will experience to death life cycle stage from decline life cycle stage rapidly, otherwise if they can choose to sell some airplanes , they may keep cash available to prepare to reduce expenditure more easily. Although, some airlines made decisions to dismiss some airline service staffs, even pilots to achieve reducing salary expenditure in this decline life cycle stage. But, it will raise unemployment rate to bring social negative challenge. If later airlines choose to sell airplanes their assets to raise cash available strategy. However, it implies that gas fuel need must be influenced to reduce, due to COVID-19 human disease will continue to occur. So, it is the right time, gas fuel manufacturers ought not only concern how to manufacture more airplane gas fuel product to satisfy airlines airplanes transport flying need in this COVID-19 human disease occurrence stage. They ought find any new gas fuel users in this gas fuel market, if these airplanes gas fuel manufacturers expect to re-grow their gas fuel manufacturing and sale business to reach the growing life cycle stage from decline life cycle stage again in the future. Otherwise, many of gas fuel manufacturers will experience the death life cycle stage from decline life cycle stage within one to two years soon as possible.

Hence, if the gas fuel manufacturers can attempt to find other new kinds of gas fuel users in this gas energy market , instead of airline airplane gas fuel market and vehicle gas market main both markets. I believe that they can re-grow to growth life cycle stage from decline life cycle stage again in possible. Although, gas price must be influenced to reduce, because excess of gas supply to airline markets before 2019 end, but when airplanes do not need to fly frequently in this COVID -19 human disease occurrence environment. The COVID-19 pandemic human disease had had a significant impact on the aviation industry, due to travel restrictions and a significant full in demand among travellers. Significant reductions in passengers number have results in airplanes do not need to fly , airplanes feel price must drop, due to oil price war occurred. Hence, due to airline fuel price falls down, it causes many gas manufacturers' gas sale number also reduces to airline market. So, it is right time , any gas fuel manufacturers ought attempt to seek other new gas users, instead of airplanes users or cars users basic both gas users market. If they expect that they can change to experience regrowth life cycle stage from decline life cycle stage again and avoid to reach the final death life cycle stage within one to two years, due to COVID-19 pandemic human disease external environment factor influence.

In fact, on early assessment of the impact of COVID-19 on airline industry, it seems to have a more serve and more rapid impact on air traffic of fuel ( oil price plummeted during the first quarter of 2020). It implies that global airline fuel price had been falling down due to COVID-19 human disease influences to global airplanes' flying times reduce. Moreover, COVID-19 impact on Asia-Pacific Aviation worsens, we have seen that first airline casually in the region, such as China , Singapore, Japan, Taiwan aviation fuel need has been influenced to reduce much significantly. Consequently, Asia-Pacific Aviation fuel price had been influenced to reduce much significantly. Then, it also influences Western Aviation, e.g. US, UK etc. Their flying times are also influenced to reduce, then fuel price sale to western Pacific Aviation can also influenced to fall down. Hence, it seems that COVID-19 human disease may also influence global aviation fuel price falls down. If the fuel manufacturers still only depend on sale aviation fuel income. I believe that the fuel manufacturers may reach to the death life cycle stage rapidly in short time. So, seeking new fuel users market is real need to any one fuel manufacturers , because global medicine scientists still can not guarantee when the kind of new medicine can be invented to kill COVID-19 human disease successfully. So, In this COVID-19 human disease threat environment, many experiencing mature life cycle stage airlines, such as US airline, Cathy airlines , UK airlines , Australia airline etc. they may be influenced to experience decline life cycle stage , even death life cycle stage within two year rapidly. Also, this kind of disease can also influence many travel agents' travelling leisure business development to experience decline stage cycle stage as well as it can also influence any airplanes fuel manufacturers to experience decline life cycle stage from mature life cycle stage in possible. Hence, it is right time , they need to change any new market users or service strategies in order to keep their businesses can continue regrow to the growth life cycle stage again.

CHAPTER FIVE

# Technology facility how improves organizational performance

Facility management influences airport and logistic employee performance

- Facility management assists employees reduce maintenance service expenditure

Facility management provides a variety of non core operations and maintenance services to support any organizations' operation. For logistic organization example, it is possible to provide effective maintenance service to warehouse in order to reduce warehouse facilities to be damaged to bring to spend to buy any new equipment facilities expenditure. So, when the logistic company's warehouse facilities can be maintenance to be the best quality. Then, they can be used these warehouses' machines facilities again. Their performance can assist workers to manufacture any products to keep the most efficiently an raising the best production performance in whole manufacturing process. Then, this logistic company's facility management department can bring to avoid purchase any new machine facilities expenditure spending. One to these warehouses' production machine facilities are kept in the best production performance environment even in long term production need.

I shall indicates airport and warehouse facilities how to influence employees performances as below:

(1) How can comfortable warehouse facilities influence workers' efficiencies in logistic industry ?

The logistic industry's facility management department can create cost savings and efficiency of the warehouse's workplaces. It's machines facilities ( production machines) are dealt with the maintenance management of the physical assets maintenance service. FM ( facilities management) has been being applied to industrial facilities in logistic and warehouse industry long term as well as maintenance plays a significant role to ensure the full service and the warehousing system, including both building components and equipment in warehouse.

Maintenance service is needed to bring a certain level of availability and reliability of a warehouse facilities system and its components and its ability perform to a standard level of quality. So , it seems that logistic industry's warehouse asset cost reducing. It depends on whether it has one facility management department to provide maintenance service to itself warehouse workplace's production machine facilities and warehouse building itself in order to let workers t feel the manufacturing machines can bring good manufacturing performance to assist them to produce any products in one safe warehouse workplace environment. Hence, the performance measurement of warehouse maintenance issue will be valued to be consider to every warehouse manager and facility manager in logistic industry.

In logistic industry, (FM) works at two level on the one hand, it provides a safe and efficient working environment, which is essential to influence warehouse workers whether how they perform to do their manufacturing tasks or logistic goods delivery tasks in warehouse. When they feel the warehouse is safe environment to work. They will not need to consider anywhere has risk to cause they die by accident in warehouse. Hence, they can concentrate on doing their every tasks . On the other hand, it can involve strategic issues, such as property ( warehouse workplace and management, strategy property decision and warehouse facility, e.g. manufacturing machine, facility maintenance and checking planning and maintenance planning development.

However, reducing the operating expense issue will be the main aim when the logistic company feels that it has need to set up one in-house facility management department to carry on any maintenance service for its warehouses' any workplace property and manufacturing machines facilities. So, when the logistic company decides to implement one facility management department, it needs to ensure its facility management department can bring the minimum level of keeping manufacturing performance and efficiency to its warehouses' any manufacturing machines and warehouses' property to avoid to be damaged in short term, such as loss of business due to failure in service, provision of project to customer satisfaction, provision of safe environment, effective utilisation of workplace space, e.g. warehouse effectiveness and communication between the workers and the logistic managers in the warehouse workplace , due to the warehouse's space is not enough maintenance service reliability to the logistic company's warehouse, responsiveness of the warehouse's worker individual negative emotion problem, due to he/she often feels need to work in one unsafe warehouse working environment. Hence, it seems that poor or unsafe warehouse working environment can influence workers feel negative emotion to work to bring low efficiency ( inefficiency) or under productive performance in warehouse. It has relationship to influence they to bring psychological negative emotion feeling to work when the organization lacks one effective warehouse management repairing service to be provided to the warehouse's facilities and properties' maintenance needs in order to avoid ineffective measurement and misleading of performance.

Hence, the logistic company's facilities management department often needs to be reviewed whether its maintenance service level is passed to achieve the lowest repair ( maintenance) service standard to its warehouse itself property and manufacturing machine or warehouse delivery tool facilities or warehouse lamps' light whether is enough to let workers to see anything clearly to avoid accident occurrence or see anything to work clearly or the warehouse space areas are enough to let they can have enough space to walk or communicate to their team supervisors or deliver any goods more easily in the short distance between the worker's sending goods location and the delivering goods destination in order to avoid because the lacking enough space to cause the accident occurrence , due to the space is not enough to let they deliver their goods to any locations in warehouse.

Hence, it seems logistic company's (FM) department can contribute to the organization's mission, such as avoiding warehouse accident occurrence, inefficiency, not enough and unavailability of the facility for future needs when the warehouse lacks enough space areas to bring poor performance of facility and dangerous warehouse itself property in warehouse, e.g. safe and reliable operations of material handling equipment and maintenance of warehouse facilities, grounds, security system, utilities, plumbing, heating , enough lighting system, air conditioning, warming heater, fire protection, security system alarm etc. facilities in warehouse.

Hence, it seems that if the logistic company expected to reduce to spend lot of excessive manufacturing machine purchase expenditure, lose of workers' life or bring workplace accidents , due to poor warehouse workplace environment, even bringing lawsuit compensation claim loss , due to the worker individual accident or death is caused from the poor warehouse facilities, or bring negative emotion to let the workers feel they are working in unsafe warehouse workplace environment. Then, it ought choose to set up on facility management department in order to provide enough maintenance service to its warehouse to avoid these non essential expenditure causing , due to these poor warehouse facilities factors.

Hence any logistic company ought choose to set up one itself in -house facility management department, it be better than outsourcing its all facilities service to one facility management ( maintenance service provider) to help it to deal any kinds of maintenance service in warehouse. Because it is long term maintenance need to its warehouse's any machines and warehouse itself properties. If it chose to find one outsourcing facilitiy management maintenance service provider to replace its in-house facility management department to deal all related facilities maintenance tasks in warehouse. Then, it is possible that it needs to pay long time facilities maintenance service fee to its outsourcing facility management maintenance service provider more than itself facility management maintenance service provision department.

(2) Can facility management influence tourism industry's human resource management influence to improve productivity in airline, travel agent, hotel tourism sectors?

In tourism industry, measuring productivity froma HRM prespective is extremely difficult and has proven to be a limitation within the tourism sector. Due to the customers are not tangible. For example, how can the travel agent measure its travel consultant individual service performance to evaluate whether the travelling customer feels or does not feel satisfactory loyalty from his/her service? How can the airline measure its pilot , airline front-line travelling passenger service attendant indiviual service performance to evaluate whether his/her travelling passenger feels or does not feel satisfactory to whose service performance? Whether airport facility management can influence airline counter service staffs performance ?

However, the complaint number whether it is more or less to the airline or travel agent's service behavior , it does not represent whose service attitude or behavior or performance is poor absolutely because there are many travelling consumers whose complaints are unreasonable , although they feel satisfactory to the airline attendent or airline front -line service staffs individual service performance, but if they feel unhappy to be caused by the airline or travel agent service staff. They will still compain their performance. For this suitation example , it is possible that the travelling passenger is delayed to catch the airplance to fly, due to the country's sudden worse weather influnce, he/she will complain the airline fron-line counter travelling customer service staffs, it concerns when the air plane will arrive the airport, if the airline counter service staff's feedback is that the airplane needs long time arrival. Then, the travelling passengers will complain to the airline counter service staffs in angry. But in fact, the air plane delays to arrive the airport, the airline counter service staffs ought not need responsibilitie to explain the reason why they can not assist the delayed air plane to arrive the country in easier. Furthermore, thy will be complained unreasonably. Hence, it is difficult to measure tourism sector's service staffs ' performance, also the complaint exact number is not one judgement factor to measure their service performance absolutely.

I assume any tourism industry's front -line service airline staffs, they must attempt to serve their travelling passenger in positive service attitude and behavior. So, any tourism industy, how to improve their front -line service staff performance in order to let they to know how to deal unreasonable complaints in sudden unpredictive suitation. Their training materials or contents my include: Teaching them how to provide positive feedback to treat any travelling passenger individual difficult problems or unreasonable complaints in order to reduce their psychological pressure to unknown how to treat these passenger individual related problems when they are facing in airports or travelling agent workplaces. The travelling agent or airline travelling service organizations can attempt to collect measures of employee performance from customers , for example, comment cards in hotel rooms, airplane, travel agent's workplace, mystery shoppers etc. more focus shouls be pleased on this form of evaluation. In order to evaluate the actually place value on the customer ratings to every employee. The all every day, the form of evaluation concerning the actually value on the customer ratings , will be gathered to strategic , it has how many customers feel good or bad ratings to every employee individual performance when every one's tasks are finishing. Due to one month, it can make statistic report to calculate how much performance marks to give to every employee in order to evaluate whether every one's performance is satisfactory to be accempted to the lowest level. If the employee's marks rating is low, his/her department manager can arrange a time and day to meet him/her to discuss whether which aspects of problems who feels in order to give recommendation how to improve his/her service attitude to let customer to give higher marks rating to him/her next time.

Hence tourism industry's service sector organizations need to have one training department to arrange courses how to improve employee service performance in order to let customer to give higher marks rating to very one as well as finding methods how to excite every front line service employee individual loyalty , they can increase their confidence to know how to deal sudden unreasonable complaints in effective and efficient positive attitude.

In conclusion, how to improve employee service performance issue will be any tourism service organization's HRM concerning problem. Airports need to arrange how to implement efficient and comfortable and available convenient airport facilities to let any airline service counter staffs feel enjoyable to serve their passengers. They need to know how to find the most effective methods to solve how improvement of front line employee individual performance problem in order to raise the airline or travel agent's quality of service to let itself further customers to feel its service performance is better than others. So, facility management has indirect relationship to influence airport airline service staffs performances.

In conclusion, to decide whether the company ought need or not need facilities maintenance service or either set up in-house facility management department or outsource one facility management maintenance service provider. It depends on whether its organization has how many facilities are used in its workplace, how many staffs are working the workplace, how much size of its workplace, its workplace is office or warehouse or factory, how long time of its facilities' useful time etc. factors , then it can decide whether it needs or does not need one facility maintenance service department or outsourcing facility maintenance service provider to help it to deal any facilities management problem in its organization.

● Facility management role in organization

When one company feels that it has need facility management service. It can choose to set up either in-house facility management department or seek one outsourcing facility management service provider to help it to arrange any facility management service need. However, this facility management role is only one for the organization. It concerns this question:

What facility management maintenance function can bring the benefits to the organization?

It can define that all services required for the management of building and real estate to maintain and increase their value, the means of providing maintenance support, project management and user management during the building life cycle, the integration of multi-disciplinary activities within the built environment and the management of their impact upon people and the workplace. In traditional, (FM) services may include building fabric maintenance, decoration and refurbishment, plant, plumbing and drainage maintenance, air conditioning maintenance, lift and escalator maintenance , fire safety alarm and fire fighting system maintenance, minor project management. All these are hard services. Otherwise, cleaning , security, handyman services, waste disposal, recycling, pes control, grounds maintenance, internal plants. All these are soft services. Additional services, might also include: pace planning, things moving management, business risk assessment, business continuity planning, benchmarking, space management, facilities contract outsourcing service arrangement, information systems, telephony, travel booking facility utility management, meeting room arrangement services, catering services, vehicle fleet management, printing service, postal services, archiving , concierge services, reception services, health and safety advice, environmental management.

All of these services will be every organization's in-house facility soft or hard services needs. So, it explains why some large organizations feel need one effective facility management department to help them to arrange how to implement facility services efficiently in order to achieve cost reducing, raising efficiency and performance improvement aims because one effective facility management control system can influence employee individual productive effort to be raised or reduced indirectly.

However, (FM) can be selected either setting up one in-house (FM) department or outsourcing its services to one facility management service provider to help the organization to solve any kinds of facilities maintain service problems. One on-house (FM) department is a team, it needs employees to deliver all (FM) services. Some specialist services are needed to be outsourced, when the service is on expertise in the company. The no expertise services will be outsourced to simple service contracts, e.g. lift and escalator (FM) department will have direct labour, but it can outsource some specialist to help it to do some complex facilities management service.

So, the team leader can of can manage whose team staffs, such as maintenance technicians run low risk operations . Otherwise, the outsourcing facility management service provider needs to help it to operate high risk operations or maintenance vital plant facility management service. Anyway, it can set up in-house (FM) department to arrange specialist direct labour and outsourced (FM) services to more than one facility management service providers to do different kinds of (FM) services. One of these outsourcing (FM) service provider, who can arrange sub-contractors to assist it to finish any (FM) services of it's outsourcing (FM) services are more complex to compare the other sub-contractors ( third parties).

● What is a facility manager's role to provide quality service to satisfy its user needs?

We need to know how quality can be defined in facility management and why it should be defined by the customer? How facility managers can find out customer (user) needs? What are the difficulties in finding out users' needs and in delivering quality services? Whether improving quality always means requiring higher cost?

In general, facility manager's major responsibilities may include these major functional areas: longer range and annual facility planning, facility financial forecasting, real estate acquisition and/or disposal, work specification, installation and space management, architectural and engineering planning and design, new construction and/or renovation, maintenance and operations management, maintenance and operation management, telecommunications integration, security and general administrative services. When the facility manager had implemented any one of these FM services for those user. How does he/she provide excellent (FM) service quality ot let whose users to feel satisfactory?

In fact, quality issues can not be considered without customer-oriented perspective service quality involves a comparison of expectation with performance. (FM) service quality is a measure of how well to service level delivered matches customer expectation. So, these issues are (FM) service user's general measurement level requirement. The (FM) manager needs to achieve these the minimum performance measurement level to satisfy whose (FM) user's needs.

However, (FM) service quality has three characteristics: Intangibility, heterogeneity, inseparability. But in fact, (FM) service delivered may be through tangible physical aspects, e.g. factory plant workplace building, machine equipment maintenance, intangible (FM) services, e.g. managing space moving in plant to let staffs to work, managing outsourcing cleaners to clean factory equipment. However, all (FM) service performance often varies, due to the behavior of service personnel. Hence, a well developed job specification and training can help to improve the consistence of services of (FM). Any (FM) production and consumption of many services may are inseparable and they are usually interactions between the (FM) client and the contact person from the service provider.

Hence, it seems that service quality is considered as hard to evaluate. In (FM) service quality, it includes physical quality and interactive non-physical service quality. Physical quality is tangibles: The appearance of the physical facilities, equipment, personnel and communication materials. Non-physical services quality means reliability: The ability to perform the promised service dependably and accurately; responsiveness means the willingness to help customers and provide promopt service to let user to feel; assurance mans the competence of the system in its credibility in providing a courteous and secure service and empathy means the approachability, ease of access and effort taken to understand customers' needs.

Hence, a good performance of (FM) manager , he/she ought satisfy the user's tangible and non-tangible both service quality needs. I recommend that he/she can attempt to predict what are the (FM) customer expects in each (FM) service needs. Then, it can make decision what aspect(s) will be the (FM) users major (FM) service need and what aspect(S) won't be the (FM) users major (FM) service need. Then, he/she can make more accurate decision to arrange time, human resource , cost spending amount arrangement whether when it ought concentrate on finishing the (FM) major service tasks as well as whether how he/she ought finish the major (FM) service tasks to be more easily, e.g. how to arrange staffs number to finish, how many the minimum staffs number is needed to be arrange the major (FM) service tasks, time arrangement is important factor, because it can influence whether he/she ought finish the major (FM) service tasks today or tomorrow or later in order to have enough time to finish other non-major (FM) service tasks. Instead of time management, staff number arrangement is also important factor , if he/she arranged the excessive staffs number to do the (FM) major services tasks, then it is possible that it will have shortage of staffs number to finish the non-major (FM) service tasks on the day. So, avoiding either major or non-major (FM) services can not finish on the day. The (FM) manager needs to predict when the major (FM) services and the non-major (FM) services which are necessary to be finished in order to have enough time and staffs to assist him/her to finish every day major and non-major (FM) service effectively. Then, the achievement of his/her (FM) major and non-major tangible and non-tangible services , it will have more chance to be performed efficiently by his/her managed staffs.

In conclusion, in any organizations , (FM) manager needs have good predictable effort to evaluate whether when his/her managed team need to finish the major and/or non-major (FM) tasks as well as whether how he/she ought arrange the accurate time and staff number to finish any major and/or non-major (FM) service tasks on the day. Then, his/her leading of (FM) service team can be managed to work more efficiently in order to satisfy her/his (FM) service user's needs.

Facility management how influences
public service transport service performance

- How (FM) space moving management brings employees efficiencies

There are interesting questions: How (FM) can bring value-add to avoid loss or earn more profit to the organization? Can it influence employees to raise performance and improve efficiency ? Some organizations' (FM) service need which is necessary in order to let employees can raise productivity.

It is based on these assumptions: I assume the organizations have completely either outsourced or in-house their (FM) facility management departments will gain more effect on added value than they have no (FM) function as well as organizations have a strong coordination with the (FM) department will gain more added value than organizations with a weak coordination. Organizations in the profit aim can gain more added value than organizations in the not for profit aim sectors.

In fact, any organization is difficult to confirm it has relationship between improving performance, raising efficiency and owning (FM) function in its organization. (FM) could have to do with the attraction of easy but incomplete indicators of efficiency rather than the necessarily and less direct measures if the effectiveness and the relevance of space moving useful management, e.g. whether building has the enough space to let employees to move to work easy in order to raise efficiency, whether the building has excessive furniture and equipment number and they are putted

on wrong places to be caused employees move difficulty in the building in order to influence productive performance.
However, how to arrange space moving management to equipment, e.g. copying machines, faxes, productive machines, they are putted on the locations where have enough space to let employees to move to another locations. For example, the building floor has more than 50 employees, but its space is not enough to let these 50 employees to move to any locations to let them to feel easily often. Then, it is possible to cause they feel nervous pressure and they can feel difficult to work , when they are working in a small office space or factory space or warehouse space. Then, the consequence will be under-predictive efficiency or poor performance to any one of these 50 employees in this office or factory or warehouse.
" Facility management is responsible for coordinating all efforts related to planning, designing, and managing buildings and their systems, equipment, and furniture to enhance. The organizations abilty to compete successfully in a rapidly changing world." ( F.Becker)
The author explains equipment, workplace internal space designing, furniture space putting location arrangement will have possible to influence employee individual productive performance or efficiency to be raised or reduced in the workplace. Hence, it seems that, in the value chain (FM) belongs to the activity part of the firm. To make the facilities cooperation with each office or factory or warehouse using space moving facility management. Facility space moving management must be linked strategically, tactically and operationally to other support activity to add value to the organization's office or factory or warehouse space moving management arrangement more effectively.
Thus, how to arrangement space moving management issue it will have possible to influence the organization's employee individual productive performance and efficiency in whose workplace. It seems that (FM) space moving management arrangement have indirect relationship to influence the organization's employee individual performance and efficiency , due to they need often to work in the workplace, if they feel moving difficulty , or excessive equipment , furniture number is putting into the small office, factory or warehouse locations, or they feel the office or factory or warehouse has excessive ( a lot of) staffs number to work in the small space of office or factory or warehouse. Then, they can not concentrate nervous on finishing every tasks in possible. In long term, their efficiencies will be poor or inefficiencies or their performance won't be improved or causing

poor performance in possible.

Instead of the not enough space moving and excessive staffs number factor, it will bring another question: Can enough information systems equipment cause a more efficient and improved performance to the organization staffs in the workplace?

I assume that the office has 100 employees and it has only ten copying machines. So it means that ten employees use one copying machine. Hence, it brings this question: Is it enough to provide only ten copying machines to average ten employees to use? It depends on other factors, e.g. whether any one of these 100 employees needs to print how many documents per day , whether the five copying machines' locations are far away to separate different locations or they are stored in one printing room in the office, whether the day has how many staffs are absent, whether the day has how many printing machine(s) is/ are broken to need to be repaired. Hence, these unpredictable external environment factors will influence whether the five copying machines number is enough to let these 100 employees to use in the office every day. Hence, facility manager ought need to spend to observe average their copying behaviors every day in order to make data record. Many employees need to use copy machines to print documents, average how many document's page number, they need to print, how much average time spending to print their documents, average how many staff absent number on the day. Even, if the all five copying machines are stored in the printing room, calculating the staffs number whether how many staffs need more than five minutes to walk to the printing room to print their documents many staffs need to spend five minute to walk to the printing room, and they have other urgent tasks to wait to finish. It is possible to influence their efficiency, due to they often need to spend more than five minutes to walk to the printing room to print documents. If there are many staffs need to often to print documents, but their printing task will have many time, e.g. 20 separate printing tasks. Then, they need to spend at least ( 20x5 ) 100 minutes to spend time to walk to the printing room to print their documents. It must influence that they should not finish the other urgent tasks on the day. If there are many staffs to spend much time to walk to the printing room in the least 20 separate printing time or more on that day. All the facility manager needs to evaluate whether all the five copy machines are stored in the printing room whether it is the best location decision or they ought need be separated to put on different office locations in their workplaces, even he/she ought need to evaluate whether it is enough copying machines number, when the office has only 5 copying machines. He/she ought need to buy more copying machines number to satisfy any one of these 100 employee individual copying task need.

In conclusion, effective office or factory or warehouse space moving facility management will be one part task of (FM) function. If the office or factory or warehouse can have accurate equipment, machine , furniture number to avoid excessive or shortage number problem to cause employees often feel moving difficult problem in their workplace when they need to move to another location to work in office or warehouse or factory as well as whether the staff needs often spend time to wait the another employee to use the copying machine to print whose document or fax machine to deliver whose document. Then, it is not that fax or printing machines number is not enough to provide the employees to use in the office or warehouse or factory workplace.

Hence, (FM) includes space moving facility management to equipment , machines, furniture number as well as choosing anywhere is(are) the suitable location (s) arrangement to putting or storing these facilities in workplace as well as decision of the staff number and the workplace area size whether it has excessive staffs number to cause these staffs need to work in the small area size of office or warehouse or factory workplace. So, the organization ought need to decide whether it needs to reduce the office's staffs number to let them to work in another more suitable locations in another workplace. Hence, all these facilities space moving management and staffs and workplace size issues will be (FM) manager's consideration issues, because these external environment factors will influence employee individual efficiency and performance to be poor to cause low valued to its organization in long term in possible .

● Predictive the choosing right
data asset and (FM) analytics
solutions to boost public
transportation service quality

Can gather the choosing right data public transportation service station facilities asset and analytics, it can give recommendation to help any organization to boost service quality? (FM) analytics data can be applied to public transportation service industry to be supported how and why the train, train, ferry , ship, air plane, underground train public transportation tools' time arrival and leaving information notice board and automated ticket paying machines facilities are putting on or stored any where locations in order to boost passengers to feel their facilities locations are convenient to let them to buy tickets and see the arrival and leaving time for the next public transportation tool from the information notice electronic board machine. So, it seems that these public transportation tools' station facilities locations can influence passengers to feel the public transportation service company how to consider to its passenger's buying ticket needs and next public transportation tool's arrival and leaving time information needs in order to boost its passengers use service quality and let them to feel better service reliable performance in any train, tram, ferry , ship, underground tram, airplane stations.

As these public transportation service organizations need to learn data analytics represent an opportunity for its ticket paying machine equipment facilities as well as the next transportation tool arrival and leaving time information notice board electronic equipment facilities anywhere the locations are the most suitable to put on or store these equipment to let passengers to walk to the ticket paying machines to buy the ticket to catch the train, tram, underground train, ferry, airplane, taxi, ship more easily. So, they do not need to spend more time to find these facilities locations and spend more time to queue to wait to buy ticket to catch the public transportation tool in stations conveniently. Instead of where is the seeking ticket paying machine location, where is the next public transportation tool arrival and leaving information notice time , these both issues will be any public transportation tool's passenger's main needs.

Hence, how to spend time to seek where the next public transportation tool's arrival and leaving time information electronic notice machine location and where the ticket paying machine location , these both factors will influence any passengers' positive or negative emotion causing. For example, if the passenger feels difficult to find the ticket paying machine in the large area size train station or /and he/she feels difficult to find the train time arrival and leaving information to let him/her to know when the next train will arrive the station. Due to he/she feels difficult to find the train ticket paying machine, he/she needs to spend much time to find any one ticket paying machine in the train station. Then, it will influence him/her to choose another public transportation tool to replace the train public transportation tool, e.g. he/she can choose to catch tram, underground train, taxi, bus, ferry, taxi, ship to replace train. So, it seems ticket paying machine and time arrival and leaving information notice electronic equipment 's location putting or stored choice will be one factor to influence the passenger to choose another kind of public transportation tool to replace train at the moment. When, he/she feels that he/she arrives the destination in the most short time. Then, the public transportation service organization (FM) manager has responsibility to evaluate whether there are enough ticket paying machines number to let passengers do not need to spend more time to queue to buy tickets to catch the public transportation tool in short time as well as there are enough time arrival and leaving for next transportation tool to let passengers to know. It will be their concerning issues when they arrive the public transportation service tool's station.

Hence, predictive passenger individual walking behavior can help the public transportation service organization to choose whether where are the most convenient and attractive locations to let the ticket paying machines and the arrival and leaving time information electronic board machines to be putted on or stored in the suitable station positions in order to let many passengers can find these essential facilities in stations very easily. So, gathering data concerns passenger walking behavior in the public transportation service any stations, which can help the facility manager to make more accurate evaluation to attempt to predict whether where the locations are common places to let passengers to choose to walk daily or where the locations are not common places to let passenger to choose not to walk daily in general. Then, he/she can apply these data of different locations in the stations to evaluate whether anywhere they will have many passengers to choose to walk or whether anywhere they won't have many passengers to choose to walk in order to make more accurate decision whether anywhere are the most suitable locations to let the ticket paying machines and the time arrival and leaving information electronic board equipment to be putter on or stored in order to let them to feel it is so easier to let them to find.

Anyway, calculating each station's passenger number per day issue is important to predict whether where , there are many passengers choose to walk or where, there are not many passengers choose to walk in these different public transportation service stations in order to evaluate whether where the stations' different ought put on paying ticket machines or time arrival and leaving information electronic boards in order to let they feel very easy to buy tickets and seeing the next arrival and leaving time information for the kind of public transportation service tool conveniently in the different stations. Moreover, if the station has no enough ticket paying machines number to be supplied to let passengers need to spend more than ten minute time to wait to buy ticket to catch the kind of public transportation service tool in every queue every day. Then it will cause them to choose another kind of public transportation tool to catch go to working place or entertainment place to replace it to on that day. Then, it will cause these passengers who often do not like to queue in the kind of public transportation service tool's any stations, who will not choose to go to anywhere of this kind of public transportation service tool's any stations again. Hence, in long term this kind of public transportation service tool will lose many passengers. Thus, calculating each station's busy time of passengers number , which can predict when it is the busy time and it can make more accurate decision whether the station has need to increase enough ticket paying machines number in order to bring enough supply number to satisfy passengers' ticket purchase need in the busy time.

In conclusion, gathering above all stations' public transportation service equipment facilities number, storing positions data and every station's passenger walking behavior data, they are necessary to any public transportation tool service industry, because these equipment number and storing locations will influence them to make decisions to choose another kind of public transportation tool to replace it's transportation service if they often feel difficult to find these facilities in its different stations. Thus, it is part of task to facility manager's responsibility if the public transportation service organization expects it won't lose many passengers , due to these external environment factor influence and it also implies cheap ticket price does not guarantee the passengers will choose to catch this kind of public transportation service tool to go to anywhere.

- The relationship between facility management and productive efficiency

It is one interesting question: Can facility management function bring benefits to raise productive efficiency to organizations? I shall indicate some cases to attempt to explain this possible occurrence chance as below:

- Facility management benefit to office workplace

In private organizations, when the firm has facility management department, whether it can bring efficient administration to influence clerks to work efficiently in office, e.g. reducing administrative time or shorten time to work in administrative processes, in order to achieve minimizing clerk number labor cost. How to design office facilities to let office staffs to feel comfortable to work and reducing their pressure to work. It seems that office working environment will influence office staff individual performance. If the office working environment could improve efficiency and creativity of services to satisfy office workers‘ comfortable working environment needs. It will reduce every administration manager's working pressure when he/she needs often to find methods to attempt to encourage whose administrative clerks to avoid to waste working time to do some non-major administration tasks.

Hence, how to design or allocate or arrange office any facilities' stored locations or whether how many equipment number is the enough to store in the locations, which will influence office employees‘ working attitude in order to raise or reduce their administration tasks efficiency indirectly, e.g. the office is clean or dirty, whether office reception has enough information telephone switchboard operation facilities, whether every clerk's table has enough computers number to supply to every to use, whether internet speed is fast or slow in order to let any employees can send and receive email to communicate or download any document from internet in short time, whether data processing and computer system maintenance service supply is enough to be repaired to employees' computers immediately when their computers are broken to wait repair, whether website editing facilities operation whether is enough to link to office every staffs in order to let any office staffs can apply internet to do their tasks conveniently in short time.

Hence, all of these general office equipment facilities whether they are enough supplied and their stored positions anywhere are the suitable to assist any clerks to work conveniently, they will influence every office employee's administrative and productive efficiency indirectly as well as all faxes, copying machines, computers, whether internet linking maintenance service time is short or long to prepare to any office employees to use conveniently any time, these different issues will also influence every employee individual efficiency in office. Hence, it concludes that office working environment, facilities supply number, facilities maintenance service and facilities location storing both factors will influence employee individual administrative productive efficiency in office.

- facility management benefits to service working environment

Can effective facility management improve service working environment to raise employee individual work performance? It is a concern about the quality of service to its customer question. The term" standards and goals" are often used to measure staff individual service performance whether he/she can serve to customers to let them to feel this staff's service performance or attitude is good or bad.

Is the service workplace working environment facilities enough, it will influence customer service staff individual performance.

For shopping center service industry case example, for this situtation, e.g. shopping center's facilities are enough or are placed to the suitable locations in order to let the shopping center's customers to feel comfortable to shopping when they enter this shopping center as well as whether the shopping center's facilities can influence the customer service staffs to serve whose shopping customers easily or difficult, due to whether the shopping center's facilities whether are adequate supplied or their locations are the best suitable positions to influence their service performance to let them to feel easier or comfortable to serve their customers in any large size shopping centers. For example, whether the lamps' lighting energy is enough to let the shoppers to feel safe to walk to visit any shops when there are many shoppers were walking to cause crowd and they feel difficult to walk to avoid any body contact to any one in busy time when the shopping center has no enough lights to let them to see anywhere in the shopping center's dark environment. Then it will influence customer service staffs to feel difficult to find any shopping center customers, e.g. when two shopping center customers are fighting in one location where is far away to the shopping customer service staffs and securities in the shopping center, because the shopping center is large and it has no enough light to let the customer service staffs and securities to find their frighting location to deal their fighting behavior and other shopping center's shoppers will feel very dangerous to walk their fighting location to avoid to close them. Then, it will has possible to cause death or hurt to any one of these two fighting shoppers ,even other shoppers' life. Because the shopping center's securities and customer service staffs who need to spend much time to find their fighting location, it will delay they can bring the policemen to their fighting location when they arrive this shopping center's destination in short time in order to solve their fighting behavior to influence all shoppers' life in this shopping center. Hence, the shopping center whether it has enough lamps number and the lamps' light whether is enough, these lighting facilities will influence any shopping center customer service staffs and securities who can spend less time to arrive any locations to deal any urgent matters.

For another situation in shopping center, if the shopping center has no enough paying telephone service facilities to supply shoppers to phone to anyone when they feel need to phone to any in the shopping center. Then, it will lead to some shoppers decide to find where the shopping center's reception's telephone to supply to them to phone call to anyone. If they are ten shoppers are waiting to use the shopping center's reception telephone to phone call to their friend or family within one minute. Thus, it will influence the reception customer service staffs feel difficult to arrange how to distribute the only one telephone to these ten shoppers to use to phone call their friend or family when they are queuing within their one minute waiting time in the shopping center's reception. If these ten shoppers can not use the reception telephone to phone call anyone. hen, they will feel dissatisfactory and complain to the reception service staffs politely. So, lacking enough facilities in the shopping center's any where, it will possible to influence their shopping centers‘ shoppers to feel all shopping center's service staff individual performance to be poor. It means that if the shopping center expects to improve customer satisfaction to its customer service staff's behavioral performance, it meets have enough facilities to be supplied in the shopping center to let its shoppers to feel it is one comfortable and safe shopping center. In conclusion, shopping center's facilities will have possible to influence shoppers' feeling to evaluate its customer service staffs to evaluate whether their service attitudes are good or poor indirectly.

- Can facility management improve productivity

The productivity means resources ( input) is therefore the amount of products or services ( output), which is produced by them. Hence, higher ( improved) productivity means that more is produced with the same expectation of resource, i.e. at the same cost is terms of land materials, machine, time or labor. Alternatively, it means same amount is produced at less labor cost in term of land, material, machine, time for labor that is utilized. So, it brings this question: How can facility management improve productivity? I shall explain as these several aspects, it is possible to be improved productivity from (FM) successfully.

Improved productivity of farm land: If the farming land has better facility management to bring advantages by using better seed, better facilities of cultivation and most fertilizer. It is in the agricultural sense is increased ( improved). So, facility management can bring benefits to any land resource to raise productivity in possible. It implies that the productivity of land used for better facility management of industrial purposes is said to have been increased if the output of products or service within that area of industrial land is increased output aim.

Improved productivity of material: If the factory has improved better equipment by facility management method to assist skillful workers to raise the manufacture cloth number, then the productivity of the cloth number is improved by (FM) method.

Improved productivity of labour: When the factory has good manufacturing equipment facilities to be supplied to improve methods of work to product more producing number per hour, then (FM) improved productivity of worker. Hence, in any workplaces, when organization has good facilities, it will influence employees to raise productivities in possible, because they need often to improved equipment facilities manufacture products to achieve higher production number aim.

- Can facility management raise bank employee productivity

Bank workplace environment is busy, the bank counter service staffs need to contact many bank clients to help them to serve or withdraw money from bank's counters. Whether does the quality of environment in bank workplace will influence the determination level of employee's motivation, subsequent performance productivity in bank working environment. For example, if the bank's staffs need work under inconvenient conditions , it will bring low performance and face occupational health diseases causing high absenteeism and turnover.

In general, bank size is usually small, it will have many bank clients enter bank to contact counter staffs to need them to help them to save or withdraw money. So, it will bring air pollution the crowd queue in every bank counter challenge when the bank has many people are queue waiting in counters to queue. So, bank working condition problem relates to environmental and physical factors which will influence every bank counter staff individual working performance to serve bank clients satisfactory. However, bank staffs need to deal many documents concern every client personal data every day. So, they need to spend much time to use computer and painting machines. This is particularly true for these employees who spend most of the day operating a computer terminal in bank workplace. As more and more computers are being installed in workplaces, an increasing number of business has been adopting designs for bank offices installment. So, bank needs have effective facilities management design because of demand of bank staffs for more human comfort.

An good equipment facility management for bank staffs to use conveniently, it is assumed that better workplace environment can motives bank employees and produces better productivity. Hence, bank office environment can be described in terms of physical and behavioral components to influence bank staffs to work inefficiently. To achieve high level of bank employee productivity, bank organizations must ensure that the physical environment in conductive to bank different department organizational needs, facilitating interaction and privacy, formality and informality, functional and disciplinarily, e.g. house loan or private loan departments, counter service department, visa card application department.

Thus, in a high safe privacy facility management working environment will let different department bank staffs feel safe to worry about privacy loss in possible. So, the improving bank facility to bring safe and high privacy to avoid bank client individual loss in working environment issue, the facility management can be results to bring these benefits, such as in a reduction in a number of complaints and absenteeism and an increase in productivity.

- Can (FM) create value to organization?

(FM) can reduce managing facilities as a strategic resource to add value to the organization and its overall performance, e.g. saving the energy in building and take care of shuttle buses and parking facilities space management for , on economic efficiency and effectiveness, or good price and value for the organization.

If the organization expects to apply (FM) process to save energy, it depends on possible input factors, i.e. interventions in the accommodation facilities services. So, it seems that the organization expects to save its energy consumption in its building. It needs have good space management facilities between parking its shuttle buses in its property's car park.

Why does space facility management is important to influence efficiency and productivity. For one school's building example, when the school decides none of the two gymnasiums student sport entertainment centers to be built in order to reduce financial cost and higher benefits. Remarkably, the use of space with the school overall strategic goals , such as creating spaces that better can support the teaching, motivate students and teachers, attract more students and increase the utilisation of existing space to accommodate an increasing number of students.

If it hopes to make high quality teaching facilities on student's choice where to study. The school will need to choose to build either one comfortable and new design facility teaching accommodation or build two gymnasium sport entertainment centers in its limited land space either for students' learning or sport aim. Due to it feels new teaching accommodation can make more attractive to increase students numbers to choose it to study more than building two new gym sport centers to let them do sport in school.

Hence, space choice (FC) management strategy will be one important considerable issue, when the organization has limited land space resources to make choose to build any constructions in order to increase many clients number. Such as the school organization has limited storage land resource to let it to build either two gymnasium sport entertainment centers or one new teaching accommodation in order to attract many students to choose it to learn. Hence, it needs to gather data to make more accurate evaluation to decide how to apply its space facility to choose to build these both kinds of buildings in order to achieve the attractive student learning choice aim, so whether the two sport entertainment activity centers or one new teaching accommodation choice, it needs to gather information to decide whether the school ought to choose to build which kind of building in order to achieve the increase of student number aim, so space facility management will be this school's land shortage problem.

● The relationship between facility management and consumer behavior

How and why shop facility management can influence consumer individual shopping behavior? If it is possible, what shop facility management factors can influence their consumption decision when they enter the shop to plan to buy anything. I shall indicate some shop case studied to explain whether how and why every shop's facility management can influence consumer individual consumption desire when any one consumer enters any shops.

● Shop's low ceiling height location (FM) influence consumer behavior

Can the shop's ceiling height influence shoppers' shopping behavior? Can the shop's variation in ceiling height can influence how consumers process information to decide to make purchase decision in the shops, e.g. for this situation, when the consumer enters the shop, he/she feels the ceiling height is low and it has a lamp will contact his/her head in possible. So, he/she chooses to move far away from the low ceiling location in the shop. It is possible that shop's ceiling low height and the lamp locates at the ceiling low height position will influence many customers' choices to leave the low ceiling height and lamp location, then the shop's low ceiling height will have possible to influenced many customers to choose to find the another shop to buy the similar kind of products , due to the lamp locates in the low ceiling height, so this lamp and low ceiling height will be possible factor to influence any shoppers who won't choose to walk to this dangerous location in the shop. If the shop's all spaces are ceiling height and it has many lamps are located at the low ceiling height spaces. Then, it will be serious to cause many shoppers do not want to spend too much time to choose any products in the shop because they feel dangerous to walk to the any low ceiling height lamps' locations in the shop.

Hence, hoe to design the different concept may be activated by the showroom ceiling if it were relatively high, as it tends to be in mall stores, versus low, as it is in most strip mall shops and outlet centers. Relatively high ceilings may bring safe shopping emotion to let any consumers to feel thoughts related to freedom, whereas lower ceilings may let consumers to feel dangerous to walk the locations in any shops. Hence it seems any shops ought not neglect whether their ceiling height is tall and the lamps ought avoid to locate in any low ceiling height locations in order to influence consumers number to be decreased.

- Can house facility management influence consumer individual purchase intention?

When one new property is built, whether the property consumers will consider how the new property is facility to influence their purchase intention to the property will the new property's (FM) influence buyers in real estate markets' preferences choice and living interest. Any new property's internal characteristics of the house unit itself , such as rooms available, when example, of external are location, accessibility to utilities services and facilities will have possible to influence the property buyer's final property purchase decision, so it seems that even the property price is cheap, it is not represent the property buyer will choose to buy the property, if he/she feels the property's facility management is poorer to compare other similar kinds of properties.

So, it can help real estate analysts better explain and predict the behavior of decision makers in real estate markets. Property consumers will search for property information, concerns the property's quality, price distinctiveness, ability, facility management, service of the property's external environment to decide whether the property is high value to choose to buy to compare other kinds of properties.

However, the external environmental forces, such as limited resources, e.g. time or financial will influence whose property consumption choice and living the property's satisfaction feeling ( represent) a feedback from post-property purchase reflection used to inform subsequent decisions. The process of the property buyer's leaving experience will serve to influence the extent to which the property consumer how to consider future next time property purchases decision and new information methods. Hence, when one property consumer chooses to buy a house, it refers house features are house internal attributes , such as quality of building, the design as well as internal and external design, which are important factors for a property consumer when he/she needs to select and purchases one house.

The other (FM) factors which can influence the property consumers' needs, include living space as features, such as the size of kitchen, bathroom, bedroom, living bath and other rooms available in the house. The environment of housing area is also important factor, e.g. the condition of the hood, attractiveness of the area, quality of houses, type of houses, type of houses, density of housing, wooded area or free coverage, slope of the attractive views, open space, non-residential uses in the areas vacant sites, traffic noise, level of owner-occupation in , level of education in level of income in, security from crime, quality of schools, religious of , transportation , shopping center, sport entertainment can be supplied to close to the house area. All these human related issue of the property's location will also influence the property buyer's living location selection. Hence, above (FM) influence property consumer purchase behavior, it is based on the relationship behavior. The consumer's house purchase intention and house features, living space, environment and distance to recreation center, supermarket, library etc. public facilities variable (FM) factors.

In conclusion, the house internal space facility management and external environment facility management factors will influence property consumer individual house purchase intention.

- The effects of in-store shelf design facility management factor influences consumer behavior

Can every store retailer's shelf design influence supermarket and large retail stores shoppers' behaviors when they visit the stores? However, currently many stores tend to build on traditional and repetitive design for their store

shelf layout, it brings results in outdated store layouts.
Another important store shelf layout design aspect, retailer should consider carefully is the allocation of products on shelves. So, it seems that efficient shelf space allocation management does not only minimize the economic threats of empty product shelves, it can also lead to higher consumer satisfaction, a better customer relationship.
Why does supermarket shelves design is important? Any retail tore will sell product category within a shelf. They can use the same nominal category , e.g. crisps next to light crisps, same food product shelf. Anyway, a goal-based shelf display can contain several product, that determine a common consumer goal, e.g. fair trade. Hence, these two categorical product structuring methods are also described in terms of how to put product, or food on shelf benefit and attribute -based product categories.
These shelf design food or product storing method will have more influence consumers to choose to buy the supermarket or retail store food or products more easily , due to products, or food put on their shelf very convenient and systematic to attract consumers' shopping consideration to the supermarket or retail store.

- Music (FM) environment influence consumer consumption desire

Is it possible that shop music (FM) environment can raise consumer purchase desire? In one shop or supermarket, it can provide soft music (FM) equipment to let consumers can listen soft music or songs in the supermarket or retail shop when the are staying to spend more time shopping and whether soft music facility can be expected to raise customer individual value-added options to the music facility shop in the supermarket or retail shop.
Can the music facilities prolong consumers to stay in the store? It is possible that tempo soft music can influence consumers to stay longer time in restaurants and supermarkets and retail shops. It is possible that the different types of music (FM) in any supermarket, restaurant, retail shop owning music listening facility shopping environment. It will have possible to influence consumers to prolong staying in their shops. For example, one wine selling retail shop has classical music (FM) listening equipment to let consumers to listen when they enter the wine shop, it is possible to cause consumers to choose to buy more expensive wine products. Some researchers indicate when the wine shop owns classical music facility to let all consumers can list classical music when they walk in the wine ship, it can evoke the wine consumers to choose to buy purchasing higher prices wine

products in the long term classical music listening environment. Otherwise, in a fitness sport center, musical fir and excite or popular music ( FM) environment can attract fitness sport players' emotion to play and kind of fitness sport facility longer time. Also, in one supermarket, the soft music facilities listening environment can persuade or attract food consumers to spend more time in the mall consuming food or beverage also purchase other products more easily, due to they will listen soft music to be influenced to choose to prolong staying time in the supermarket. It seems that it has relationship between retail shop's music facility environment and consumer's emotion will be influenced by these different kinds of soft music or songs to raise consumption desire in the supermarket, if some consumers like to prolong to stay longer consuming time in the owning music facility environment's retail shop.

In fact, some researchers indicate the owning background music facility selling environment's ship , it can affect consumer decision making, memory, concentration consumption desire. So, classical , jazz soft music facility ought be installed in restaurants, retail shops, restaurants' environment. Otherwise, popular , exciting, noise, pop music facility ought be installed in fitness sport centers, theme park entertainment parks business places in order to influence fitness sport players or theme park entertainers to prolong playing or entertaining time to feel real sport or entertainment theme park playing machine facility's entertainment enjoyable feeling as well as attracting restaurant or supermarket or retail shop's consumers to prolong their staying time to make consumption decisions. Hence, it seems that music facility environment can raise consumers' consumption desire in possible.

● University bookstore atmospheric factors how to influence student's purchase book behavior?

Any university bookstore how to do international control and structuring of book internal environment to raise students' purchase book desires in university itself school's bookstore, it will be one popular question to any universities. Hence, whether the university bookstore internal (FM) factors include: lighting, music, colors, scents, temperature, layout and general cleanliness as well as university external factors include: the university bookstore shape/size, windows, university parking facility for students availability and location, which can play an influential role of the university bookstore image in order to influence the university itself students to choose to buy books from themselves bookstore or university outside bookstores.

Whether the university student needs to spend how long individual learning time and how much learning nervous to spend time to choose any kinds of book in the universiity bookstore or outside bookstores, this issue , he/she will consider. Because he/she does want to expect spend much time and nervous to choose to buy books in any bookstore. If the university's bookstore physical location and internal (FM) image can let its target student customers to feel it's all book products are stored in any attractive internal book shelves places, e.g. the cheapest and the most expensive different subjects of text books are stored in one system method to bring the positive image of value and quality in order to let university target student customers can find their books‘ choice location to spend less time to search any books to read in the unviersiity bookstore easily.

However, due to learning time is shortage to every university student of the university's book shelves can display all text books in the attractive right locations in the university bookstore as well as the university's bookstore ought has an adequate space to let university students to walk to anywhere and find any subjects of text books and compare their book sale prices in the bookstore's any shelves' locations easily when they walk to the subject of book shelf location, then they can make accurate decision either to buy the right kind of subject book or not buy it to read in the short time. They will feel their book choice purchase decision making process won't influence their learning time in themselves universiity. Then, the university students will be influenced by themselves university's bookstore's attractive external university facilities in the university's any teaching places and the university's bookstore internal attractive environment facility image which can influence the students to make final choices to buy their liking books to read from their university's itself bookstore. Hence, the university's bookstore internal and external building environment (FM) design factors will influence its students whether choose to buy from themselves bookstore or another outside general bookstore.

● How and why does retail atmospheric environment influence consumers behavior in retail shop?

Any shop's internal facility management design can influence atmospheric environment to influence consumer individual shopping desire, e.g. colour, lighting, music, crowding, design and layout factors, which internal shop (FM) environment can influence the first time shopping visiting client ‘ cognitive process how to feel the shop store image. Such as if the store's

(FM) environment can bring enjoyable and fun and happy image to let them to feel shopping's enjoyment.

In conclusion, when consumers will like to stay longer time in the store. Due to the store's internal (FM) atmospheric environment can attract them to stay longer time in the store. Then, the customer's shopping value will raise and it can bring purchasing intention and shopping satisfaction. How can (FM) influence retail atmospheric physical (FM) environment ? Can (FM) bring indirect relationship to influence how the consumer individual causes positive or negative purchase intention when he/she has influence to prolong staying desire in the store, when the shop has good (FM) , it will bring long time to make consumption chance in the shop.

- Facility management influences consumer satisfactory service level

Can facility management (FM) quality influence consumer satisfactory service feeling? Any organization's facility management can improve the effectiveness of the maintenance organization. It can provide improved operational and maintenance functions to maintain the physical environment to support the overall mission. However, any organization will consider whether it improves its facilities, it will raise consumer satisfactory feeling when it provides the service to them, e.g. education service industry, when students need to often to attend any school's classrooms or lecture halls, computer rooms, libraries, all these facilities will be student's learning environment. If these school facilities can be maintenance to let students to feel comfortable to enjoy to study in their schools' any learning locations. Then, it has possible that to bring their enjoyable learning feeling in theirs schools.

- How school's facility management influences student's learning satisfactory feeling.

However, in education industry case, the school's facility management has those criteria can be used to measure effectiveness. Student individual response time between the student's request for computer use service in school computer rooms, library reading service in school library , classroom computer facilities and tables, chairs etc. furniture supplies service and the facility management supply number and available to useful time. If the student believes that the response time is too long when he/she feels need to use any school facilities, the actual number of seconds or minutes, he/she needs to wait how long time to queue to use his/her school's any facilities in library, classroom, computer room. So, the student's queue waiting time to use any his/her school's facilities, it can measure the school's facility management effectiveness.

- Scheduling of preventive maintenance activities.

It schedules of any maintenance activities are not arranged effectively to the school. Then, it will influence students' poor learning facility service to their school. For their situation, when the school's first floor has two men toilets are damaged. They are needed to be required. However, it is one week period, the first floor 100 students can not use the first floor men toilets. Hence, in this week, all 100 students need to go to other floors toilets to often use. They will feel busy and time is not enough when they need to attend to any classrooms to listen the first floor classrooms teachers' lesson. If he/she arrives the first floor classroom too late, due to he/she needs to go to another floor male toilets to queue to use. Then, he/she will feel angry and worries about whose absent or late attending classroom behavior when the lesson's teacher has attended early in the first floor classroom , and he teacher will need him/her to explain why he/she will go to this classroom lately, if his/her explanation won't be accepted to attend to the first floor classroom too late in the week. So, arrangement maintenance schedule to any school's facilities issue is importnt to influence student's satisfactory feeling to the school. Also, lacking of preventive maintenance activities will bring results in unscheduled shutdown of critical equipment can have an unrecoverable impact on the school's good learning environment providing to student's mission.

In fact, however in any organizations, such as school, ship, office etc. organizations, achieving balance of effectiveness and efficient difficulties and takes time and effort on the part of management and staff. It is not enough to establish an optimal relationship between these two parts. It has another factor that organizations need to consider costs. In today's budget tightening environment, decreasing expenses requires accepting a lower level of efficiency and effectiveness. The goal is to determine the point at which decreasing efficiency and effectiveness is no longer acceptable before that point is reached.

It brings this question : How to apply facility management knowledge to rise efficiency and effectiveness in order to improve quality standard of service to satisfy consumers' needs in short time? Such as school's facilities service case. What factors can influence student's level of satisfaction with regards to higher educational facilities services? It seems that any school's facilities will influence its students how to satisfy its education service indirectly. Because they need often to go to school to learn. So, any school's facilities, e.g. classrooms, computer rooms, libraries, toilets, lecture halls, canteens, sport and entertainment centers, research laboratories, school car parks, student enquiry counters, all these places to the school's any students will attend. So, how raise schools' facilities improvement to satisfy students' learning needs in the school's any locations which will have help to influence it student individual satisfaction level to the school's service, instead of every teacher individual teaching performance service to the school's students.

For any service organizations , such as hotels, restaurant, financial institutions, retail stores and hospitals etc. The physical environment can influence how customers' evaluation of their service. Due to service has intangible nature, so customers will rely on evaluate service quality.

Any higher education institutions are education service providing organizations. They need have comfortable and enjoyable educational environment to be provided to the students to attend the school's any places in order to meet whose learning expectations and studying experience needs. So, the school's facility management will be one factor to influence student's learning satisfaction when they expect to attend the school's any locations or places to let them to feel the school's learning environment have good facility management feeling.

In fact, if the school has comfortable classrooms or lecture halls educational environment to let its students to feel, it will bring assistance to raise their learning satisfactory feeling. So, comfortable learning facility management environment is one kind of school's facility service characteristics, it includes intangibility, perishability, inseparability and variability. So, they are every student individual learning feeling when they are attending to the school's any learning locations. So, school's facility management service feeling will influence whether they expect to choose this school to study. If the school's facility management learning environment is more comfortable and teaching facilities are better to compare other schools' facilities. Then, it will have possible to attract many students to choose this school to study. Such as any educational organizations, instead of the teachers ( lecturers and professors) whose educational level is influence students number. The university's building environment will influence students' learning feeling, when they attend in the university. The facilities include laboratories, lecture theatres an offices, but also residential accommodations, catering

facilities, sports and recreations centers because university students need have university life feeling to let them to fell the university can give welfare services , e.g. medical services, career guidance, sport entertainment, residential accommodation etc. service, instead of educational learning service in classrooms and lecture theatres. Hence, university's diversification facilities services are needed to satisfy university students to choose it to study, instead of university teacher's educational performance.
When one student can enroll the university to study from secondary education institution. The admitted student will usually consider two aspects to decide to choose the university to study. One aspect is the academic programs, of sequence of courses choices and the another aspect is the university's facilities whether they can satisfy their university life need, e.g. library, dorms, bookstore, food canteen , gym's sport entertainment, education technological facilities in the classrooms and lecture theatres to let the students to feel the university's teaching facilities are achieved his/her learning demand.
So, these two factors ( teaching and learning and facilities) are linked to each other to influence student's total school learning experience and attitude towards a particular institution and this is termed as value chain in the student's learning process in the university. Hence, student individual evaluation variables will include teaching staff, teaching method, enrolment and facility enough supply actual service need.
However, the university's facilities, such as any residential accommodation, canteen, library , classroom, lecture theatre, sport gym, entertainment center will be their useful facilities need to satisfy their learning, entertainment and eating ,even living need in residential accommodation in the school's learning life experience every day. If one student chooses to live in the university residential accommodation . All of his/her learning and eating and living time and spending will be calculated to the university's any facilities to let him/her to feel it can provide enough facilities to let him/her to enjoy.
Hence, the facility management factor, such as overall campus environment, library, laboratory, classroom, lecturer theatre size and facility supply of on campus accommodation, welfare right service, parking areas, cafeteria , sport center etc. They will be every students facilities service needs from the university supplies choice. So, any university ought not neglect how to improve itself university's space area facilities to achieve satisfy their needs after they choose this university to study. Hence, any

university's facility management will influence how the student's satisfactory learning service feeling when he/she chooses the university to study.

In conclusion, better facility management will attract more students to choose the university to study. Otherwise, worse facility management will not attract more students to choose to study the school. Hence, it seems that the school's facility management factor has relationship to influence student's satisfactory feeling, instead of teacher individual teaching performance factor to the school.

- Property facility management influences householder buying behavior

One new property's low price is attractive factor to influence property buyer individual preference choice. Does the new individual's facility management factor influence the property buyer's preference choice decision, if the property buyer feels its facility management is better than other similar properties, even it's price is higher than other properties. I shall indicate some cases to analyze this possibility as below:

Some properties' facility management service quality has possible to create true value for any property buyers when they consider the calculation ingredients to make decision whether to new property has higher value to choose to buy. The factors may include: price, natural environment, transportation tools convenient available, shopping centers supplies, the neighour quality, and the property's internal facility management etc. factors.

In fact, car or house purchase buyers, they have similar behaviors. It is that car's buyers will consider the car's machines whether they are safe to drive on roads, instead price, manufacture loyalty factors. It is possible that the car's machines quality factor will be preference to any car buyers when they make preference decisions to choose which brand its cars are the suitable. However, if the car's brand is famous and its appearance beautiful and price is cheap. But the car consumer feels its machine qualities are unsafe to let the driver to drive on road. Then, the car's poor machine quality factor will influence the car buyer's decisions to choose to buy this car. It can influence the car buyer individual car purchase decision.

The car buyer's behavior is similar to property buyer's behavior. Although, the new property price is cheap, good neigh ours are living near to the new property's location, shopping centers and transportation tools are available to near to this new property's area. But if the property buyers' feels its facility management is poor quality to compare other similar properties.

Then, the poor quality of facility management factor will have possible to influence the property buyers whose final buying decision to choose to buy this new property. It brings this question: How and why can the facility management poor quality factor influence property consumers' preference choice?

In general, all property consumers won't know whether the new property's facility management is good or bad quality , they need to spend time to visit to the new property in order to observe whether its internal facility is satisfactory to his/her acceptable level. In simple, their purchase decision will regard to how to allocate household budget, how the household's economic resources are influenced, e.g. for travelling, visits to restaurants, comparing the different similar types of property product groups, e.g. apartments or houses or houses of a givn size data. For example, if one property's room(s) size is (re) small to compare other kind similar product type of room(s) size. Although the prior property's price is cheaper to compare to the later properties. But, if some property buyers hoped the property has large room(s) size, then the later larger room(s) size which will be possible to some property buyer's preference choice. Even, their property price is more expensive to compare the smaller room(s) size of properties. Thus, the property's room size which will be one major factor to influence property buyers' purchase decision. room's size had relationship to facility management issue. Moreover, if the room's quality and design is attractive, then it will bring more attractive to persuade some property buyers to choose to buy them to live in preference.

Hence, whether the new property is good durable product feeling which will influence householder's choice. If the householder feels the new property has long term durable life to avoid to spend much maintenance expense when they have been living in the new property for a long term period. They will believe it has better facility management, quality to let them to live longer time and the most importance is that they do not need to spend any maintenance expense , due to the property 's any internal facilities are damaged easily.

The external factors may include: culture, reference groups, family, social class and demography of lifestyle as well as internal factors may include: feelings, past property buying and living experience , property knowledge, motivation of the property buyer individual psychology. These both factors can influence any property buyer individual decision making process to do final house purchase behavior. However, internal factors, such as: property knowledge of facility management and property living experience, e.g. how to evaluate to choose to buy the property , due to the property buyer's past living experience for the past property's facilities whether its facilities can satisfy its property buyers' comfortable living needs. This internal factor will be more important to influence any property buyer's property purchase final decision. If he/she feels whose prior old property's facilities are satisfactory. Then, he/she will compare this new property and old property's facilities to decide whether this new property is value to buy. So, the old property's facility will be the measurement standard to compare his/her next new property purchase choice. So, the property purchaser will compare these new and old property's property facilities product knowledge to similarities among property alternative which will influence his/her final decision to choose to buy the new property to live.

It seems that property low price factor must not guarantee to attractive many property buyers' choice. Otherwise, it is assumed that many property buyers like rent or buy to live the property for themselves for long term intention. There are less property buyers expect to sell the first property to earn profit intention. So, they will usually consider whether the property is long term durable product to avoid to pay maintenance expense when they had been living in the property in long term.

Some factors that taking consideration are proximity to the specific location, housing prices, developer's brand, the payment scheme, reference group, which are not the main factors to influence any property buyer individual choice. Because property buyer's need is that the property has good facilities to supply to them to live, e.g. good heater equipment can provide hot water to them to bath in winter or good air conditioners can provide cold temperature to let them to feel cool comfortable feeling in summer in their homes. Good electric tools facilities , when they have need to use electricity in safe environment at home, e.g. car park accessibility facility , level of security facility , surface area facility and housing types, bedroom, bathroom facilities, quality of housing manufacturing raw material, house design , house durable guarantee, speed of complaint responsiveness, specification accuracy, confirmation of building plan service, showing legal file property purchase process service, finance instalments process assistance, speed of responsiveness, officers' skills of presentation. All of above these concern property facility management issues will influence any property buyers' final choice to decide whether the property is value to buy. So, facility management will influence property purchaser individual final decision in possible.

● Hotel facilities influence hotel consumer choice

Travellers choose hotel to live. They will consider price, room comfortable feeling, hotel location , gum sport or entertainment service facility supplies , hotel room booking service etc. factors to decide whether the hotel can achieve every traveller individual minimum living need. However, whether hotel facilities factor will be the main factor to influence travellers' living needs. How and why do travellers consider hotel facilities whether are enough supply or facilities of quality to satisfy their demand to cause their living choice to the hotel final decision.

Usually, hotel's customers won't plan to live too long time, e.g. more than three months in the hotel. Because they are travelling aim. It will bring this question: Does hotel facilities quality consider to influence their hotel living choice if the traveller is short-term traveller to the country? However , some travellers who have effort to spend money to live high class hotels, even their journey is short trip. Hence it seems that short trip , hotel living reason can not influence the high class hotel travellers' living comfortable demand to the high class hotel room. Hence , the high class hotel room's facility management quality is also needed high performance. Even, when they need to eat breakfast, lunch , dinner in the high class hotel canteens or playing any sport equipment, or gum equipment or wathching movie in the hotel's small cinema room . They must need high class hotel can supply more entertainment, restaurant , sport facilities to satisfy their comfortable needs in the high class hotel. Moreover, they must consider safety issue when they are living in the high class hotel. So, thy must demand the hotel have enough five fright equipment in their rooms, or corridors and the stairs to let them can leave the dangerous locations to arrive the most safe locations immediately when the hotel has fire accident occurrence in any where . So, it ensures that the high class hotel's customers must ensure the high class hotel's facilities can satisfy their any one of above these needs before they decide to live this high class hotel.

In fact, high class hotel's room price must be more expensive to compare the low class hotel. So, it explains why high class hotel's consumers will need the hotel has safe and good quality of facilities to let them to feel it is one reasonable price, safe , good service and good facilities' high class hotel to live. Usually, when the traveller arrives the country to travel, the travelers chooses the hotel to live, it is whose first time visit in common. So, he/she ought consider that the hotel environment seems it is good or bad to let the traveller to select to live. If the hotel's facility environment is new and beauty and design colorful to let the first time travellers to feel. Then, it is possible that good facilities environment can influence the first time travellers to select to live, even the hotel's room price is more expensive to compare other similar hotels in the travelling living places. Hence, it explains why hotel facilities can influence traveller individual room booking choice. When he/she is the first time to visit the hotel to select whether to live or not.

- How and why facility management can influence workplace productivity to bring customer satisfaction

Facility management is one part of manufacturers or retailers as their productivity in workplace as their input and functionalistics within physical environment. In fact, facility management in workplace may include: site selection, property disposal, site acquisition, workplace space allocation, space inventory, space forecasting facility management, interior furniture change planning, interior furniture installation, moving maintenance, inventory, design evaluation, employment satisfaction evaluation plan, external maintenance and breakdown maintenance, preventive maintenance, landscape maintenance, energy space facility management, hazardous waste disposal, capital , operating furniture budgeting. So, it seems that one workplace considered whether the workplace's facility is enough to let employees to work in order to raise efficiency and improve productive performance more easily. Then, it will bring this question:

- How and why workplace facility management can influence consumer individual satisfaction?

Strategic FM delivery is essential for business survival. I shall explain why for delivery is important to influence customer satisfaction. In business process view point, an effective and meaningful service to their customer , i.e. the user. For logistic industry, the product's delivery time will influence when the product can be sent to the user's arrival destination. If the product is delayed to sent to the user's home or office or any location destination. The reason is because the logistic product sender has no efficient facility management (FM) arrangement in its warehouse . Then, its warehouse lacks efficient (FM), which will cause users to feel its delivery service is poor and they will complain its delivery service staffs. Then, they will find another delivery service company to replace its service. So, it explains that logistic industry's warehouse (FM) service arrangement can raise efficient time to send any products to their customers in order to let they feel satisfactory service. For example, Amazon online logistic company's warehouse has applied artificial intelligence robotic tools to assist warehouse workers to arrange the different kinds of products to deliver to the right shelves . Then, the warehouse robotics will follow their right product shelves locations to follow the right products to deliver to US domestic or overseas product buyers in the short time and it can avoid the wrong products to deliver to the wrong buyers' risk. Also, the (AI) delivery tools can raise time efficiency to assist Amazon warehouse workers to reduce their work load, and tried to work in large warehouse environment. Although, its warehouse's area is large, the (AI) tools facility can help them to deliver the different products to different shelves in the right locations , e.g. exact product number and the kinds of product to be delivered to the right country' client's shelf location in the warehouse. Also, it implies FM is very important to influence Amazon warehouse delivery efficiency and avoiding delivery wrong occurrence chance. For example, the shelf location belongs to US domestic customers, or the shelf location belongs to Japan customers, or the shelf location belongs to Hong Kong customers, or any other Asia or Western countries' different customers' locations. The warehouse's facility needs have different countries' shelves enough space to put and it also need enough space to let the (AI) tools, robotic delivery workers and human workers both to walk to different shelves locations easily and the different countries' shelves number needs to be calculated accurate. For example, it has how many client number will buy Amazon's the kind product per day. If it has above 5,000 to 10,000 China clients to buy the kind of product. Then, it will need to make judgement how many shelves are placed in the warehouse. So, it can avoid to lack enough shelves to put any different kinds of products to prepare to delivery to China clients in efficient time and it won't avoid to delay to deliver to their homes or offices or any locations in China.

Hence, such as Amazon logistic case, it explains why warehouse's space shelves number and area or locations facility management can influence workers or (AI) delivery tools how to move convenient and avoiding the delivery to the customer's wrong destination chance occurrence and shortening time to deliver products to its clients efficiently. Then, due to the delivering time is shorten and the wrong delivery destination's occurrence chance is also reduced , even it can avoid to deliver the product to wrong client's destination occurrence. Then, the logistic firm's clients will feel more satisfactory to its product sale delivery service and their complaints will be avoided. Hence, it explains effective warehouse (FM) space management service arrangement is essential to any logistic businesses nowadays.

- Facility management brings departmental benefits

Why do organizations need have facility management (FM) service? As above examples indicate that (FM) can improve workplace environment facilities, e.g. warehouse environment to let workers to raise efficiencies or improve performances, even it can influence consumers to raise satisfactory to it's services indirectly, also it can help organizations' equipment to be used long term to cause old and are needed to spend expenditure to maintenance or change new equipment in order to improve better quality . So , it can assist organizations to avoid to spend more expenditure for new equipment purchase or maintenance. All these issues will be facility management service's benefits to an organizations, which can concern raising customers' service satisfaction, raising efficiency or improving productive performance, raising productivity, reducing equipment or property maintenance or new alternation much of expenditure spending, office or warehouse or any workplace space planning arrangement .

However, every organization will need a facility manager or manage whose team effectively . When a facility manager begins to apply FM techniques to solve business problems. The case for FM is made. It is a simple matter of demonstrating a qualified return on the investment required. Every organization's success, FM operation of three key activities: they include: needing a proper understanding of the organization's needs, wants, drivers and goals and knowing when needs to review its changing circumstances, developing an effective facilities solution o support the organization's needs, wants , property drives and contribute to achieve its goals both short term and long term, achievement of reliable delivery of that solution in a managed, measured manner.

So, it bring one question: What are the influential factors to be followed the right direction to FM manager's strategic FM operational decision? The influencing factors may include: ownership, governance sector, complexity and perhaps of most significant, the size of the organization's property portfolio.

In fact, major occupiers feel FM service need, they are large corporate organizations and public service organizations. Their aims usually are to raise. The most marginal improvement in efficiency or effectiveness, these aims are the great significance. Major property occupiers will already have a facilities department or individuals performing the FM function with another department like property, finance or human resource, sale and marketing's facilities.

Usually these FM need occupiers who will encounter this problem: How can apply FM service systems and processes to be developed to improve reliable service delivery making use of the economies of scale, not suffering because of the size of the problem. This question will be facility manager individual concerning question: How to apply (FM) technique to solve the improvement reliable service delivery making use of the economics of scale problem for whose organization?

In reality much of external facilities management benefits to organizations, instead of raising efficiency, improving performance, raising productivity, reducing maintenance expenditure, e.g. energy saving, reducing natural resource waste, increasing local employment, improving supply chain management are all elements of the FM contribution to every organization's need. Hence are the work life balance argument and provision of an effective and safe working environment that supports why some organizations feel need (FM) service to support their organizational development.

Moreover, on cost benefit of space saving efficient view point, space service cost reduction is a key driver for all organizations and the medium, or large sized players will benefit directly from a well coordinated facilities strategy. For example, application FM technique to help warehouse or office space area to save 50% space vacancy to let employees can move easily or putting enough furniture or equipment or many stocks can be putted in warehouses . So, paying more rent expenditure to rent or purchasing another new warehouse or office to satisfy workers or employees' working environment to be better need. If the organization has effective (FM) technique, then it has enough space vacancy to supply to the increase stocks number to be putted inside in warehouse and it can let workers to move safety in available to let staffs to move easily and equipment have enough space to be stored in the limited warehouse space problem.

For greater space savings benefits will bring either long term renting or buying of increasing offices or warehouse number expenditure problem to any organizations, when the organizations' cost or renting or buying accommodation probably accounting for 60 to 70% of total occupancy cost . So a strategic program to release space or the prevent the acquisition of moves can be the most significant consideration to any facility manager, with between 40% and 60% of the workplaces are unoccupied in most offices or warehouses at any given moment in time.

Hence, how to apply (FM) technique to save space occupied areas for employment moving or stocks or equipment saving need in offices or warehouses. This issue will be any facility managers' seeking methods to solve problem. However, the important major advantage of facility management to organizations is that the application of management principle to keep the organization's property assets with the aim of maximizing their potentials. Thus, any organizations' facilities have become important, due to the property facilities' worth will increase if the organization's facility management technique can protect the organization's facilities have good performance. Then, the organization's maintenance expenditure will reduce and it won't need to spend expenditure to buy any new facilities to replace old facilities , due to they often damage factor when they are used old.

In conclusion, it explains why effective FM combines resources and activities can raise work environment improvement, which is essential to the raising employee performance aim. For hotel living service case example, this industry must need have good facility management service because hotels must need to fully equipped in term and facilities for effectiveness to satisfy hotel living clients' demand , hotels ought need good facilities asset management style lead to effectiveness in service delivery, there are benefit derivable from the adoption of facilities management from which other hotels can learn from for their effective operations. Hence, it explains why effective FM can bring benefits to hotels' properties to be more comfortable, beautiful appearances to attract many hotel customers to choose to live the hotel. Because hotel's building industrial kitchens, rooms facilities, equipment , halls of categories, restaurant facilities, gum sport entertainment centers' facilities, fans, elevators, lifts, electrical installation, escalators, baking equipment, recreational facilities, including golf courses which will be important factors to influence hotel clients' comfortable living feeling, if the hotel can keep its all facilities in the best living environment often. Then, it can raise chance to attract many hotel customers to choose it to live. So , hotel industry has absolute need to implement effective FM strategy to keep its properties more attractive to satisfy its clients' living needs.

Instead of hotel industry, logistic transportation industry also needs effective facilities management in warehouse, because of the logistic company's warehouse 's facilities are good, then it will assist to raise employee individual efficiency in the safe and system shelve stored facilities in workplace environment and improving performance.

Consequently, it will bring the shorten time to deliver any products to clients to avoide the delaying time delivery in order to let customers to feel more satisfactory to their services. In simple, it seems that some industries need have effective facilities management techniques to help them to bring long term customer satisfactory feeling, worker individual efficiency raising and performance improvement benefits. Hence, it seems facility management techniques' demand will be increased to some industries in popular in the future because it has help to raise employee individual efficiency , productive performance and client individual satisfactory level consequently.

Facility management how influences employee Psychology to raise productive efficiency

- How to impact of workplace management on well-being and productivity

In facility management strategy, design can lead promotion, the value of offices that are enriched, particularly including warehouses, shopping centers to raise their market value. Moreover, effective organizations, such as raising powering workers when giving the effective design of office space. I assume that a good design of an interior office workspace environment seems a psychological department to influence staff individual emotion to bring positive power in order to raising productive efficient influence, such as in a commercial city office. So, it brings this question: How workspace management strategy can impact on staff's working behaviors in office.

In fact, office tasks general include various forms of productivity, e.g. information processing, information management and any clerical tasks by computerization. Hence, office productivity concerns how to influence each office white color worker applies computers to work in office. The office space can impact on white color workers‘ performances in these several aspects: feeling of psychological comfort, organizational physical comfort and job satisfaction and productivity, efficiency. So, it seems that office workspace design strategy can influence white color workers' working behavior and attitude and performance indirectly.

The office space management includes: how to removal from the workspace of everything except the materials required to do the job at hand, how tight managerial control of the workspace, and how to implement standardization of managerial practice and workspace design. So, these key ideas will influence how each white color worker's efficiency and productivity in office working environment.

For this office space design situation, a large unseparated small space size's space design can accommodate more people and so brings itself to economies of scale. As a result, space occupancy can be centrally managed with minimal disruptive interference from office workers. Indeed, many businesses now adopt a clean and fresh air office working policy because they have more employees than they have spaces at which they can work. This desks are either taken on a first -come first -served basis. ( hot desking) or can be booked in advance. So , when a company has many employees need to work in a small space working environment. It must concern how to let staffs to feel more comfortable in order to reduce high psychological pressure to work in this uncomfortable working environment. Hence, it explains why workspace design can impact on office workers' performance in some offices. All these issues are assumed that empowering workers to manage and have input into the design of their own workspace, then the effective office or any working places space management will enhance wellbeing to bring workers' positive emotions and improving productivity. I also assume the space working environment design have relationship of these depend variable factors to influence office worker individual productive efficiency. The variable factors may include psychological comfort, organizational comfortable, job satisfaction, physical comfort and productivity.

However, office furniture , facilities will influence office white color workers' performance ,e.g. the room size whether is big or small for manage office worker, a high backed, comfortable leather chair is needed for office staffs to sit down to let more comfortable, the door and most of the walls need glass, the office room environment needs have sea-grass rug beneath the desk covering the immediate working area, the office also needs have plants and pictures, mail boxes, telephone and computer facility is needed. When one staff needs to send email or phone call or send letters or deliver documents conveniently. These office elements are essential in order to increase physical well-being and feeling of satisfaction to white-color workers. Hence, geren office and office working space design management is needed in order to influence white color workers' productive efficiency in long term.

● Effective workspace design can influence communication to raise productivity

Office white-color workers often need communication between their managers, supervisors, and themselves. Office communication extends from the way that a user experiences a service. An effective office communication can bring these benefits; Providing positive influence on decision making by presenting a strong point of view and developing mutual understanding, delivering efficient decisions and solutions by providing accurate , timely and relevant information, enabling mutually benefit solutions, building health relationships by encouraging trust and understanding between the high level, middle level and low level staffs.

Effective office communication needs to clearly communicate its nature and purpose. Good communication ensures that all service staffs are sending out the same messages. Communication is also important for ensuring the service understands what users requires and why he/she talks about understanding users' needs and communication receiver can have effective communication skill to understand what he/she needs the another to do and the another knows he/she ought how to work by his/her task demand. Then, it will shorten much time. If the office has 100 staffs need to often communicate. However, if the office has good space management arrangement to let every staff can communicate easily and walks to anywhere to find the right staff to communicate conveniently. Then, they can spend less time to waste on communication issue. Then, their productive efficiency will be also influence to raise.

● Health and safe work environment influences productivity

Is a health and safe work environment can raise employees' work productive efficiencies indirectly? How and why it can influence employees' productive performance? Some occupations' working environments are easier to occur occupational accidents and diseases risks when the workers are working in the high health and safe risk's working environment. Hence, health and safety issues at these high life risk workplaces can be considered as a key to influence employees' overall performance. The idea that health and safety management program have positive impacts on productivity.

When one worker needs to work in this high risk of health and safe workplace. He/she will consider whether how his/her work behavior will bring suffer serious injuries for shorter or longer time from work related causes in possible. So, he/she will work carefully in order to avoid injuries occurrence chance. It is possible to influence whose work performance, low productive efficiency in order to avoid any occupational accident occurrences in the dangerous workplace.

If the employee feels danger when he/she needs to stay in the warehouses stable location to work often. Then his/her absenteeism day number will have increase, due to he/she feels that workplace accidents and occupational illnesses and can lead to permanent occupational disability, when he/she needs to attend the stable dangerous workplace to work in the warehouse. Hence, he/she will choose to apply holiday often in order to avoid injuries chance increasing when he/she needs to stay in the stable workplace location in the warehouse. It explains why companies increase need qualified, motivated and efficient workers who are able willing to contribute activity to technical and organizational innovations. So, healthy workers working in healthy working conditions are thus an important precondition for organization to work smoothly and productively. Hence, a health and safety workplace environment can bring these benefits to organizations as below:

It can prevent among workers of learning work, due to health problems caused by their working conditions, the protection of workers in their employment from risks resulting from factors adverse to health. The placing and maintenance of the worker in an occupational, environment adapted to his/her physiological and psychological, capabilities, mental , physical and social conditions of workplace and adequacy of health and safety measures are needed to any employees in order to bring positive impact not only on safety and health performance, but also productivity. However, identifying and quantifying these effects will difficult to be measured as well as the quality of a working environment has a strong influence on productive efficiency.

For one aviation air plane manufacturing factory, where workplace can environment will have high risk to occur occupational related accidents to cause employees' injuries. Hence, employees will be consider themselves safety when they need to work in high accident occurrence workplace. The bad consequence will influence such as absenteeism day number increases, leaving this kind of aviation air plane job of employees number increases, low productive efficiencies, due to there are many proficient experienced employees who choose leave this kind of high accident risk occupation. Consequently, any high accident occurrence risk workplace environment , employers need have good safe and health strategy to let their employees have confidence to work in this kind of high risk accident occurrence workplace if they expect low productive efficiencies effect is caused by high accident occurrence risk workplace factor.

- Employee personal empowerment factor influences performance

Is empowerment one good method to raise employee himself/herself effort in order to improve productive efficiency in organizations. Empowerment often consists of support groups, e.g. management's effective leading or trainer's training, course educational opportunities. Employee self-management education may impact to improve himself/herself job performance, e.g. increased self-empowerment, self-management skills and job treatment satisfaction.

Only organization's empowerment strategy can lead every employee to through improvements in the employee individual decision making efficacy, improvement task performance behavior by reviewing whether what are the employee himself/herself errors when he/she encounters any job difficulties, after he/she reviewed his/her task error and his/her manager feels his/her performance can be improved. Then, it can enhance satisfaction with the employee and his/her manage relationship and better access and raising efficient performance in possible . Hence, empowerment can let every employee to discover whether what task related difficulties he/she faces or encounters every day. When his/her manager give ideas to let him/her to know how he/she ought review his/her task error in a supportive education working environment, it aims to let the low performance or low inefficient employees to increase confidence to continue work in the organization. So, the employee turnover number will decrease , if the inefficient employees can feel that they can attempt to solve their task-related difficulties successfully by themselves. So, empowerment can increase social support, leadership and advocacy development , it has resulted in greater employee individual performance psychological empowerment, autonomy and authority to let every employee to feel to achieve to improve themselves efficiencies more effectively in any organizations.

For hospital organizational efficiency measurement empowerment influence case, how empowerment can influence hospital's efficiency raising? Efficiency is one of the most important indicators of hospital performance evaluation. Why do some hospitals' efficiencies poor? It is possible that mis management of resources, lacking health plan packages, e.g. coverage of basic health insurance, poor quality of care service, more payment demand for out-of pocket payment , quality of primary healthcare , healthcare providers neglect to concern potentially about service efficiency issues.

In fact, low hospital efficiency is the major problem to influence patients number to choose the hospital's medical service, e.g. when the hospital often needs patients to queue to wait for doctor's care medical service. They need to wait on hour at least or more when the hospital has many patients are waiting for its medical service. Then, it will influence them to choose another hospital to replace it , if the hospital 's medical fee is cheaper and it does not need patients to spend long time to queue to wait its medical service. So, service efficiency is important to influence patients consumers' positive or negative feeling to choose the hospital's medical service. Even, the hospital's doctors are famous or they own many medical working experience, if patients often need long time to queue to wait its medical service . Then, it will cause its patients number to be reduced .

These are variable factors to influence the hospital's inefficiency. They may include old speed hospital information system and medical record documents based on inefficient input and output variables. Input variables may include the number of hospital admissions, the number of nurses and the number of available beds. The output variable may include average of length of stay and bed turnover interval inefficient paper document record in the patient record administrative department.

However, to evaluate the hospital efficiency indicators may include technical, scale and managerial efficiency the out-based data development analysis approach and the variable returns to scales assumption was used. Based on the out-input based approach ( maximizing the factors of medical service production), to increase efficiency the organization should be increased outputs.

Hence, when the hospital has good efficient evaluation method to measure every staff's performance , e.g. ward administrative clerk, patient registration clerk etc. Then, it can base on an put-put based approach and assuming a variable return to scale, there is capacity to improve technical efficiency and managerial efficiency in these any hospital different administrative units without an increase in costs and use of same amount of resources in relation to technical efficiency and managerial efficiency and scale efficiency of hospital's administrative labour individual task.

In conclusion, factors, such as modification of managerial practices, use of modern technologies tailored to the cultural, political and formulation of clinical guidelines to standardize the medical processes in order to reduce medical errors and increase the empowerment of health care buyers ( insurance organizations), length of stay, management hospitals by specialist managers, administrative requirement, full time hospital physicians, limiting the authority of decision makers in relation to the recruitment of staff in accordance with the needs of the hospital and optimal allocation of beds, conducting economic evaluations and the type of hospitals ownership had an impact on the hospital efficiency significantly. By increasing the number of beds the hospitals efficiency decreases. Otherwise, optimizing the bed size can increase hospital efficiency.

However, the important factor to raise hospital overall staffs efficiencies empowerment is needed to let every hospital staff to review whether why and how himself/herself error is caused and he/she needs to review his/ her errors to avoid to be caused from any negligence again in order to avoid patients' complaints again or reduce the patients' complaint number aims. So, empowerment of staff himself/herself error review factor is one major raising efficient good method.

● How organizational facility environment factor influences new and old employees long term performance

In psychological view ,in any organization's environments, they depend on the types of social and physical environment factors to influence employee personal behavior how to be caused. How and why does the employee select to do whose behavior? If the organization's physical and social environment is better, then it may influence its employees select to work hard. It is possible to bring productive efficient raising consequence.

In fact, when one new employee enters the new organization to work, he/ she needs to learn how to adapt to cooperate with the organization's old employees to work together. So, it explains how and why organization's physical and social environment can influence the new employee individual motivation of behavior to work. In regarding new employee individual behavior by new employer's culture expectations as well as new employees need to adapt of actions that are likely to productive positive outcomes and generally discard those that bring unrewarding or puniishing outcomes by new employer's treatment.

However, anticipated material and organization environment co-operation outcomes between the new employee and the organization old employees' cooperation, which are not the only kind of incentives that influence the new employee behavior of the new employee actions were performed only on behalf of anticipated external rewards and punishment from the new employer. In actuality, the new employee concerns considerable self-direction in the face of the new employer's organization's old employees competing influences. However, when the new employee has adopted an intension and an action plan. When, he/she works in the new organization for a period, he/she can't simply not back and visit for the appropriate performances to appear.

The new employee's new job goal will be motivated by enlisting self-evaluative engagement in activities rather than directly. By making self-evaluation conditional on matching personal new job standards, the new employee will give direction to his/her new job pursuits and create self-inventions to sustain his/her efforts for new job goal attainment. The new employee will select to do new task behavior to give him/her self-satisfaction and a sense of pride and self worth for the new job chance.

Efficacy beliefs also play a key role in shaping the new employees' behavior to do their tasks by influencing the types of new organization's activities and working environments, the new employees choose to set into any factor that influences the employee's choice behavior can affect the direction of employee personal career development in the new organization. This is because the organizational working environment influences operating in the employee how to select working environments continue to work. Thus, by choosing and shaping the new organization's working environments, new employee can have a hand in what they expect.

In conclusion , when a new employee chooses the new organization to work. He/she must need to adapt the organization's new working environment. If he/she feels difficult to adapt or accept to the organization's new working environment, then he/she will be influenced to work inefficient or poor productive performance , due to he/she feels unhappy to work the new organization's working environment and the new organization's manager will dissatisfy his/her performance and complain or give verbal warning to dismiss him/her. Then, it will bring the poor consequence to let the organization's inefficient productive performance effect. If many new employees feel difficult to adapt to work in the new organization. Then, inefficient productive performance will be influenced to keep a long term. So, it implies that the organization will need to change its organizational culture in order to let many new employees can adapt and accept this new organizational culture to work happily if the organization expects new employees work to raise productive efficiency successfully.

● Raising efficient and effective
interview psychological methods

In human resource department, interviewing and selecting the most right applicants to do different kinds of positions, it is one part of HRM function. If the interviewer need to spend more time to interview to decide whom is the most right applicant to do the position in one day, e.g. 50 at least , even more applicants number as well as he/she can also make the more accurate personal selection decision to choose the most right applicant to do the position after the interview day. Then, the interviewing process needs to be avoided to spend more time to choose the most suitable applicant to do the position within the day. It is difficult to judge whether whom ought be the most right applicant to do the position, if there are more than 50 applicants , they are needed to be interview in the day. The consequence will bring HR department can spend extra time to do the interview task, but it can have enough staffs and time and resource to do other urgent or important task at the interview day. It will bring this question: How to apply psychological method to raise interviewer's efficiency to shorten to spend extra time to do interviewing tasks ? I shall explain some psychological methods to attempt to let interviewers have more confidence to select the most right applicant in short time as below:

1. Behavioral interview skill

The interviewer can apply the actual behavioral interview method to let the interviewee to answer how he/she deals the matters, he/she feels that it is the best decision in order to judge and analyze whether whom applicant is the most suitable to be selected, e.g. describing the situation, he/she needs or the task that he/she needs to accomplish. The situation may be from a previous job, any relevant event, describing the action he/she took and be sure to keep the focus on him/her , e.g. discussing a group project or effort in the team; explaining what results he/she achieved, what happen?

How did the event and what dis the applicant accomplishes? What did the applicant learn?

In the behavioral-based interview. the interviewer can need the applicant to attempt to explain examples clearly in order to judge whose analytical skill whether he/she is the suitable applicant to do the position. The interviewer may ask the applicant to identify some examples from whose post experience where he/she demonstrated top behaviors and skills that employers typically seek. To judge whether his/her examples should be totally positive, such as accomplishments or meeting goals, the other half should be situations that started at negatively , but either ended positively or he/she made the best of the outcome.

This behavioral interview test aims to review whether the applicant's every example answer, he/she can provide an appropriate description of how he/she demonstrated the desired behaviors. In the behavioral interview, the interviewer can attempt to judge whether the applicant has good imagine effort to mind any relatively small set of examples to respond to a number of different behavioral questions to satisfy the right example are applied to the right situations in the limited interview time. Hence, behavioral interview can let the interviewer to make more accurate analysis to judge whether whom applicant(s) has ( have) good analytical effort to solve any work-related situational problems in the most reasonable way or attitude in order to select whom is the most right applicant to do the position.

2. E-mail interviewing in qualitative research

E-mail interviewing is another good interview method to select right applicant to do the managerial level position. E-mail interviewing can be in many cases a viable alternative to face-to-face telephone interviewing. Internet-based qualitative research methods may include online personal interview and virtual focus groups. However, it brings two questions: What opportunities and challenges does online in depth interviewing present for collectively qualitative data? How can in depth e-mail interviews be conducted effectively?

The applicant targets may be the top-level manager, advertising executive , sales manager, human resource manager etc. management position applicants. They need to answer any complex or difficult interviewing question by email in the limited time, e.g. how to solve one case study problem , how to give recommendation to solve the situation problem. The interview participants may be recruited by tool/method of psychological test questions, the interview questions may be interview guide in a single e-mail and follow yp, length of email data collection period may be up to 10 weeks, the number of e-mail or follow up exchanges may be several number. The electronic formal and require little editing or formation before the applicants are processed for analysis all e-mail interviewing questions. So, they need to answer any managerial case study problem in limited time. It is one good managerial interview test method to evaluate whether whom applicant has the best analysis cffort in order to the managerial position, because they need to find the best solutions to give recommendations to attempt to solve any situational problems in any un predictive case study problems. For example, when the applicant or a focus group of discussion applicants whom need to spend the maximum half hours to give recommendations to discuss to solve one complex or difficult case study problem either between the interviewer and the another interviewee applicant or between the group of five to ten interviewees ( job applicants) themselves. Thus, after the interviewer sent the one case study question to let the applicants to know by every email channel. The interviewer needs to judger whether whom one applicant or one of the focus group applicants their recommendations are the most reasonable to solve the case study managerial situational problem within half hour to one hour. Then, the interviewer can make more accurate judgement to select whether whom has the best analytical effort to do the managerial position.

3. The effectiveness of motivational interviewing for young or older adult applicants selection process

How can apply case management skills to be effective to prepare any interview motivation? How to do the most effective and efficient to meet the objectives of the interview? Some interview techniques used may vary the based on the individuals involved in the interview. For an interview with the young age applicant more require a different approach than an interview with a senior adult applicant. The following are one pointers to assist with preparing for the interview as below:

Knowing the purpose of the interview and what needs to be accomplished . What is the expected outcome? Gathering all forms that need to be completed or signed having the interview and making list of questions that need to be asked, knowing the key facts and topics to be discussed, during the interview. Gathering factual information that may be helpful. Opening mind is needed in the whole interview process. Making an appointment for the interview and arranging sufficient time to set fully participate in the interview. Taking notes during the interview, let the participants know in general terms the reason notes are being made and how they will be used, opening ended questions invite the applicant to provide more information usually begin with other words who, what, where, how, asking one question at a time and keeping wording simple and specific, defining any terms that may be unfamiliar to the applicant , giving the interviewing participants in the interview an opportunity to ask their one questions or to clarify anything that was discussed, closing the interview with a review of the information discussed and facts gathered, reviewing any follow-up that is to be done by the case manager or others involved in the interview.

In an efficient and effective interview, the interviewer needs have good body and spoken word communication to the interviewee or the position applicant. Because a good communication can reduce waste time or avoid the extended longer interview time if the interviewer can make good communication to impact good message to let the applicant to understand what is the mean to his/her interview question. What he/she wants to know, the total impact of a message includes ,e.g. 7 % verbal ( words), 38% vocal /volume, pitch, rhythm etc. and 55% body movements ( mostly facial expression). The interviewer's body and verbal behavior can make more clear message to let the interviewee( job applicant) to understand what answers are he/she wants to know mostly. Hence, an efficient and effective interview can let the interviewer to control and manage the whole interview to evaluate whether whom the applicants' answers or feedbacks are more reasonable to be acceptable to be better to compare other applicants to apply the position more accurately.

- What is efficient achievement of technological inputs factor in construction industry

What is organizational efficient raising actual mean? I shall indicate construction industry case to explain technological factor is the major factor to assist construction organization to raise efficiency. For construction industry example, improved productivity could be attributed to advances in and increased usage of information technologies, increased competition, due to globalization and changes in workplace and organizational structures.

For construction efficiency, the construction process can reduce waste in coordinating labor and in managing, moving and installing materials, loss avoidance. It can achieve efficient aim. The construction productive efficient concept can be defined efficiency improvements as ways to cut waste and labor. So, one construction organizational efficient achievement means that it implemented through the capital facilities sector, these activities would significantly advance construction efficiency and improve the quality, timeliness, cost effectiveness of projects in construction processes.

On construction industry technological factor influence hand, it can influence that construction productivity how well, how quality, and at what cost buildings and infrastructure can be constructured, directly affects prices for homes and consumer products and the robustness of the national economy. Construction productivity will also affect the outcomes of national efforts to renew existing infrastructure systems; to build new infrastructure for power from renewable to renew existing infrastructure systems; to build new infrastructure for power from renewable resources to develop high-performance " green building" and to remain competitive in the global market. If the construction organization expected to achieve effficient aim. It ought consider how to change in building design, construction and renovation and in building materials and materials recycling, will be essential to the success of national efforts to minimize environmental impacts, reduce overall energy use, and reduce greenhouse gas emissions.

However, construction industry analysts differ on whether construction industry productivity is improved by efficiency outcome. They indicate construction efficiency needs to reduce 25-50 percent waste in coordinating labour and in managing, moving and installing materials. This is the most minimum standard efficient achievement level to any construction organizations.

What are the factors influence efficiency to any construction organizations? An efficient construction task process is made possible by a range of information technological tools and applications, including computer-aided design and drafting, three and four dimensional visualization and modeling programs, laser scanning, cost-estimating and scheduling tools and materials tracking. So, high technological tool will assist to raise efficient construction process to any construction organizations. It can help them to shorten time and avoid materials waste and control cost effective estimation for any construction projects.

Effective use of interoperate technologies requires effective team cooperative processes and effective planning up front and this it can help overcome obstacles to efficiency created by process fragmentation.

Interoperable technologies can also help to improve the quality and speed of any construction project related decision making, integrate processes, managing supply chains, sequence work flows, improve data accuracy and reduce the time spent on data entry, reduce design and engineering conflicts and the subsequent need for rework, improve the life-cycle management of buildings and infrastructure.

All of these factors will influence whether the construction organization can implement efficiency in success. For example, interoperable techcholgies include legal issues, data-storage capacities and the need for " intelligent " search applications to sort quickly through thousands of data elements and make real-time information available for on-site decision making. How to improve job-site efficiency through more effective interfacing of people, processes, materials ,equipment, and information. The job site for a large construction project is a dynamic place, involving numerous contractors, subcontractors, trades people and labors, all of whom must require equipment, materials and supplies to complete their tasks. So, they need to know how to manage activities and demands to achieve the maximum efficiency from the limited available resources. Time, money, and resources will have possible to be wasted when projects are poorly managed, causing workers to have to wait around for tools and work crews are not on-site at appropriate time or when supplies and equipment are stored in complexity or difficulty, requiring that they can be moved multiple time ( time waste).

How to improve job site safety and improve the quality of projects, significantly cut waste? The use of automated equipment, e.g. for excavation and earthmoving operations, pip installation, concrete placement, and information technologies, e.g. radio-frequency identification tags for tracking materials personal digital assistants for capturing field data. These high technological tool can help any construction projects to raise efficiency to process improvements and the provision for real -time information for improved management at the job site.

Moreover, on mannal research and development tools hand, instead of data technological tools hand, any construction organizations also need to consider how to take a variety of forms: How to test field on a job site? How to arrange lecture shows in efficient way, seminrs, training and conference, and scientific laboratories time, human resource available arrangement, spending expenditure budget to finish. Moreover, effective performance mearements are enablers of innovation and of corrective actions throughout a construction project's life cycle. They can help any construction companies or organizations understand how processes led to success or failure, improvements or inefficiencies and how to use that knowledge to improve construction products , processes and outcomes of active projects.

The nature of construction projects, the industry itself, any construction organizations ought consider the construction working environment how to influence construction workers' emotions. For example, when the construction site is high levels, of noise, dust and airborne particles, adverse weather conditions,and other factors that can cause injuries and thereby reduce efficiency and productivity. New types of equipment can make an active physically easier to perform, easier to control, move precise , and safer for construction workers. Similarly, changes in materials can reduce the weight of construction components, make them easier to handle, move and install. Manufacturing building components off-site providers need more control conditions and allow for improved quality and precision in the fabrication of the component, One study that examined the relationship between changes in material technology and construction productivity based on 100 construction a related tasks, the study found that labor productivity for the same activity increased by 30 % at least when higher materials were used and labour productivity also improved when construction activites were performed using materials that were easier to install or were pre-fabricated. So, it seems material heavy can influence construction worker individual productive efficiency in site, if the material is higher , then the construction worker's productivity will be influenced to improve ( Goodrum et al. 2009).

Thus, the factors influence construction organization's efficiency. It focuses on whether the construction firm applies how advanced construction technologies to assist its construction workers to work as well as whether its construction environment can let workers to feel safe to avoid life danger or accident occurrence. When the workers do not worry about whose life safety as well as they can apply advanced construction technology to assist them to work. Then, their productive efficiencies ought need to be improved easily. Thus, facility management and advanced technology will be the main factor to raise construction workers' efficiencies.

CHAPTER SIX

# Technology how assists organizational development

Investing in office technology can bring what advantages

Management Science Dependency Theory Solves Macrosoft and IBM software cooperational success method

● Macrosoft or Microcorp and IBM software cooperational strategy

What is information technologic game strategy? How and why information technological game strategy can influence economic growth? I shall explain as below:

Nowadays, Macrosoft and Microcorp are the global information technological big companies. They own much market share in global information technological industry. Whether what factors influence they can still be global information technological products leaders. Why does computer software consumers still choose their products to compare other software products in preference? I suppose that Macrosoft and Microcorp, their hypothetical any software games have developed a clever new computer game that is certain to be very popular. Although Microcorp have the unique competitive advantage with its own software game engineers and compete against Macrosoft, but it can so it cheaper and better if it can hire any Macrosoft's software game engineers. So, in economic view, it needs to pay high salary ( higher cost) to hire Macrosoft's engineers ( labor), but Macrosoft's engineers can help Microcorp to invent any new kinds of software games to compete Macrosoft. Although, Microsorp needs to pay higher labor cost, but when it can raise its any software games' design and game playing methods to attract any game players. Then, these new and exciting software games can help it can bring many game entertainment players and then it can sell cheaper price to raise more attractive effort to win its competitor ( Macrosoft). So, higher software game designing engineers ( skill labor), their game designing effort will be the major factor to influence any one information technological companies in success. If one software designing company can employ one high software game designing effort profession to help it to design any kinds of attractive software games. Although, it may pay high salary ( labor cost), but it have much chance to attract many software game buyers to compare that if it pays less salary to employ one poor game software designing profession. Because the poor software game designing profession may need to spend long time to research how to design any kinds of attractive game software to excite game players' playing desires in this playing software game industry market. Long time research to the poor software game designer may be one none any reward to compensate to the software game designing firm when it needs to pay long time salary to employ him. Otherwise, if the software game designing firm can accept to pay higher salary to the higher software game designer, he will have higher chance to help it to design any more attractive software games to influence game players' playing game entertainment desires. So, any software game designing companies their game designers ( labor) must be the major factor to influence their business succeeds or fails in this software game entertainment market.

On the employing method hand, Microcorp can choose to include in its contracts with its software engineers that from working for another Macrosoft software company for a certain period of time if they resign from Macrosoft. A move such as this is sometimes called a preeptive move. Its propose is to alter its rivals' payoffs in order to alter their employing strategies. Preemptive moves are usually costly (high slaary), and this one is no exception. In its employment contracts makes Macrosoft a less attractive to let its old game software engineers want to leave their current employer, such as Macrosoft. As a result, Macrosoft must pay its software game designing engineers above the going market salary if it hopes their employment contracts can be continue between Macrosoft and its software game engineers.

Should Macrosoft must need to decide how to react. It can choose to fight Microcorp by aggressively advertising its game, which is costly high, but gives it a larger market share in the game player entertainment market, when Macrosoft had any one profession game software engineer(s) leave(s) his company and he/they change(s) to the another Microcorp software game designing company to work, or it can forego the expense of an advertisement campaign and simply share the market 50/50 with its major competitor, Microcorp to be partners.

Their competition has close relationship to influence economic growth because it will have many game players number to be increase if they can cooperate to be partners in success when they can design any new kinds of software game products to satisfy software game players' entertainment feeling. Otherwise, if they can not be one good partners and they only consider their every business benefits and neglect themselves business benefits. Then, their software playing games sale price can either to be reduced in order to attract any software game players when their software games can not be designed to have much new playing methods to attract many game players. Consequently, the GDP income to this software game entertainment market must reduce because any kinds of entertainment software games prices are reduced as well as the game players number is also decreasing. Due to they are the major software entertainment game suppliers in global. Any game players will only choose either Microcorp or Macrosoft to buy their any kinds of entertainment software game products to play majorly. So, their software game manufacturing and sale number must influence global GDP income increases or decreases in macro economy view. It implies that any countries technological software game industry's GDP income will depend on these both Microcorp and Macrosoft software game's cooperation relationship whether they have good or bad cooperation relationship. If their cooperation relationship is good, then they can manufacture high quality and attractive entertainment software games as well as raising sale price and exciting many game players' entertainment desires to achieve the increase to game players number aim more easily.

How to achieve their cooperation relationship more easier. I suppose that, in the software game entertainment industry, over its lifetime, the computer game will generate $500,000 in new income ( income minus production cost) for all the firms producing it or its clones. Macrosoft must pay its software engineers an additional $100,000 to get them to agree to accept a contract containing an anticompetition clause. It costs Microcorp $100,000 to develop the software if it can hire Macrosoft's engineers and $200,000 otherwise. Aggressive advertising costs Macrosoft $70,000 and has the effect of giving it a 80% market share if it restricts its engineers' employment and a 72% market share if it does not. So, the fall in total market share is caused by the fact that without some of Macrosoft's advertisements. If however, Macrosoft passively acquiesces to Microcorp's entry and shares the market, then both firms can still achieve a 50% market share fairly. Hence, they must need to achieve 50/50 market share if they hope to achieve the cooperation relationship in success. Otherwise, they will not achieve cooperation relationship in success.

However, the spending advertisement factor will also their cooperation chance in success. For example, it would be more realistic to recast the Software Game as one in which Macrosoft chooses how much to spend on advertising with sales depending continuously on the amount spent. Other examples of continuous cooperation choices may include: the productive capacity of an electrical power plant; the salary to offer a prospective employee; or the insurance premium to charge a prospective policyholder. So, the amount to any of these expenditure factor will influence whether they will decide to cooperate to sell their software games products in global game entertainment market.

How and why Macrosoft and Microcorp's cooperation can influence global economic growth? It is significant that Macrosoft and Microcorp both technological software game designing companies are global the largest firms, they are doing international software game trade business to many countries and they have large market share in the software entertainment game sale market. Aside from trade based on technological gaps and software game product cycles, software game entertainment industry is dynamic in nature or game players' entertainment taste will change any time in completely static in nature. That is, given the nation's game players' playing taste and game entertainment factor, such as game playing designing technological method and game player individual playing game taste both. We proceeded to determine the nation's comparative advantage and the gains from the different kinds of entertainment software game designing supply factor and the game player individual game taste changing factor. So, any nation's software game players number will depend on these both factors to influence whether their number will either increase or decrease in the year in this global software game entertainment market. However, these factors can be changed by time, technology usually can improve any software game playing methods and game player individual playing taste will also change any time. As a result, the nation's comparative advantage also changes over time, such as when the nation has many game players lose their interest to buy any software games to play, then the nation ought not only consider how to develop its software entertainment game in the technological industry, it is right time to research any other new technological industries to develop if it still hopes its GDP income can rise in the technological industry overall aspect. Such as dynamic trade theory is still in its infancy. However, our comparative statics analysis can carry us a long way in analyzing the effect on international trade resulting from changes in factor technology, and tastes over time, such as entertainment software game case.

The growth of factors of production will also influence the software game entertainment industry development, through time, a nation's population usually grows and with its size of its labor force , such as China and India. Similarly, by utilizing part of its resources to produce capital equipment, e.g. India needs to utilize its technological resources, technological engineers and technological material can need to be used to manufacture either new software game products or computers. But, its technological resources will be shortage ( both labor and technological material). So, many technological companies choose to apply more technological material and technological engineers to use much time and money to manufacture any new software game products. Then, these labor and material resources will be reduced to be spent time and material to manufacture any new computer products in the year. In this technological industry case, capital refers to all the man-made means of production, such as machinery, factories, communication and education and training of labor force, all of which greatly enhance the nation's ability to produce either computer products or software game products. So, the national will also continue to assume that it can experiencing economic growth is producing two commodities, such as software game and computer both kinds of technological products under the constant returns to scale. So, if India can not raise the rapid technical process to skill labor and supply technological material supplying number to satisfy to manufacture the enough software game and computer products to supply them to sell to any countries' playing game players and computer users every month. Then, its technological industry will lose many clients, due to it can not supply enough software games and computers number to sell to any countries.

Several empirical studies have indicated that most the increase in real per capita income in technological industrial nations is due to technical progress and much less to capital accumulation. However, the analysis of technical progress is much more complex than the analysis of factor growth because there are several definitions and types of technical progress, and they can

take place at different rates in the production of either or both commodities, such as software game and computer.
Technical progress is usually classified into neutral, labor saving , or capital saving. All technical progress , regardless of its types reduces the amount of both labor and capital required to produce any given level of output. So, if India could have good technical progress to raise its technological labor skill and reducing the technological material to be used to manufacture the software games and computers. Then, it will have chance to keep the maximum manufacturing level number to software game and computer products as the same time.

Why ought any kinds of businesses need to invest in technology to offices when businessmen began to do businesses? The reason is simple, such as any offices need email to communicate to let different departments staffs can contact to do any tasks in short time. So, email can replace telephone calling communication channel between departments in offices. Moreover, for paper files, electronic files may replace to keep to save any office confident documents or general memos, letters, reports etc. documents. So, paper printing number may reduce. Even some businesses began to sell their products from online webstores to let customers to pat visa to buy their products from their webstores conveniently. Hence, computer technology is essential to nowadays any kinds of businesses offices.

The best are developed with the entire project-focused organization in mind. For example, a question on resourcing could involve looking a cariety of systems and files with no way to automatically generate the rught combination of data. Hence, any business offices ought need a single, centralised database which keeps accounting, project and even HR information and can integrate data when required.

ON the office investing in technology web-based system with mobile access benefit, due to investing globalization and pressure on fee rates means staff are in the office less
frequently than ever. A web-based system means data can be accessed from PCs and networked laptops with no other software needed. So, instead of offices can apply laptops and intra-internet communication technological tool, which can also offer the option of a mobile applications suite which means personnel working on -site can enter timesheet and expense reports from laptops, even when not connected to the central data base. This helps

minimise time delays, streamlining the billing process and improving cash flow. So, office mobile onlinesite technology may help thme to bring real-time , easy access benefits. For exmaple, if a staff is
still making decisions based on information that is seven or eight weeks old, the staff will be surprised by the power of having real-time information at the
staff's fingertips. At any time this will give the staff an accurate "snapshot" of the health of the staff's
project, enabling the staff to take preventive action if the problems arise before it is too late.

This visualisation ensures that all key stakeholders can identify project problems immediately they happen . It's also an ideal way for directors or other managers to
grab headline information before a short notice meeting, for example, all of office laptop, mobile intra-internet, onsite technology may help to ensure more targeted decisions and better project control. Hence, office technology may help any business offices to save more time deal urgent tasks daiuly. It means that office technology may help any offices to save much time in long term.

For some businesses office technology may help their businesses to manage on projects to achieve rapid finishing in short time, such as all projects of harbour construction business aspect, some projects may face complex to prolong time to finish. SO, defining a discipline as " complex project management assumes that one can find projects cause of complexity". Also, any the harbour business projects do not really exist. The term project is a contract used to describe a particular human activity. Hence, if the harbour construction company managers can let its all harbour construction managers to apply mobile onsite technology, intra-internet communication channel to do daily communication tasks in short time between their different construction teams. Then, these new harbour onsite mobile intra-internet communication technology ought help all
onsite harbour construction managers can supervise all harbour onsite workers to construct all harbour construction projects in short time efficiently and effectively.

Sp, on-site mobile intra-internet communication technology may be future construction industry which a kind of essential onsite mobile intra-internet communication
technoogy.Moreover, on-site mobile intra-internet communication

technology can bring future construction industry on time to save cost and construction quality improvement benefits. Due to increasingly construction industry and clients demand more for less and this is in a traditionalty high risk industry. The problem of construction and its relatively slow pace of change seem to stem from its competive building living demand role in providing building buyer value. With its attendant professions, it is often too remote from the customers' experience of their buildings.

When if the construction company really knew how to add value for building clients? What if the construction firm could improve productivity among those using the building? How much is that worth? What if the school could improve performance of students in shcools and the recovery of patients in hospitals? Such improvements represent much cost benefits that could mean that the building pays for itself. However, nowadays building technology can bring these key benefical features to any construction companies, such as value success are committed leadership providing the vision, suitable values and effective shared processes.

How office technology brings intelligent thinking to office staffs? Finally, I beleive that if the company can invest technology in office. It will bring intelligent thinking to office staffs in order to improve efficient and performance, because investing in office technology , which is a way to reduce risk without going over the top through effective use of the company networks. Why can office technology working environment can help staffs to bring intelligent thinking in order to improve performance and raise efficiency?

The reason of office technology working environment can excite staffs their intelligent thining to be raise. What's lacking is a way of mitigating against these risks and doing so cost- effectively. Because more recently, a new stage has been reached where office staffs rely not only on their technical and business knowledge, but now have methodologies and tools so sophisticated that they can forward predict and control any office projects to finish before due date more easily.Hence, with good technical knowledge, sound business underatanding, a good way of methodologies, and training in the very latest software technology to hand, these are the not investing in office technology staffs, those who still find it impossible to deliver projects successfully more easily before any their office projects finishing due date. What needs to be addressed to change this situation?

The main factors critical to improve office staffs performance and improve efficiency, the non-investing in office technology working environment ought to

changed to invest technology to office working environment in order to excite staff individual working emotion to bring raising efficiency, even improve performance effectiveness.

ON conclusion, any offices need to invest technology to offices in order to bring " improving technical skill to staffs their working environment", because

they need to know that skill does not equate to competence , and there fore, a competence and therefore a competency based assessment is essential so that a

prospective office employee knowledge and understanding, attitude and skills can be evaluated. So, technological office can help managers to evaluate office employee

individual job skill more easily in order to make decision whether skill is high or low to let high skillful staffs can continue to be trained to work

in offices as well as fire the low skillful staffs. So, when the office can attempt to spend more money to invest to its office working environment, it means that the organization should be investing in training for permanent staffs in the scarce skills working markets. A small

investment in office technology can reap significant benefits further down the live, such as planning for skills scarcity on investing nowadays office technological working environment.

Why do some organizations need to implement outsourcing technoogical strategy? If the organization does not implement outsourcing strategy, what disadvantages to the organization ? The fundamental elements of outsourcing, it is necessary to have a picture that incorporates all of the elements include its nature, services, strategies management of relationships and particularly its theoretical models.

Firstly, we need to understand why the organization ought choose to implement outsourcing strategy. We need to know that service providers need to implement effective strategy in order to let its employees can feel comfortable to work in the organization's office, e.g. facility management outsourcing service, property management, office clearning, maintenance , securty and catering services.

All of these services are elements to any organizational environment. Hence, if the organizatios can attempt to implement outsourcing strategy for above element services. Consequently, it is possible to help this organization to reduce much extra expenditure to compare it chooses to set up cleaning department, security department, property management , facility managment departments, catering department to deal itself daily element services for itself employees working environment in its office building.Hence, it seems that any one of these any one element office service ought be implemeted outsoucing service from outsourcing service provider.

Why outsourcing service may help this organization to reduce cost expenditure to compare it implements to set up different departments ? The main benefit to this organization, it must not need to employ many employees, e.g. cleaning, catering, property and facility management, security employees hen it decides to outsource these services from outsourcing service providers. Hence, it must reduce to spend salaries expenditure when it decides to outsource service providers to help it to do these any one office services for its office benefits.

In fact, outsourcing service may be improved service performance, e.g. cleaning , security, catering, Fm, property management service performance, due to this outsourcing service provider hopes this organization can continue choose its services for long term among of many same service providers in the outsoucring office service competitive market. Otherwise, if it only employs cleaning, security, catering, FM , property management service employees. They may leave this organization when they feel low salaries, or change their career, change another new employer. Otherwise, when this organization chooses outsourcing services to outsoucring service providers, it won't need to worry about these employees.

Outsoucring is clearly quite common in many companies around the world. Outsouring from " out"and " service". which together " describe an external source is a management approach that delegates to an external agent the operational responsibility for processes or services previously delivered by the enterprise itself. It can be defined as the purchase of a product or a service that was previously provided internally" ( Bailhelemy , 2003 ( p.92),

eLMUTI & Kathawala, 2000 ( p,114), Lankford and Parsa, 1999 ( p,312).
However, there is much debate in the managment, literature regardly the definition of outsourcing ( Gilley & Rasheed, 2000). resolve this confusion by providing a broad finition for outsourcing that includes the following arrangements and concepts: internal vs external sourcing ( Scheuing, 1989); Strategic make -or - outsourcing decisions ( Virolarinen, 1998) and make-or-buy and focus decisions ) Knight & Hurland, 2000).

In fact, in transaction cost economic theory, it can explain why outsourcing office service which can earn more benefit to compare employing service employees. The reason is indicated Williamson ( 1985) considers the relative advantages of handling transactions through internal ( hierarchy) or external ( market) organizational forms. Outsourcing offers an organizational solution what can reduce production costs by leveraging on market economies, though this must be balanced against associated transactions costs.

So, the author explains that why organizations ought need to outsource service during this stage, companies outsourced noncore business processes basically to cut operational costs. Outsoucing which was a tool to make organizations more efficient economic units for profit maximization mainly occurred domestically.

He believed that the relationship were managed in an arms-length manner, relying on contracts. Moreover, the level of transaction costs incurred depends on characteristics of the outsourced activities, in particular, asset specificity, uncertainty and transaction frequency,

However, typical commercial buildings, every organization 's office must need to implement saving of costing strategy for improving competitive edges and outcomes some functions, for example maintenance works critiically consideration on performance in terms of technical knowledge, skill, equipment, speed, flexible manpower to outsourcing service providers as well as outsourcing service providers can manage more effective and efficient building maintenance serving jobs for the office owner, such as air-conditioning, mechanical ventilation, fire services, life/escalators, plumbing/drainage, lighting , laundry and catering installations, even simple service jobs, such as cleaning and security deliver higher level of quality services to compare the organization ( office owner) employs these service employees for itself office services.

On conclusion, it seems that any middle and large size organizations ought choose to give outsourcing service jobs to outsourcing service providers to finish and they do not need to employ service employees in order to improve service performance and reduce salaries expenditure for itself organization office and employees their working environment long term benefits.

Technology demand and supply relationship

Can technology influence human shopping behavioral change?

Nowadays, technological development has reached mature stage, whether technological mature stage may bring positive or negative shopping emotion influence to global consumers. I shall aplly internet inventin or ecommerce shopping channel tool to explain whether internet technology can bring postive or negative influence to global consumer behavior in behavioral economic view.

Internet is a good technological tool, it brings e-commerce business chance. In fact, commonly, global has have many businessmen choose to use internet channel to carry on their products transactions between global online-buyers and their electronic websites. So, global many shoppers had begun to feel online shopping is more convenient to compare visiting shops shopping. Their shopping behaviors have been changed from internet technological tool. Global has many shoppers choose to buy any products from any overseas or local businessmen their web stores. They only need to spend time to find any businessmen their webstores to choose the most suitable products to pay visa to buy from their webstores. at homes. So, in general, global had have may shoppers had changed their shopping behaviors from visiting shops to visiting webstores at homes often.

So, it seems that internet technological tool had influenced global many shops disappear, but internet webstores will be replaced their actual shops on streets. Some of businessmen either they choose webstores to replace shops or choose websotes and shops both or still keep shops only. Hence, internet tool influences global businessmen have three kinds of products sale channels to let globa local and overseas consumers to choose how to buy their products.

However, in fact, many of global shoppers, youngers and olders had begun to accept to buy any products from webstores. They feel to spend time to leave homes to visit shops , their shopping behaviors will be wasted time to not essential part to their daily lives. Hence, since internet technological invention, it had changed many consumers their traditional visiting shops shopping habit to change to buying products from webstores channel.

However, on the one hand, internet creates webstores ecommerce shopping channel to let global many consumers do not need to leave homes to go to shopping. It brings negative visiting shops shopping emotion to global general consumers nowadays. But on the other hand, it also brings positive visiting internet webstores shopping emotion to global general consumer nowadays. So, it seems that global many consumers feel that they often do not need to spend much time to go out shopping. Many global consumers feel convenient and enjoy to choose any products to buy from different internet webstores, when the online buyer chooses the most suitable product, he she only needs to pay visa card to buy the product from the online seller's webstore conveniently at home.

Hence, online shopping can bring economic benefit to online buyers, e.g. avoiding walking time or spending transport fare to visit the shop to go to shopping, shortening or reducing shopping time to do another important matter.

On conclusion, global many consumers began feel online shopping can bring more economic benefits on shortening shopping time, avoiding transport fare spending aspect. So, online shopping will be popular shopping behavior for future long time. It may encourage global many shoppers can make rapid shopping decision in short time in order to carry on any products buying transaction to global any one online shopper in short time easily in behavioral economic view. So, global many businessmen had begun to build themselves one attraction webstore in order to persuade different countries consumers to choose to click themselves webstores from internet channel to buy any kinds of products in short time easily.

So, internet technology had changed consumers traditional shopping behaviors to build positive online shopping emotion as well as raise online sellers' any products sale chance easily in behavioral economic view.

Why and how human behavior may influence the country's economic growth or recession?

When one country has many people choose to do the same matter for one period, whether their behavior may influence the country's pvera; economic growth or recession . I shall attempt to indicate cases toexplain their relationship as below:

For flowing rubblish behavioral case example, do you feel that when the country has many people often flow rubblish on the streets, instead of their flowing rubblish behavior may bring streets dirty? But, their flowing rubblish behavior may explain that this country has people may have enough money to buy food to ear, or enough cloths to wear, enough bottles of water to drink, even they may have enough money to buy new television, radio, refrigeraters , washing machines, desktops or laptops electronic home products from old to new to use in order to satisfy their living needs. So, when they flow old electronic home products, their flowing old home electronic products behaviors may seem that they have enough money to buy other new home electronic products to replace old home electronic products to use at homes.

However, it seems thaat this country ought have many people have jobs to do. So, many of them, they can easy to make purchase decison to flow any old home electronic products and buy any new home electronic products to use . Because this country has many people have jobs to do. So, they can often not use old home electonic products to become rubblishs to flow on streets after they had bought any kinds of new home electronic homes.

In fact, it also implies that this country's economy grows rapidly. So, many businesses can glow up rapdly. When they expanded their businesses, they must need to increase employees number in order to let they help themselves to raise productivity or serve their clients absolutely. So, when the country has many businesses can grow up, it seems that its economy must be better or it is improved to compare past. Due to many different kinds of home electronic products had been often bought to use by this country people in this period. So, this country's any streets can be observed that expensive electronic home products were flowed on streets anywhere. then, this country will have many electronic home products sellers can sell their home electronic products very easily. When this country has many people can find any kinds of jobs to do easily. So, due to unemploymen rate had been decreasing.

In behavioral economic view, as this many electronic home products rubblish country case, we can observe this country may have many people have jobs to do. So, consumption number has been increased long time. So, cheap food, or expensive home electronic products may be rubblish on any streets. This country's people , their flowing rubblish behaviors may be explained that many of people have enough jobs to do, so they have ability to buy any good taste food to eat or buy any kinds of expensive electronic home products to use. So, this country's economy may be improved for this long period. So, in behavioral economic view, when this country can have many electronic home products rubblishs are flowed on anywherer in streets frequently. It seems that this country will have many people have jobs to do, so it causes they often change old home electronic products or replaced them easily, when they have enough income to spend to buy any kinds of new home electronic products to use at homes easily. Moreover, their flowing old electronic home products behaviors also indicate that this country has many people their salaries may be increased in possible from their emplyers. When this country can have many different kinds of home electornic products are sold. It means that this country's electronic home products needs or demand had been increasing, due to many people have jobs to do and income increases to excite their living of needs also improve. Consequently, this country may seem have better economic improvement. We can observe from this country's electronic home products rubblish increasing income in theis period.

On conclusion, this country ought experience economic growth at this period. So, " flowing expensive electronic home rubblish increasing number " may seem that this country's economic growth is rapidly in this period, due to many people have jobs to do as well as salaries increase in this period.

Technology how impacts human behavior changing?

Technology how influences human behavior to bring changing? For example, online share purchase and sale transaction from smart phone brings share investor can do share buying or selling transation in any where and any time conveniently, non manual driving auto vehicle, bring car owner feels comfortable and spends free time to do other matter, e.g. reading, listening mucis in himself or herself car freely. electrical energy vehicle can help car owner to reduce air polluton and it can brings the drivers do not feel drive long time in any journeys in order to avoid air pollution for environmental protection responsible car drivers in our societies. Thus, they will drive long time in any journeys when they can drive electronic energy cars to replace oil energy cars.

However, online technology can also bring consumers can choose to stay at homes to buy any things from seller individual online webstore conveniently. Such as online technology can bring shoppers do not need to spend much time to visit shops to buy any things. They can choose any kinds of products from any online sellers individual online webstores conveniently at homes. Online technology excite busy consumers can make purchase decision easily as well as it can help online sellers sell any kinds of products from internet easily.

In behavioral economic view, technology can change human behavior to be improved, it can let human feels comfortable, more free time ro use, rapid making any decisions, such as apply smart phones to make share purchase or sale transaction decision, online shopping decision, even travelling any where decision in short time, when the traveller finds the most cheap hotel accommodation room price and air ticket price frm any travel agent online tourism webstore, then the potential travel customer can follow the online hotel accommodation price and air ticket price data to make decision when to buy the air ticket from the airline travel agent or make decision when to prebook which hotel accommodation room to go to the country to travel from online travel agent tourism webstores. So, technology can encourage global any country travelers to make anywhere to trvel rapidly. If the traveler can find the country's general hotel rooms and airline tickets prices had been decreasing more sightly. The traveler may make travel decision to choose the country to travel in short time, then he/she can prebook the country;s any hotel room and airline ticket to pay by visa fraom the country's any hotel and airline travel agent webstores., before one week, even one month or more easily. Hence, online technology can also encourage traveler individual frequent travel times to be increased, due to global travelers can find any hotel rooms and airline tickets prices from internet conveniently at homes. They do not need to spend time to visit any airline travel agent to enquire travel choice country's hotel rooms prices and airline ticket prices. They can compare global travel of countries choices ' all hotels rooms and airline agents air tickets prices to make prebook airline seat and hotel room decision before one week, one month even six months early.

On conclusion, online technology can encourage global travelers can make travelling any where and when traveling time desicions easily. It can excite tourism industry develops in long time. Also, such as electricity cars invention can encourage environment protection car owners do car purchase decision easily, because they can choose to drive electronic energy cars to replace oil energy cars in order to avoid air pollution occurs easily. So, electronic cars can increase electronic car purchasrs number, due to many of environmental protection attitude of car owners can choose to drive electricity cars to bring air cleans, even non -manual driving cars can encourage lazy driving and free time driving car owners to choose to buy non-manual ( artificial intelligent) cars to drive , because they can spend much free time to read, listen music or do any matters in themselves cars, they do not need to drive cars, robotic (AI) auto driving machine is such one non-manual driver to help them to drive themselves cars confidently.

So, non-manual driving cars can attract lazy and enjoying free time driving car owners to choose to buy to replace traditional manual cars to drive easily. Moreover, online share transaction can help any share investors to make share buying and selling decision in short time easily. When they can apply smart phones technological tool to carry on share buying and selling activities easily. They can observe any share rising or falling price suitation from smart phones in any where any any time easily. So, smart phone technology can help global any shareholders to make share purchase and sale transaction easily. So, technology can encourage human makes decision in short time rapidly.

How and why employees behaviors may influence economy development?

In behavioral economy view,I believe the country's any organizational employees behavior may bring indirect relationship to influence the country's long term economic development. I shall indicate past manufacture industry social development period to explain their relationship. For many countries' past business activities had belonged to manufacturing industry, such as US, UK past before 1980 year, it focused on steel manufacturing and steel manufacturing related machine products. So, US, Uk developed countries manufacturing industries may be past main country's economic income sources. I assume US , UK past had one million number different kinds of industries. They ought had about seven houndred thousand number organizational businesses were belonged to manufactured industry. They may include:

Steel manufacturing and steel related machine manufacturing, e.g. vehicle manufacturing, home appliances, e.g. washing machine, television, radio, refrigerate cooler, heater, air condition etc. different kinds of different kinds of steel -related manufacturing machine, they were manufactured from US, UK steel machine manufacturers. So, US, Uk the other three hundred thousand number industry may be general service industry, e.g. hotel service, restaurent, cinema, public transport service, tourism lesiure , wine bar, supermarket etc. different kinds of non-manufacturing industries business organizations were operated in UK, US past before 1980 year.

So, in UK, US developed countries industry development history, they ought have high percentage of businesses belonged to steel related manufacturing machine and steel products. Also, in the past before 1980 year, US, Uk business employers , they employed many workers are manufacturing workers. They needed to spend long time to work in factories. They were skillful workers, and they are trained to manufacturing cars, washing machine, television, heater, etc. even steel itself different kinds of steel related products to prepare to deliver to their shops to sell to US, Uk local or overseas clients.

So, I believe that past UK, US ought employ many employees, they belonged to skillful manufacturing workers, manufacture increasing steel machine or steel related machine number of products rapidly daily. So, if UK, US had had many of these manufacturing factories owned high skillful workers, then their manufacturing steel-related machine or steel both kinds of products number must be influenced to raise rapidly. Consequently, their steel machine manufacturing products would been exported to overseas or would been sold to local both markets , they may be influenced to raise sale number. They ( these manufacturing workers) needed to be trained to know how to manufactur these different kinds of machine products in the efficient teams and they ought to be trained to raise their efficiencies in order to shorten time to manufacturing many kinds of steel related manufacturing machine or steel itself products rapidly. So , if their efficiencies and manufacturing performance was improved, these US, UK any one manufacturing worker and their teams ought achieve raising productivities significantly.

Hence, when past UK, US manufacturing industry development period, if these two countries' any manufacturing factories could have many manufacturing workers could be trained to be skillful and proficient manufacturing workers. Then, in past every day to these factories workers, they ought help their steel or steel related manufacturing employers to raise any kinds of machine or steel products number in every team. So, when past in the manufacturing industry development, US, UK could have many factories' manufacturing workers themselves steel or steel related machine products manufacturing skill could be trained to to improve to any kinds of these machine or steel manufacuring products quality as well as their products number could be influenced to raise by themselves skillful improvement significantly every day.

Then, what would be influenced to occur to past UK, US manufacturing industry period? In behavioral economic view, when these two manufacturing industry developed countries, such as UK, US , if they had many factories workers can be trained to improve their skill in order to achieve any kinds of steel or steel-related machine products quality could be improved as well as products manufacturing number could be also increased absolutely.

In consequence, past UK and US both countries ought increase themselves any kinds of steel and steel related machine products number to be supplied to themselves local shops to let local clients to choose any one kind of machine manufacturing products to buy easily as well as they could also export to supply overseas any countries to buy their different kinds of steel or steel related machine products to let overseas steel or steel related manufacturing machine product buyers, they can have many of these different kinds of these steel or steel-related different kinds of manufacturing machine from UK and UK these both countries easily to compare other countries.

On conclusion, I believe that past US, and UK macro manufacturing industry income GDP would increase significantly. So, they would have good economic growth performance because when many of these manufacturing workers themselves manufacturing effort could be improved. So, it explained when employees manufacturing abilities can influence economic growth indirectly.

Robots invention whether they can help organizations to raise efficiencies or inefficiencies?

In behavioral economic view, in any organizations, when the organization hopes its worker teams can raise efficiencies , the organization may choose to increase more workers number and/or it can provide training to improve these workets themselves skills in order to raise their efficiencies. For one warehouse example, when the warehouse increases many goods , they are needed to delivered these goods from the shelves to the delivering destination locations. If this warehouse supervisors feel these workers themselves goods delivery speeds are slow, which is possible due to this warehouse's workers number is not enough. So, this warehouse supervisor ought increase workers number in order to increase their goods delivery speed in order to deliver goods from the shelves to every indicated goods delivery destination in order to let any one lorry driver can transport the right kinds of goods and ensure the accurate goods number to transport to any one client home rapidly.

However, if this warehouse supervisor planed to buy several warehouse goods delivery robots to assist these warehouse workers to find the right kinds of goods from shelves and then deliver to the right destination location in the warehouse. So, these warehouse orkers can concentrate on counting the accurate goods number and ensuring the right kinds of goods in order to prepare to let lorry drivers to transport these goods to these goods of buyers themselvers homes rapidly. Consequently, in the first step, robots can concentrate on finding th right goods from shelves and delivers them to the right goods transportation of location destination. Then, in the second step, these warehouse workers can concentrate on counting the accurate goods number and ensuring the right kinds of goods in order to prepare to put them to the lorry. Consequently, when warehouse robots and warehouse workers can cooperate to work together, the most important, robots, can deal on finding the right kinds of goods and deal on delivering the accurate number of goods of job duty as well as these warehouse workers can only concentrte on counting the right kinds of goods number in order to avoid it has none any mistake of wrong kinds of goods and inaccurate goods of delivery number to be transported to the lorry and to deliver to any one buyer's home.

So, it seems that warehouse robots ought help any one warehouse worker to raise himself efficiency and avoid goods delivery of mistake occurrence easily as well as their help to warehouse workers that can let any one goods buyer feels their goods can be delivered to their homes rapidly. Moreover, warehouse robots can also help these warehouse workers to raise efficiencies because warehouse robots can help them to shorten goods delivery time between any one shelf and any one goods delivery destination of location in the warehuse because robots may help them to find the right kinds of goods from the right shelf in the short time. So, any one worker does not need to spend long time to seek anywhere is the right shelf location for the kind of goods when the kind of goods are needed to deliver to the buyer's home from lorry. Warehouse robots can help them to do this aspect of " finding the goods from the right shelf in short time job duty". So, any one warehouse worker only needed tospend less time to do the counting of any right kind of goods number and ensuring the right kind of goods job duty. Consequently, this warehouse 's any one worker, his any one kind of goods delivery time may be reduced, because robots' assistance and they may have more confidence to avoid mistake to deliver the wrong number of goods and/or the wrong kind of goods to any one goods buyer's home.

On conclusion, it seems that warehouse robots ought may help any one warehouse worker to raise efficiency for any one team in the warehouse as well as the warehouse any one supervisor does not need to spend much time to observe any one worker individual performance for " goods delivery job duty aspect" because their goods delivery job duty that had been replaced to do by these several warehouse robots. Robots can achieve the more accurate of right kinds of goods and the right number of goods delviery job performance to compare any one of human warehouse worker themselves right kinds of goods of delivery and right number of goods of delivery job performance. So, when robots can participate to cooperate with this warehouse's any one worker to do their goods of delivery job duty in this warehouse every day. Then, robots can raies any one of supervisor individual confidence in order to let they do not need to spend time to observe any one of worker individual whose goods of delivery job performane. They can concentrate on supervising any one worker whose goods transport to lorry in the final step in order to avoid to deliver wrong goods number and / or wrong kind of goods to any one goods buyer's home every day. Consequently, this warehouse's overall teams of their delviery of goods performance many be improved by robotss' participatin to goods of delivery task as well as this warehouse's oveall teams themselves efficiencies may be influenced to raise by robots' goods of delivery task participation.

Why social behavior may influence organizational strategy needs to be changed ?

Why any organizations need to know whether nowadays social behaivor how has been changing in order to implement the kind of the most right strategy to achieve the profit aim pursue in possible. I shall indicate nowadays ecommerce or online, customer shopping behavior to explain above question concerns they ought have close relationship between social behavior and organizational strategic choice or organizational behavioral changing need.

On nowadays ecommerce business, or online shopping model, this kind of shopping model in global many young and old age consumers like to apply internet tool to choose any country sellers website stores in order to stay at home to buy any kinds of products from themselves webstores in global societies.

In fact, online shopping model had been popular for long time above to twenty years. Most of global sellers will make decision to design themselves webstores in order to attract global many online buyers to choose to buy their products from themselves webstores. So, it seems that social consumers purchase behaviors had been changed to online shopping from internet invention.

Hence, social consumers purchase behavioral changes may influence any organizations' strategies need to be changed from visiting shops purchase strategy model to online purchase strategy model, if the seller still concentrate on concentrate on considerate how to design itelf , but neglects to considerate how to design itself webstore, e.g. how to design attract product photos to put on itself webstore, how to arrange sale price information location to be putted on webstore and visa card payment location on itself webstore in order to let any one online buyer can feel very easier to buy itself any kinds of products from itself webstore. Then, its potential online buyers will be influenced to increase number when they can find this online seller itself any kinds of products photes and every kinds of product sale price information and visa card payment channel locations easily from itself webstore.

So, it implies that nowadays any one seller ought need to design one webstore to let any one online overseas and domestic consumers can have chance to click itself webstore to choose any one kind of product to buy conveniently when he/she does not hope to leave him/her home to go to shop, because nowadays social shopping behaviors had been influenced to change when internet invention, them it gives another online purchase method to replace visiting shops purchase method to global any one buyer in nowadays societies.

So, if nowadays any one seller still concentrate on how to design itself shop display in order to put any kinds of product on shelf in order to let any one visiting shop customer to find the kind of product to buy, but it neglects to change to choose to pursue another new technological shopping method, such as webstore purchase method in order to implement effective strategy to design the most right webstore as well as in order to attract global overseas and local consumers to find itself webstore easily from website and find its any one kind of product phots and sale price and visa card payment button in order to choose to buy itself any kinds of products in the short time. Consequently I believe that the seller will lose many customers from overseas and local when its other same or similar product sellers choose to design themselves webstores in order to let global any one product buyer can buy themselves any one kind of product when they can pay visa card to buy their products from them webstores conveniently when they stay at home habitly. Then, the seller will lose many global potential customers in long time.

On conclusion, in behavioral economic view, any consumer behavioral social changing, which will influence any in order to avoid customers number loses significantly . In future time, organizations need to make rapid decision in order to implement the most reasonable and the most useful strategy in order to avoid global potential customers number reduces or lose them in long time. So, social behavioral changing environment ought influence any global organizations need to decide how to change themselves strategies in order to avoid customers loses significantly in future time.

How and why human behavior may influence economic growth or recession?

May ourselves daily behaviors influence our global societial continue economic growth or recession? Do they have cause and effect close relationship between human behaviors and global economic growth or recession? I shall apply behavioral economic theory to analyze and explain whether ourselves daily behaviors and our global societial economic growth or recession which have close cause and effect relationship as below:

Every country itself economic development must depend on any business activities, otherwise, any kinds of business activities must need ourselves business activities or behaviors in order to achieve any business activities as well as achieve the country's overall economic development in macro view. However, any country's overall business activites or behaviors which must depend on any kinds of individual businessmen, themselves employees daily working behavior or activity or performance in order to help them to attract or increase many clients number to acieve " earning profit" aim. So, it seems that any individual business, itself overall every department individual working behavior is one main factor to influence the company's overall business performance.

For agricultural fruit and meat food farming industry example, such as New Zealand is a farming main target industry country. It had had many New Zealanders were daily themselves own farming businesses for many years. Their farming businesses include growing fruit, sheep, cow, pig pork, meat etc. food sale business. If the New Zealand farmer owned a large size farming land, then he will choose either growing fruit or feeding sheeps, pigs, cows to be meat to to transport to New Zealand supermarkets to help them to sell to their farmers meet to New Zealanders in order to earn profit. Thus, if the New Zealand farmer owned large size of farming lands, then he needs to employ many farming employees ( farming workers) to help him to carry on farming business daily tasks, e.g. picking up friuts, feeding pigs, cows, sheeps to eat food daily. These daily farming jobs are very important to influence this New Zealand farmer's meats or fruits sale number whether they can be easy or diffcult to sell in New Zealand supermarkets , if these farming workers can own encough farming knowledge or skill to know how to pick up fruits method and make judgement to know whether it is right time to pick up the kind of fruits from the trees , as well as know how feed this pigs, sheeps, cows to eat food in order to let they are better health. Consequently, their farming behaviors which can let these animals can provide the best taste and enough meat from these animals to let New Zealander to buy to eat from New Zealand any one supermarket. Even these New Zealand farming workers can know whether the kinds of fruits, e.g. oranges, apples, gapes etc. fruits whether they ought be picked up from the trees at the right time. Consequently, they can make judgement to decide to pick up any kinds of the best taste fruits to let any one New Zealander to buy to eat from any one supermarket in New Zealand. Otherwise, if they do not make judegement to know whether the kind of fruit ought not be picked up because they still need longer time to continue grow up to increase fruit size and better taste from the trees in order to let any one fruit buyer can feel better taste when they eat this kind of fruit later. If they can buy this kind of fruit to eat later, then this New Zealand farmer's his fruit buyers can buy the best taste of this kind of fruit to eat from an yone supermarket in New Zealand. Consequently, many New Zealand supermarkets will choose to buy any kinds of fruits from this farmer fruit supplier when they feel this farmer's fruits can provide more better taste fruits to compare other farmers‘ fruits.

Thus, due to New Zealand is one farming main income source country. It's any kinds of fruits and meats need to be export to overseas to sell , instead of local sale. It's GDP percent is very high to whole country 's overall income source. So, any one New Zealand farmer individual and any one farming worker individual working behavior will influence its economy whether it is influenced to grow or recession possible. Moreover, it also seems that farming workers' farming knowledge and skill will influence themselves farming daily activities to achieve the aim of the number of increase or decrease to any kinds of fruits whether they are better taste or the number of increase of decrease to any kinds of meats whether they are better taste to supply to any one New Zealand fruit or meat buyers to eat from any one New Zealand supermarket. So, it implies that any one New Zealand farming worker individual farming behavior may influence any kinds of fruits or any kinds of meat taste because they are transported to any one supermarket to sell in New Zealand.

Consequently, if New Zealans had many farmers can teach god farming knowledge and skill to let their any one farming workers know how to decide judgement to decide when it is right time to pick up any kinds of fruits from trees , or how to grow them on soil in order to let they can grow rapidly. Then, many different kinds of fruits can be provided to let any one New Zealanders can eat the best taste of fruits when their fruits are supplied to any one New Zealand supermarkets. Even, if they knew how to feed foods to pigs, cows, sheeps to eat daily. Then they can be more health and they can provide the best taste of meats to let any one New Zealanders can buy their meats from any one New Zealand supermarkets. Moreover, their fruits and meats can be transported to overseas to let any one country fruits or meats buyers can choose any kinds of New Zealand meats and fruits to buy to eat from themselves countries supermarkets. Then, many overseas fruit and meat buyers will perfer to choose New Zealand any kinds of fruits or meats to buy to compare other countries fruits or meats to buy when they go to any one local supermarkets.

On conclusion, it seems that New Zealand farming workers themselves farming behavior may influence their farming employers any kinds of fruits or meats sale number and income because their farming task behaviors must influence whether their fruits or meats taste are the better taste or worse taste to compare their other local farmers ( the farmer competitors) whose fruits or meats taste. If tthe farmer's any one farming worker can be trained to learn how to know to feed animals skill and when is the most right time to pick up any kinds of fruits from trees or how to grow them on the soil methods. Due to these farming worker individual farming behavior may influence his different finds of fruits and meats sale number to be increase or decrease, so these any one New Zealand farmer must need to depend on any one farming worker whose farming working methods, if their farming working behaviors can be the best to influence any kinds of fruits to grow rapid or any kinds of pigs, cows, sheeps animals grow up rapidly , then their sale number may be increase significantly and their taste can be improved to let any New Zealand or overseas meat or fruit buyer to buy to eat to feel from any one New Zealand or overseas supermarkets, then New Zealand's agriculture industry must be influenced to increase. In the world, any one fruit or meat buyer must choose to buy New Zealand's fruit and meat to eat in prefer to compare other countries' fruits and meats. So, New Zealand's

GDP may be influenced to raise from any one New Zealand farming worker individual farming working behaviors. It seems that New Zealand farmer fruit and meat sale number is depended on their eatting consumers demand more than their meat and fruit supply because if these NZ farmers can apply high technology method to grow good taste fruit or feed good taste meat to let global eatting customers to feel, their demand will increase, then NZ farmers will need to increase good taste fruit and good taste meat supply number to satisfy global meat and fruit eatting customer taste need.

www.ingramcontent.com/pod-product-compliance
Ingram Content Group UK Ltd.
Pitfield, Milton Keynes, MK11 3LW, UK
UKHW022028190726
13853UKWH00005B/2154